7/11/94

Happy Birthday—

Skip.

Good hunting

Love

marc

& Leslie - Sarah

HENRY HOLT AND COMPANY / NEW YORK

A HUNTER'S ROAD

A Journey

with

Gun and Dog

Across

the American Uplands

JIM FERGUS

Henry Holt and Company, Inc.
Publishers since 1866
115 West 18th Street
New York, New York 10011

Henry Holt® is a registered trademark
of Henry Holt and Company, Inc.

Published in Canada by Fitzhenry & Whiteside Ltd.,
195 Allstate Parkway, Markham, Ontario L3R 4T8.

Library of Congress Cataloging-in-Publication Data

Fergus, Jim.
A hunter's road: a journey with gun and dog across the American
uplands / Jim Fergus—1st ed.
p.   cm.
Includes bibliographical references.
1. Upland game bird shooting—United States.   2. Hunting stories,
American.   I. Title.
SK323.F47   1992
799.2′42′0973—dc20   92-5722
                                                                    CIP

ISBN 0-8050-1619-8
ISBN 0-8050-3008-5 (An Owl Book: pbk.)

Henry Holt books are available for special promotions and
premiums. For details contact: Director, Special Markets.

First published in hardcover
by Henry Holt and Company, Inc. in 1992.

First Owl Book Edition—1993
Printed in the United States of America
All first editions are printed on acid-free paper. ∞

3   5   7   9   10   8   6   4
1   3   5   7   9   10   8   6   4   2
(pbk.)

To Barney

ACKNOWLEDGMENTS

I regret that space does not allow thanking individually the many generous hunters who took me afield in the course of my travels around America, who showed me the countryside and allowed me into their favorite cherished bird coverts. I owe each of you an unpayable debt of gratitude and thanks. You know who you are, and where I can be found, and you are always a welcome guest in my country.

Special thanks to Colleen Daly, the first to learn the particulars of this unlikely scheme, for her invaluable early support and suggestions. Ditto to David Seybold, who is always performing unpaid favors and kindnesses for his many writer friends, and to whom I am greatly indebted for his help all along the road.

It is impossible to modify the word "thanks" with any adjective adequate to the tireless efforts on my behalf of my agent, John Ware, without whose unflagging faith, enthusiasm, and encouragement this project would never have come to pass. So thanks, John. And to you, too, Bill Strachan, my editor, who took a flyer on this at the beginning and made it better than it would have been at the end.

Now, how to thank you, Dillon, for loaning me your dog and sending me out on the hunter's road?

CONTENTS

AUTHOR'S NOTE

Although this is essentially a work of nonfiction, certain fictional devices and techniques have been used. In some instances the names of characters, places, towns, regions, and states have been changed, and situations and events altered or otherwise disguised. In the same manner, some of the characters in this book are composites of two or more real people, while others are entirely the creation of the author's imagination. Even the narrator—the hunter—of this book may occasionally slip into the guise of a fictional persona. Sometimes this fictionalization and intentional obfuscation is undertaken simply to protect the privacy of the individuals involved. At other times, it serves to obscure this hunter's trail, to brush his tracks, as it is not the author's intention to serve as chamber of commerce, to promote the sport of bird hunting, or to advise the reader where, or with whom, to go bird hunting; there are plenty of organizations, publications, and individuals already in that business. It may seem somewhat anachronistic in this age of information to withhold such specifics, but there was a time, not so long ago, that a favorite fishing hole or hunting covert was a carefully guarded secret. The author adheres to such old-fashioned discretion.

One of the principal advantages of hunting, my dear readers, consists in its forcing you to be constantly moving from place to place, which is highly agreeable for a man of leisure.

Ivan Turgenev, A HUNTER'S SKETCHES (1852)

Without his meaning it to, the hunter's soul leaps out, spreads out over the hunting ground like a net, anchored here and there with the fingernails of his attention. Now everything is imminent and at any instant any figure of the countryside can become—as if by magic—the hunter's prey.

José Ortega y Gasset, MEDITATIONS ON HUNTING (1942)

THE HUNTER

The hunter is the alert man.

Ortega y Gasset

I can't tell you what makes one man a hunter and another not. But I can tell you how this all happened for one hunter.

It began when I was a boy growing up in the midwestern suburbs. I was small for my age, asthmatic, quiet and somewhat timid, solitary and frequently afraid; at night I would make a tent of my covers and read sporting magazines by a pen flashlight, while my parents battled downstairs, saying things to each other that this boy simply could not bear to hear. My mother had dark troubles with drink; only a few years later she would die young, a hard death, alone on another continent.

Under the covers in my den with my flashlight I was safe; my dog, Sugar, a little Welsh terrier, nestled beside me. Under there, enormous fish leapt on mirrored lakes and huge coveys of game birds blackened the sky over field and forest, while jocular, self-reliant outdoorsmen such as I longed to be cooked hearty meals over an open fire and slept in bedrolls under the stars. These were my companions, all superb shots and incredibly proficient anglers. Of course, later I would learn that many of their tales of sporting triumphs were pure fabrication, but I didn't need to know that yet.

I had a slingshot that I used to hunt squirrels with in the ravine near my house, although for a long time I never actually hit any. I did kill a few robins with my slingshot, and one time I made a campfire in the ravine and roasted a robin on a stick as a kind of sacrament. Even then I believed in eating what I killed and not killing what I wouldn't eat. I plucked and drew the bird first, and it was quite delicious. But a neighbor saw the smoke from the campfire and called the fire department and that put an end to my robin roasts. I got in a good bit of trouble at home.

One day I finally hit a squirrel with my slingshot, but I only wounded it and then I had to kill it with a stick; it was a nasty, messy business and the squirrel suffered. This made me feel terrible. I still, all these years later, feel terrible thinking about it, and to this day I remain squeamish about killing things. I hate suffering of any kind, human or animal. Don't think because I'm a hunter that this is not so.

I had a cheap spun glass fishing rod, too, and I often fished for perch in Lake Michigan. The lake was only a few blocks from my house, and I would walk down there with my rod and tackle box. Already I wanted a bamboo fly rod, and I had my eye on a Daisy BB gun at the hardware store, but I wasn't old enough to have that yet.

Frequently my parents gave cocktail parties and I would be sent off early to my room. I would lie in bed and listen to the revelry downstairs— the chatty, animated voices of the grown-ups, the tinkling of glasses and ice cubes, and my mother's peculiar shrieking laughter which became dangerously higher pitched and more hysterical as the evening wore on.

There was a woman friend of my parents' who always used to come up to see me in my room during these parties. I believed she was a drunk, too, but she was very nice, and she would sit on the edge of my bed and smoke and sip her drink and talk to me—sometimes for hours—and eventually I would fall asleep while she talked on and on. In the morning I would find ashes from her cigarettes and sometimes burn marks on my blanket. Though I was only a boy, she would confide in me, tell me strange adult things that I wouldn't understand until many years later. But I did understand some of what the woman told me, and I understood that she had a very unhappy marriage. I liked her and felt sorry for her in that instinctive way that children do.

One time while she was in my room talking to me, the woman's husband came in looking for her. He told her to go back to the party and then he sat down on my bed. He was very drunk and he breathed heavily and gave off an unpleasant sour smell. He asked me if his wife had tried to have sex with me. I wasn't altogether sure what the man was talking about; I knew what sex was but I didn't see why his wife would want to have it with me. So I said by way of answer, "I'm only ten, sir." Then the man asked me if I wanted to have a pillow fight. I said no thank you, that I was supposed to be asleep. But the man insisted, and he grabbed the pillow from under my head and started striking me with it. "C'mon, fight back," he said, "fight back," and he hit me harder and harder with the pillow.

"Fight back, you little shit!" I covered my head with my arms and I did not fight back, because, you see, he had my pillow.

Sugar was under the bed and I could hear her growling. Finally she could take no more of this, and she sank her teeth into the man's ankle. He hollered and jumped up, but terriers are notorious for not letting go, and the man dragged the dog out from under the bed at the end of his leg; he was dancing around the room and trying to shake her loose. It was quite comical. My trusty companion Sugie hung on tenaciously, growling all the while, until I told her to let go. How I loved that little dog.

After that the man left my room, promising darkly that he was going to talk to my father about this, but I think he just went back down to the party and had another drink because I never heard any more about it. The very next week, the man died in a car wreck on the expressway while driving home from work. He had "fallen asleep at the wheel," which was the euphemism parents used in those days for drunken driving. I still held a fresh grudge against the man, and I was secretly glad that he had died. I knew that this was a terrible way to feel, but I was an angry boy, and even then I understood the need for a tonic to my anger. That is the point of this story, in case you're wondering, the beginning of my plan, the seed of my life as a sportsman. When you're an angry boy, sport can offer some real measure of peace and escape—not just escape from something bad, but escape to something wonderful: grace.

That night of the one-sided pillow fight, Sugar and I firmed up our plan, made our pact under the covers with my pen flashlight and sporting magazines. The plan was a simple one, universal perhaps to boys—to girls, too, for that matter—which may account for all the runaways in our society, the difference being that most of the runaways have no place to go and no resources once they get there. But this boy and his dog did: we were headed for the open country. There was a giant oak tree outside my bedroom window; its branches would scratch at the glass at night, beckoning us. This would be our escape route when things got really bad at home. I had already climbed down it many times in preparation, had even carried Sugar down to make sure I could do it; she was not crazy about this part but she trusted me.

We would travel across the country, Sugie and I, with my fishing rod and that Daisy BB gun which I now intended to steal—desperate measures, I knew, but I was a desperate boy. We would hunt and fish and live off the land, a vast storybook land of beauty, goodness, and bounty, a land studded by farms and ranches and villages, inhabited by fine upstanding, honest folks. In this fantasy, we would trade our abundant harvest of game to the locals for produce and pies, or whatever else we needed, or simply for a spot in the barn to spend the night, and sometimes along the way someone would invite us into their home to have dinner with the family, a family that bore no relationship whatsoever to my family. We would eat fried chicken with mashed potatoes, gravy and biscuits, prepared by a kindly mother in a white apron, a woman I am sad to recall now, who bore no relationship whatsoever to my own mother. Sugie and I would spend the night curled together in the hay in a corner of the barn, warm as toast, and the next morning after a hearty farm breakfast we would be on our way, off to a new unknown destination, another day of sport and adventure.

It would be nearly thirty years before I actually implemented this plan, and, of course, Sugar would be long gone by then, tragically struck by a car the year after my parents both died. This is a difficult thing to acknowledge, but her death was harder for me in an immediate way than theirs had been. That little dog had protected me from so much harm.

I would, over the ensuing years, lose interest in hunting in favor of organized sports; indeed, this dwindling interest had started with my inept dispatching of the wounded squirrel. I would maintain a keen lifelong interest in fishing, though even that would be superseded periodically by other interests and concerns. And I would travel widely and live in several different regions of the country and parts of the world. Eventually I would make my home in the countryside of the American West.

At age thirty-nine, I suddenly developed a strange, overpowering obsession with bird hunting, an obsession childlike in its single-minded intensity. I had started doing a bit of hunting again over the preceding few years, but this newly discovered passion was no longer casual or even particularly gradual. I started buying all the sporting magazines again, something I had not done since I was a kid, and I bought an old double-barreled shotgun, the possession of which seemed somehow to placate finally my boyhood desire for that Daisy BB gun—which I never did own. I bought books about bird hunting, both contemporary and classic, books about shooting technique, and bird-dog training books—even though I didn't own a bird dog. Then one day I brought home a yellow Lab puppy, ostensibly as a gift to my wife, who had lost her beloved old dog the year before and pined for a replacement. Of course, I had designs of my own on that puppy.

I am well aware that such an obsession, standing as I was on the precipice of middle age, might easily be mistaken for a "midlife crisis," although it hardly seemed like a crisis situation to me. Rather it seemed like a conscious attempt to complete some unfinished business from the past, to keep an old pact, to put into action a dusty plan that had been stored away all these years in an ancient trunk in one of those attic garrets of the mind, put away so long that I had nearly forgotten it was there. At the same time, it still seemed like a reasonable way of diffusing old childhood angers. Sometimes just knowing that we can always climb out that bedroom window and down the branches of that old oak tree and head for the *big* country actually keeps us alive.

Midlife crisis or not, my new obsession seemed pretty harmless, and except for the fact that I had appropriated her dog for my own nefarious purposes, my wife hardly even remarked upon it. She just watched patiently as packages arrived at the door—more books or gear, yet another shotgun. Pretty harmless even to the birds, in fact, given the size of my bag from the nearly daily hunting excursions that first season. "Did you get anything?" my wife, tolerant and vaguely amused, would inquire of us every day upon our return. She had named the new puppy Sweetzer after a summit in Idaho on which we had once been stranded in a blizzard. That's right, *Sweetzer.* Over the next year, I would take a lot of abuse from hunting companions about this apparently sissified name, but secretly to me it seemed like a kind of magical coincidence that Sweetzer sounded like the name for a Sugar substitute.

By the time I had turned forty, Sweetz and I had our first hunting season together under our belts—not a complete success, but not a total bust, either. We had hunted hard in Idaho where my wife and I had moved recently, and in late January after the season there closed we took a trip to Nevada to hunt chukar partridges alone in the high, desolate rimrock around Battle Mountain. It was there, on a cold, clear winter day, having climbed for several hours up the steep face of a rocky, barren mountainside, having finally gained the top of a broad, snow-covered, wind-whorled plateau, all alone on what seemed to be the very top of the world, that Sweetzer flushed a covey of chukars—grayish birds, with intense black and white stripes on their flanks. I can still see that covey rise in my mind's eye, as if it's happening right now: the vast, empty, somehow prehistoric country stretching away below, the wild cries of the birds on the wind, and those black stripes stenciled against the snow. I shot and killed a chukar, my first of the species, and Sweetzer proudly retrieved it to me. Then I sat in the snow with my gun broken in my lap, and opened the bird's crop to see what he had been eating before he died. The crop was packed tight with a fistful of bright green cheatgrass blades. I held the still warm bird in my hand, and put the grass up to my nose and inhaled deeply; it reminded me oddly and intensely of my childhood—exactly the smell of mowing the lawn on a warm summer day in the midwest. I opened my fist and let the grass blow away on the wind.

We had many preparations to make that spring and summer before heading out on the first day of September. I won't deny that a large measure of the romance of the sporting life lies in a certain suspension of the "real world"—the world of commerce, industry, mortgages, bills, net worth—the endless money blather of the age. Nor will I deny that sportsmen as a whole are a childlike, if not precisely childish, bunch. But personally, I prefer the great Sioux seer Black Elk's concept of the "real world behind this one," and I like to imagine that I was not so much escaping reality as creating it out of whole cloth. I envisioned the trip as a kind of seasonal life migration, and I was going, among other reasons, out of simple curiosity, to find out what it was really like on the other side of that young boy's dream.

Still, certain grown-up sacrifices were made. At least partly to fund this fancy, my wife and I put our house in Idaho on the market and moved back to our old spartan cabin in northern Colorado, where we had lived for nearly ten years and which we owned free and clear. I rigged up a deal with the bank and went out and bought an elaborate camper affair to live in on my travels, a compact but self-contained motor home built on a small truck chassis. The quizzical salesman told me that the average age of his customers was sixty-five. I explained that I was getting a jump on retirement. In the fall my wife went to stay with her mother in Florida, and I was off, my copilot Sweetzer sitting up in the passenger seat.

It would be almost exactly a year to the day of my epiphany on a mountaintop in Nevada that Sweetz and I would come full circle, pulling back into the drive of the cabin in Colorado on a snowy winter evening, the first day of February. We had been on the road for 5 months, driven over 17,000 miles, hunted in 24 states, and spent over $700 in hunting license fees. In her mouth, young Sweetzer, who turned 2 years old during the trip, had carried 21 species of game birds to me (including one Central Park pigeon).

But those are simply statistics, of interest perhaps only to diehard hunters, many of whom, I discovered on my travels, had always dreamed of a journey such as mine. And although the diligent reader may find a snippet or two of useful "how-to" information about the sport of bird hunting herein, this book is not intended to be instructional, nor is it, by a long shot, the work of an "expert" hunter. There have been many excellent books written by *real* experts on bird hunting, and by way of compensating the unsuspecting reader who may have shelled out his money in the mistaken notion that this was one such book, I have included at the end a partial list of what I consider to be some of the best on the subject.

If this is not a "how-to" bird hunting book, written by an expert, then what is it? Fair question. First of all, it's a book about country and people—the former of which we seem to be in increasingly short supply, while ever long on the latter—as much as it is about hunting. I saw so much extraordinary country on my travels—the mountains, plains, prairies, forests, hollows, marshes, deltas, and deserts of America—and spent time afield with so many fine, wonderful, strange, and sometimes insufferable companions along the way, people of all occupations, ages, and classes. Then, too, it's a book about dogs—of hundreds of miles walking alone with my own trusty Sweetzer, and behind dozens of other dogs of every conceivable sporting breed. Finally, this is a book about birds: the pointed covey, the stunning explosion of wings, the perfect arc of flight; birds—dead and alive, large and small, single and in flocks, in the field and on the table—haunt this hunter's dreams.

J. F.
Ayn, Colorado
September 1991

1

MY LIFE AS
A DOG TRAINER

Preserve wild game, use a trained dog.

Common ad slogan of
state fish and game agencies

I live in a small town in northern Colorado called Ayn (as in Ayn Rand; local boosters have tried to make a case: that the noted writer actually came here once and that our town is the model for a town in *The Fountainhead*, but I can find no evidence for either claim). It is a tiny community (population 13), not even on most maps. There aren't too many shotgunners around and certainly no skeet range at which to practice, so last summer my rancher friend Billy Cantrell and I formed our own skeet club at his ranch dump. We called it the Ayn Gun Club and we were the only members. We had different stations set up in various parts of the dump. One of the most challenging stations from a shooting standpoint was the one we called the "hole" down at the bottom of the dump next to an old upended chest freezer; here the clay targets would whiz directly over your head. Billy shoots an old Ithaca Flues model 20-gauge double-barreled shotgun that he inherited from his beloved aunt, Effie, who died some years ago and is buried in the tiny cemetery on a windblown ridge overlooking town. He calls the gun "Old Effie," which I find lovely. I was shooting my little Belgium side-by-side which I bought cheaply from a dealer in Texas. Manufactured in Liège by a small company that didn't survive World War II, the gun has no collector value but is in excellent condition—a plain gun, but I think rather elegant. It has an initial plate on the stock and came with the original muttonchop leather case, both engraved with the initials DAB. It also has sling clips attached; before the war in Europe, bird hunters used to sling their shotguns over their backs and ride their bicycles outside town for a little shooting. I like to hold that shotgun in my hand and imagine young DAB pedaling away in the Belgian countryside on a fine fall morning. Anyway, by the end of the summer when it was time for me to leave on my trip, Billy and I were breaking targets pretty regularly, even from the hole. Maybe it wasn't exactly the Orvis shooting school, but we had a lot of fun.

Though Cantrell never went to college and hasn't been down to the city in nearly twenty years, he is possessed of that innate brand of rural wisdom and humor, hard earned through a lifetime of close attention to his surroundings and a familial understanding of the country. The first time he watched me working Sweetzer on hand signals when she was just a puppy, he smiled his generous tobacco-flecked smile, spat a stream of tobacco juice on the ground, and said, "Why Jim, she's just like a fool a fuckin', she don't know where to begin!"

Billy used to hunt sage grouse around here as a boy. He tells a story about driving down a dirt road one day with his uncle. They came across a flock of sage grouse crossing the road. His uncle told him to grab the shotgun behind the seat and shoot one for supper. Billy reached around, got the gun, and aimed it out the window. Then he waited. "Well, what are you waiting for?" his uncle finally asked. "I'm waiting for them to fly," Billy said, thinking that was the sporting thing to do. He'd read the sporting magazines, too. "Billy, we can watch them fly *after* you shoot one," his uncle explained. "Tonight I want to eat sage chicken for supper."

There are actually two other fellows in town who shoot shotguns: my friend Don Reed, who runs the general store, and another rancher named Marvin Labatt, who owns a nice-looking English setter. Actually, Marvin found the dog in a campground in the national forest, either a runaway or abandoned by its owners, and though he advertised in the newspaper, no one ever claimed it. So I loaned him a couple of my dog training books and he set out to make the dog into a bird dog. For the most part, people up here still lead a kind of close-to-the-bone existence and there is no question of going out and buying a fancy thousand-dollar finished bird dog, or even a hundred-dollar unstarted bird dog for that matter.

Let me say right off that I believe in training your own dog, rather than buying a finished dog or sending it off to a professional trainer. It's hard work but fun—for you and the dog (though there are people with temperaments clearly unsuited to dog training, in which case it's no fun for anyone). So one day early that same summer I went down to the local general store to ask my friend Don if he was a competent wing shot. I had acquired a couple of pheasants from a game bird farm, and I wanted to shoot them over Sweetzer in order to teach her steadiness to wing and shot. I intended to eat the pheasants, too. Both Billy and Marvin were busy with irrigating and other spring ranch work and I needed a gunner while I handled the dog.

For those readers unfamiliar with the vocabulary, steadiness to wing and shot simply means that when the bird flushes and you shoot, the dog is to stop, sit, and wait until you send it for the retrieve rather than chase wildly after the bird. This is important partly as a matter of safety and also because the dog is better able to mark the location of fallen birds for the retrieve from a stationary position than when running. And the better able your dog is to mark and find dead and crippled birds, the fewer will be lost in the field.

Reed and his wife, Sandy, run the general store, which is the only business in town. Besides being one of those consummate jack-of-all-trades so important to the life of a small town, Don serves another invaluable function as the local skunk buster. The skunks get underneath the houses, many of which have no foundations. At night they tend to quarrel amongst themselves and squirt each other. Many times I've woken up in the middle of the night with my eyes watering from the skunk juice wafting up through the floorboards. That's when I call Don, who, when he can't shoot them, traps them.

"Don's an excellent shot," Sandy interjected proudly on the day I went over. "I bet he's killed fifty skunks around town so far this year."

"Yeah, but do you shoot them on the wing?" I asked skeptically.

"On the wing?" Don asked.

"Yeah, you know, are they flying or do you ground-sluice them?"

"Oh," he said, nodding. "On the wing. Definitely. Wouldn't be sporting to shoot them on the ground, would it?"

So that evening Don and I met up on the sage flat above town next to the cemetery for our controlled pheasant shoot. I rigged up my release cage with the pheasant inside, positioned Don, and put Sweetzer on the check cord. Reed wanted to shoot three-inch magnum shells in his 20-gauge Winchester automatic, his gun and load of choice to bring down flying skunks, but I insisted that he use light field-load shells which I provided. I wanted to eat that pheasant, not have it blown to bits. Don seemed a little nervous to me. I explained that the pheasant was likely to be a bit faster off the ground than your average skunk, and I tried to calm him by telling him that it was no big deal if he missed. Still, he knew that the pheasant had cost me five dollars, and that it would be a wasteful thing if he were to miss, like letting a package of perfectly good "pick of the chick" go bad in the refrigerator. This kind of conscientious thrift still exists in the heartland.

"Just take your time and say 'Pull' when you're ready," I told Don.

"Okay. . . ." He settled himself. "Pull!" I pulled the cord attached to the lid of the cage, the pheasant saw daylight and rocketed out the top. Just as I had hoped—a perfect release, offering Don a perfect crossing shot. He swung on the bird. I had been worried that he might be overanxious and fire too quickly, not letting the pheasant get out far enough and thus damaging the meat with too much shot, but Don kept his cool and let the bird get out a bit, and then he let it get out a bit farther, and I began to think that he'd better shoot now, that pheasant was really gaining airspeed, and soon it would be out of range all together. "Ah, Don . . . ," I said.

"Oh, shit!" he hollered suddenly, "shit, my goddamn gun misfired!" Sweetzer seemed to have a certain puzzled look on her face as the pheasant sailed, unmolested, over the ridge, heading for the dense willows of the creek bottom below. "That's never happened before," Don moaned, flustered and embarrassed. "I've shot hundreds of skunks, and this gun has never misfired!"

I wondered if maybe in the heat of the moment, Don hadn't had a small attack of what is known as "buck fever" and possibly forgotten to take his safety off. I've done it myself, pulling helplessly against an unyielding trigger as the birds dispersed in the air. But I would never suggest such a thing to Don. If he says his gun misfired, then it misfired.

Still, he was terribly upset about it, and apologetic, and later that evening he called me at home and asked if he could have a second chance, could we try again tomorrow with my other pheasant? It wouldn't happen again, he assured me. He had taken his shotgun apart, cleaned and oiled all the moving parts, and it was now working perfectly. Having just watched one five-dollar bill fly over the ridge, I admit I was reluctant to risk the other one so soon, and I stalled Don, told him that I wanted to get ahold of some pigeons for us to practice on before we tried the second pheasant. "Okay," he agreed reluctantly, "but I want another chance."

The next day I took my pigeon trap and set it up in the warehouse of a feed store in the county seat, a town called Thoreau (no relation to Henry David), twenty-two miles up the road from Ayn. They had some pigeons hanging around eating their spilled grain and generally making a mess, as pigeons do, and they were delighted to have me trap them.

I had the trap down there for several days but for some reason I caught only one pigeon. It was hardly worth a forty-four-mile round-trip drive for just one pigeon, but the girl who called me from the feed store said I'd better get over there because it was the "weirdest-looking pigeon you ever saw."

I went to pick it up and, yes, it was easily the weirdest-looking pigeon I'd ever seen. It appeared to be some sort of show pigeon, a foppish-looking thing with mottled reddish brown and white plumage and a lavish crown on its head. But the most extraordinary thing about it was that it had fully feathered feet, like little white booties. It looked kind of like Nancy Sinatra in the old days of go-go. When I brought the pigeon home, my wife took one look at it and said, "Jim Fergus, you are not going to shoot that pigeon, are you?" She had already expressed her disapproval of our abortive pheasant shoot and made no bones about the fact that she was delighted the bird escaped unharmed.

"It's all for a good cause," I explained. " 'Conserve wild game. Use a trained dog.' "

I called Don and that afternoon we met back up at the cemetery. He had a determined, no-nonsense look on his face. I had Sweetzer and the feather-footed pigeon with me.

"That's the weirdest-looking pigeon, I've ever seen," Reed marveled.

"I know, that's what everyone says."

We set up. Don called Pull. I flipped the lid but, unlike the pheasant, the pigeon didn't fly out of the trap. It looked calmly at the open door and then hopped up and sat on the top.

"Don't shoot!" I said. "I'll take the dog in and flush it. Then it'll have to fly." I walked in with Sweetzer on the check cord—this would be good practice for her—but the pigeon just sort of hopped off the cage and flapped over to land on the hood of Don's truck. "Don't shoot!" I repeated, afraid that Don would be overanxious.

"Don't worry, Jim," Reed said, calmly, "I'm not going to shoot my truck."

"I don't think we're going to be able to shoot this pigeon." I went over to the truck and picked the pigeon off the hood. He was so tame he hardly resisted. "The dog's not getting much training out of this at all," I said.

"Throw the son of a bitch up in the air, then he'll *have* to fly," Don suggested. He really wanted to shoot that pigeon to redeem himself, and I really wanted to have a bird shot over Sweetz. She was beginning to wonder what the purpose of these trips to the cemetery was. Now I'm not proud about this part, but I'm going to tell it anyway. I held the pigeon in both hands, put him between my legs, and catapulted him in the air for all I was worth. Still the pigeon was not having any part of this and he kind of fluttered back down to about five feet off the ground and flew a clumsy circle around us. He wasn't a very strong flyer. "Don't shoot!" I hollered again, as Sweetzer and I hit the deck. My concern was unfounded, for Don is not careless with firearms. We watched the pigeon fly around us and then he landed back on the hood of Don's truck.

"Must be a homing pigeon," Reed remarked.

"This pigeon shoot is over," I announced, gathering up my bird.

"Guess we'll have to shoot that other pheasant," Don said hopefully.

"I'll call you."

When I got home, my wife was on the couch reading a magazine. "If you shot that poor pigeon I'm not talking to you."

"Then I guess I'm in luck."

That evening I made a few phone calls trying to track down the owner of the strange pigeon, so I could give it back. I learned that there was only one old man in the entire county who kept pigeons and he lived in a town thirty-five miles away. He was known locally as—what else—"Pigeon Man" and evidently he had several hundred of them, each of whom he knew individually and by name. I phoned Pigeon Man and described the feather-footed pigeon. There was a long pause on the end of the line before the old man spoke in a soft, reverent voice. "No," he said, "that ain't one of my birds, but I sure would give about anything to have a pigeon like that. I never seen one with feathers on its feet."

Imagine my wife's amusement the next morning as I drove off to deliver the pigeon to Pigeon Man's house. But before I left, I put a little harness on the pigeon, planted it in the bushes, and let Sweetzer find and retrieve it a couple of times. So far our training sessions with live birds had been a complete bust and I was desperate to show her some action. She has a very soft mouth and the pigeon didn't seem to mind having her carry him around. In fact, he was so relaxed about it that I think maybe he enjoyed it. I'll be honest, I was glad we hadn't shot that pigeon. I named him Rocko, to compensate for his effeminate, feather-footed appearance. Sweetzer and her new friend, Rocko. Seemed like a nice balance. I almost didn't want to give him up.

Pigeon Man lived in a broken-down old trailer house in the flats outside a town with the inelegant name of Cowpy. His place was easy to find, due to all the pigeons soaring above it or sitting on the roofs of a motley collection of outbuildings in various stages of collapse. He was a tall, cadaverous eighty-four-year-old, with a long chicken neck, rheumy eyes, and a vicious wet cough. His skin had the ashen gray, oxygen-deprivation pallor of the lifelong smoker. He led me inside the trailer which had a variety of wooden lean-to additions tacked on; they looked somewhat like a litter of mongrel puppies hanging on their mother's teats.

Mrs. Pigeon Man was sitting at the kitchen table, smoking an extralong cigarette and watching a game show on TV. She was emaciated, too, wiry and just as tough looking as old shoe leather, her face wizened with a network of deeply etched lines. She was wearing a housedress and she sat with her legs sticking straight out. She had a pair of worn Indian moccasins on her feet, the kind with the laces stitched around the top, and the big toenail on each foot protruded through holes in the leather. They looked like small, dangerous stilettos, astonishingly long and pearly. Suddenly I was overcome with the bizarre notion that she was going to leap up from the table and perform a series of high-kick karate moves, slicing my face to ribbons with those toenails. "You come for pigeons?" she asked. And before I could answer, unable to take my eyes off her toenails, she said, "You can take every goddamn one of the filthy things. I hate 'em." She took a long disgusted pull on her cigarette and went back to her game show.

We sat down at the table and Pigeon Man expertly rolled himself a smoke out of a pouch of Bugler tobacco. He held the cigarette up between long, skeletal, weirdly translucent fingers, and regarded it thoughtfully: "Waaall," he said, slowly, "they ain't killed me yet, but I'm gonna give 'em one more chance." Then he popped the cigarette in his mouth and lit it. The air in the trailer was already dense with smoke. An ex-smoker myself, I figured that five minutes in here was equivalent to a pack-a-day habit, and I was anxious to get back outside to conduct our pigeon business. However, in the country there is an obligatory enforced "visiting" period, during which you are required to sit around the kitchen table like this, visiting. "This fella brought the pigeon with the feathers on his feet," said Pigeon Man to his wife, but she ignored him, her attention riveted to the television set. "I ain't seen it yet. I thought we'd visit for a bit first."

I didn't get the feeling that Mr. and Mrs. Pigeon Man received many visitors and, given his wife's dour nature, I think that he was a lonely old man. He was a sociable fellow, as talkative as she was silent, and now that he had a captive audience he wasn't about to give me up too quickly. Like many country eccentrics, Pigeon Man shared a deep hatred of the government and after he had vented his ire at local, state, and federal officials alike, he asked me what I did for a living. When I told him, he wanted to know how much money I earned at it. He clearly distrusted anyone who made a lot of money. I gave him a modest ballpark sum representing my average yearly income, and he seemed quite pleased. I had passed the test. Finally, I suggested that we go have a look at my pigeon. At no time during our visit did I take my eye off those toenails.

"What would you take for that pigeon?" Pigeon Man asked, trying to appear only casually interested, like a canny horse trader. In truth, he was clearly having difficulty containing his excitement. This was certainly the fanciest pigeon he'd ever laid eyes on.

"I need some pigeons to train my dog," I explained. "Just regular old pigeons that don't have feathers on their feet and that are strong flyers."

"Oh, hell, I got plenty like that!" he said. "I'd trade you a dozen of my pigeons for that one there."

"Done."

Now I was in the pigeon business and I went home and built a coop for my new birds. My wife watched quizzically through the kitchen window as I worked on it. Later she accompanied me up to the store where I went to organize yet another pigeon shoot with Reed. She had stopped worrying about the pigeons. I guess they seemed safe enough in our hands. Indeed, before we were through, Don and I would populate Ayn with pigeons escaped from our shoots. By the end of the summer they were roosting on roofs all over town. People were beginning to complain. Somehow my wife seemed able to anticipate all this. "Who are you going to get to shoot the pigeons for you?" she asked me that day as we were walking to the store.

"Why, Don, of course, that's why we're going to the store. And I might shoot a few of them myself, once I get Sweetzer lined out," I added.

"Yeah, right, but who are you going to get to actually *shoot* the pigeons?" Then she just laughed.

SEPTEMBER

Wyoming

Colorado

Idaho

Montana

2

OPENING DAY

Hunting with a dog and a gun is delightful in itself, but let us suppose you were not born a hunter, but are fond of nature and freedom all the same; you cannot then help envying us hunters. . . . Listen.

Ivan Turgenev

I hunted opening day of sage grouse season in Wyoming, blue grouse season in Colorado, and chukar season in Idaho. I shot the sage hen on the high windy plains near Saratoga, Wyoming, on the first day of September; its crop was full of this fall's harvest of fresh alfalfa, studded with tender young sage buds. The aroma was indescribable and suggests a possible recipe. I killed the blue grouse on the eighth day of the month in an aspen grove atop a mountain from where I could see the speck of my cabin below in the valley of Ayn. The bird had a crop packed with tart, scarlet vaccinium berries, which grow low to the ground above timberline; its breast meat was stained red by the fruit. The chukar I shot on the steep rocky slope of a narrow canyon outside Picabo, Idaho, on the fifteenth, its crop full of pungent wild watercress leaves that grew in a small spring flowing at the base.

I ate each of these first three birds of the season, simply seasoned, roasted in a very hot oven, slightly pink at the bone (and in the case of the sage grouse, rare). Eating them brought back the country where they lived and the particular day afield, and the intense bittersweet feelings of the exact moment when each died at the end of my gun.

I see no reason to apologize for being a hunter, particularly in this age. What comparable sweetness, mystery, and wonder can be found in the Styrofoam-dished, Saran-wrapped, boneless, skinless chicken breasts at the meat counter of the supermarket? As modern consumers we tend to think of this bloodless product as something manufactured, not a flesh-and-blood creature once actually alive. The hunter cleans the birds he kills, tears them open gently at the anus and reaches in with his fingers to pull out still warm intestines, the liver, and the heart. Later, even after washing, he can still smell the pungent scent of entrails on his hands. This terrible intimacy of killing, drawing, and eating anchors him to a real earth, a place he can believe in.

September 1, Saratoga, Wyoming: On the opening day of this long season, it seems appropriate to be hunting with my old childhood pal Higgy. We grew up together in the Midwest and lost touch for many years until we accidentally ran into each other at the airport in Denver a few years ago. We repaired to the airport lounge and ordered martinis (the last time we had seen each other we drank cherry Cokes at the drugstore soda fountain), our friendship instantly renewing itself as if only a few days, and not more than a quarter century, had passed. We share the bonds of checkered childhoods, early deceased parents, and a fondness for gin. My wife refers to us collectively as "the boyz from Illinoiz."

As kids, Higgy and I, ceremonial blood brothers, roamed the wild dark country of the local suburban ravines; armed with slingshots or bows and arrows, we pretended to be intrepid explorer/hunters in the Amazon jungle. Sometimes, as proof of our courage, we played an incredibly dangerous game of "chicken" in the backyard. We shot arrows straight up in the air and then ran under them to see how close we could be standing to where they landed. Once I judged one a hair too well and it clipped the beak of my baseball cap, pierced it, and pinned it to the ground right between my legs. We both looked down at my impaled cap, and then we looked at each other and it occurred to both of us at the same instant, and I think for the very first time in our young lives, that one day we were going to die. We never played that game again, though sometimes I think Higgy is still running under the arrow.

Higgy is a large, gregarious man, never married, who lives by his wits, an incredibly complicated and frequently mysterious existence. An entrepreneurial juggler of schemes, he lives the kind of teetering, house-of-cards life (personal and financial) that threatens to collapse at any moment, and, in fact, periodically does collapse of its own sheer density, at which point Higgy vanishes, sometimes for months at a time. Neither irate girlfriends, at whose houses he has been living for months or sometimes years, or creditors (and sometimes these are one and the same) can find him during these disappearances. I don't mean to suggest that Higgy is some kind of sleazy con man, for there is never anything precisely illegal about his activities. His is simply a world in which misunderstanding and confusion bloom like fungus in the sunless, murky corners of his cluttered affairs. Often it isn't even his fault, as if he's merely the innocent host vehicle for the spore.

After these hiatuses, Higgy eventually returns to construct a brand-new life, more unworkable, more complicated, and more precarious than the last. Once a couple of years ago in the middle of one of these vanishing acts, I got a strange report that Higgy had been spotted in a nightclub in Costa Rica where he was helping the prostitutes organize a union. I never doubted the story for a minute. A few weeks later, I got a confirmed Higgy sighting from a woman newspaper reporter friend who had actually met him in Nicaragua; Higgy happened to turn up and introduce himself just in time for the reporter, several other Americans, and Higgy to be pinned down in the midst of a street gun battle between the Contras and the Sandanistas (Higgy is a magnet to such situations). They all thought they were going to die, but Higgy, the only one fluent in Spanish, distinguished himself, displaying great grace under pressure and rescuing them all. Rumors persist that Higgy works for the CIA, but these I discount.

Higgy is also an extraordinarily fine shot; he and his brother used to be skeet hustlers as kids, the way that some urban kids become pool hustlers. Their father would take them down to a local skeet range and challenge the rich guys to a round, and like pool hustlers they learned when to lay back and miss a few and when to come on and shoot twenty-five straight.

I know that you're not supposed to mix alcohol and firearms, but the evening before, I had witnessed Higgy dust a dozen micro-skeet (about the size of a silver dollar) in a row off my deck after two martinis, shooting a .410 shotgun that he'd never picked up before. Ordinarily I wouldn't allow such a thing, but Higgy had recently recovered from open-heart surgery ("They laid me open like a gutted deer," he reported sadly), which took some wind out of his sails, and he was anxious to prove that he could still shoot.

Our other companions this opening day are the rancher on whose property we are hunting and one of his hired men. Both are former urbanites who recently threw in the towel against city living to move to Saratoga. The rancher, Dave, a tall, lanky man, was a successful contractor in Boulder, Colorado, where he built large stylish homes for young professional people. "Grew weary of the yuppy lifestyle," he says simply of his decision one day to pack his family off to a working cattle ranch here. The hired man, with the unlikely spaghetti-western name of Giorgio, is the son of an Italian diplomat, just graduated from Yale, where he studied the classics. Giorgio had disdained the "get-ahead" ambitions of his college peers to come to Wyoming to work for a year, hard work from dawn to dusk for ranch hand wages, which on average are well below the starting pay scale at any fast-food chain in America. He lives alone in a tiny shack separate from the bunkhouse, abhors television, and carries around a dog-eared copy of Rimbaud's poetry in his back pocket to read when things get slow. He is a bright, friendly, open, cheerful, talkative young man whose dark Latin looks seem a bit out of place on the spare plains of southern Wyoming.

Although you might not guess it from his white-toothed, good-natured smile, Giorgio is a little down in the dumps this morning. Evidently his American girlfriend from New Haven has just broken up with him over the telephone; expressing disappointment with his current career choice, she thinks he isn't "going anywhere." Actually, Giorgio explains with wide-eyed enthusiasm, he is pursuing avid interests in photography and cooking and has a specific plan for this part of his life, which he calls "creative drifting." "After my year here is over?" he tells us in the distinctive way he has of ending nearly every sentence with a question mark, "and I've saved up enough money? I plan to buy a round-the-country bus ticket and see the rest of the United States?" We all like Giorgio and suspect that his girlfriend is wrong about him.

As it happens, only Higgy and I out of the group have any actual bird hunting experience. Dave, our host, is still fresh from the city, and though he's been telling me all summer about the huge flocks of sage grouse that he sees in his alfalfa fields every morning, he has never hunted them before. Our most immediate problem is a shortage of shotguns and Dave suggests that we stop by a neighboring rancher's place to borrow one for Giorgio. The neighbor is an old reprobate with a local reputation as a hard drinker who has gradually run his place into the ground over the years. We can see it as we drive in—the broken-down fences and the last cutting of hay, which has been mowed but left to rot in the fields. The ranch house and outbuildings are in a similar state of decline, and the rancher, who comes to the door to meet us, doesn't look so hot himself this Saturday morning.

Noticing a skinny yellow Lab bitch with a litter of young puppies underneath his front porch, I bend down to look at them. "She dropped a dozen pups," says the rancher, "but I drowned four of 'em when they was a day old. I figured she didn't have enough tits to go around, so I threw the extras in the river." He chuckles deeply. "Son of a bitch, if one of them pups don't try to swim for shore! Oh, hell, that was a sight, I'll tell you—his goddamn eyes weren't even open yet!" It breaks my heart to think about that day-old puppy with such a strong instinct for survival, an instinct already as a water dog, trying to swim for his life while the current of the river swept him away. I'd like to have had that dog.

The rancher disappears into the house and returns a moment later with an ancient, single-shot 12-gauge hammer gun with a beat-up stock. Higgy checks it out and pronounces it sound, and we give Giorgio a short, abbreviated hunter's safety course. Under most circumstances, I avoid going into the field with people I don't know who have never handled a shotgun before, but I make an exception in Giorgio's case. He seems a smart, sensible lad and pays close attention, listening carefully to our instruction and nodding politely, smiling all the while. We, too, will watch him carefully. Seasoned outfitters and bird hunting guides who deal regularly with inexperienced shooters will tell you that the best place to be is right at their elbow, where you can keep an eye on them.

And so we set out on this cool Wyoming morning, the sun just clearing the mountains in the distance. It promises to be a lovely day, the last bit of summer hanging on in the thin, clean air.

I have Sweetzer with me, quartering ahead, and we all fan out and walk at a leisurely pace across the sage plains, bordering the irrigated fields. The alfalfa, about to be cut for the final crop of the season, is heavy and bent with morning dew which intensifies its deep green color.

Someone must have tipped off the sage grouse that the season is open because the first flock we see—twenty-five birds or so—flushes wild on the edge of the alfalfa field far out of range. Perhaps a coyote, hunting for his breakfast, has put them up. Giorgio raises his eyebrows in astonishment. "I've been irrigating this field all summer," he says, "and I've had to practically kick these birds out of my way? Sometimes I'll be walking along in the alfalfa and all of a sudden they fly up at my feet? They scare the hell out of me!"

As the largest bird in the grouse family, sometimes running to five pounds or better, sage grouse are often disdained by sportsmen for being rather ponderous off the ground once they do decide to fly. In my opinion the species gets a bum rap, both as sporting game and table fare. Especially after they have been shot at, they can be a wary bird, hard to approach, and though they may be a tad slow on liftoff, they're strong flyers once they gain airspeed and are capable of flying long distances. Because of their propensity to fly farther, and more often, than most other species of upland game bird, sage grouse also have larger heart muscles and denser, redder meat.

While he isn't saying so, I have a suspicion that Higgy, who has never hunted them before, is expecting the ungainly sage grouse to present an easy target. Indeed, it stands to reason that if you can't miss a micro-clay pigeon roughly the size of a child's tea saucer, launched from a spring-loaded contraption that wings them out to forty yards in a matter of milliseconds, you surely won't miss a bird the size of a plump roasting chicken that lumbers up directly in front of you like a troop transport helicopter.

Even I, middling shooter on my best days, am feeling a bit cocky about my gunning skills as matched up against *Mr. Sage Grouse*, as they used to say in the old sporting magazines of my youth. Haven't I been practicing all summer, powdering skeet up at Cantrell's dump, the winner of our final shoot of the summer, breaking five straight from the "hole" and edging Billy out by one target? Yes, the proud champion of the Ayn Gun Club!

Later in my trip, after I have shot abysmally at least once in every region of the country, humiliating myself in front of some of the great wing shots in America, it will be difficult for me to recall the sense of confidence I feel on opening day. Later, compared to the Hungarian Partridge of Montana, exploding from the ground like so many cherry bombs, or the solitary ghostly ruffed grouse flushing wild in the dense timber of the Minnesota northwoods, or the bobwhite quail in Georgia—like a dozen whirling egg-beaters—or the darting, shrieking tangents described by the snipe on the delta of Mobile Bay, or the incredible accelerating rising flight of the Mearns' quail (which, in fact, put one in mind of micro-skeet) in the high desert mountains of Arizona—compared to these birds, the sage grouse will seem in memory as big as a condor.

We mark the covey down in a creek bottom against the bluff some distance away and have to cross several fences to get there. "Unload your gun, Giorgio," Higgy instructs our neophyte shooter. "Oh?" says Giorgio in that open, inquisitive way of his. "For safety reasons," explains Higgy. "Never cross a fence with a loaded gun, in case you were to trip or get hung up."

"Ah!" Giorgio says, nodding and smiling pleasantly.

"And never shoot skeet after two martinis," I caution.

"At least not for money," adds Higgy.

We walk up on the birds. They're not exactly where we expect them to be, but close enough. A thousand covey rises later, I think I will never be ready for this moment, even when—especially when—I know it's coming. Later, I will remember it all as if it were in slow motion—a decidedly mixed blessing, this ability to recall the specific flight of each flushed bird in each covey rise, a catalogue of thousands. Every now and then, I hear the unsettling whir of wings as one flies through my mind at unexpected times. When I am too old to hunt, I will simply play these scenes back like a built-in video library. I have an elderly French grandmother in the final throes of senile dementia who has lost the ability to speak or to recognize anyone, but who is far from brain dead. She lives now in some inaccessible back room of her unconscious mind where at night in her sleep she chatters away fluently in two languages and laughs gaily like a young girl, evidently reliving the high points of her life. Faced with such a fate, the hunter might hope to watch the flight of game birds, thousands of them, millions. And hopefully even make a few good shots in the process.

A volley of gunfire in response to the first covey rise of the season: Higgy, fastest on the draw, shoots first as the birds get up out of the tall grass on the edge of the creek; both barrels in rapid succession, the same way he shoots a double on skeet—*boom-boom*. I'm a split second behind him, slower and more deliberate. *Boom. Boom.* No flight of any individual bird is interrupted; not so much as a feather floats in the air. The enormous, lumbering sage grouse have leveled off and begun to gain airspeed by the time Dave, the rancher, futilely fires his two barrels. *Boom. . . . Boom.* And even the stragglers are altogether out of range by the time Giorgio pulls the trigger of his borrowed antique single-shot; presumably he is politely waiting to see how we experts do it first. Giorgio has impeccable manners. *Boom?* his shot comes as an afterthought, timid and questioning. Better than fifty yards in the distance, a sage grouse plummets from the sky, stone dead. We all look in wonder at Giorgio. "I did a little shooting in Italy when I was a boy?" he admits with a sly smile.

"I have to go now," announces Higgy suddenly. "Great shot, Giorgio!"

"What do you mean, Higgy?" I ask. "We just got started." I wonder if maybe Higgy's heart is bothering him, or perhaps he's just embarrassed by his double whiff and has decided to quit, though I know he isn't a bad sport.

"I have a bit of a tax problem," he says.

"A tax problem? What the hell are you talking about, Higgy? It's Saturday. It's opening day. We're hunting. What kind of a tax problem?" It is then that I notice the car bouncing slowly down the rutted dirt road against the foothills, a clumsy late-model sedan entirely inappropriate to the landscape, in the same way that a rancher's pickup truck would seem out of place in Manhattan. There appear to be two men in the car.

"It's kind of complicated," Higgy says.

"What kind of a tax problem?"

"The tax boys want to ask me a few questions."

"*The tax boys?* Jesus, Higgy. Why don't you refer them to your accountant?"

"My accountant's in jail."

"Of course he is."

"I'll be in touch," promises Higgy, hurrying off. He moves rather spryly for a large fellow with a recently rerouted heart. "I want you to meet the woman I'm dating," he calls back over his shoulder. "You'll really like her. She's twenty-three years old! I'd like to bring her up to your place some night for dinner."

"That'll be fine, Higgy," I say. We watch him disappear over the nearest hill, jogging briskly. By the time the car reaches us, Higgy is well out of sight.

The vehicle comes to a halt and the man in the passenger seat rolls down his tinted automatic window. Both men wear suits and sunglasses. "Which of you gentlemen is Jack Higginbotham?" he asks in an official tone, and not a very polite one.

"None of us," says our host Dave, squinting laconically at the men. "And we have identification to prove it." He smiles pleasantly and looks out across his fields. "Furthermore," he adds, "we're armed, you're trespassing, and this is opening day in Wyoming."

We haven't seen or heard from Higgy since that opening day, but various rumors about his purported whereabouts have filtered back through mutual acquaintances. Someone said he was running an antipoaching squad for the Kenyan government, tracking down and executing elephant poachers, but we haven't been able to confirm it. Someone else suggested that he was serving a short prison sentence on a tax rap, but no one really believes that. Then we heard he had had another heart attack. I'm not worried; I figure he'll turn up one of these days.

As to the rest of that opening day, Giorgio made two more spectacular shots before limiting out well before lunch. I didn't shoot anything until Dave and I were on the way home late in the afternoon, crossing the last alfalfa field of the day, as an enormous reddening sun dropped down into the North Platte River basin below; Sweetzer flushed two single birds, one after the other, and I killed them both, in what is sometimes called a delayed double. I don't shoot that many doubles, delayed or otherwise, so I remember it quite well. Sweetz had a terrible time deciding which bird to retrieve first, and kept running back and forth between them, picking one up in her mouth and then changing her mind and dropping it to run over to the other. She was still pretty green.

But what I remember best about that day happened just a bit later. After shooting the two sage grouse, I didn't reload my shotgun. Two birds were all I needed. Three's the limit these days, as sage grouse populations are depressed in Wyoming and elsewhere in the West. But Sweetzer got on a strong scent, and though I had worked with her all summer on this, she started running out ahead of me across the alfalfa field and would not stop on the single blast of the whistle as she had been taught. I blew and I blew. The sage grouse must have been running on the ground in front of her, and at the edge of the field, she busted them. They got up all at once, a huge flock, close to a hundred birds silhouetted against the brilliant red sun. And

Sweetzer, drunk with bird scent and disobedience and puppy exuberance, leapt straight up in the air after them, as if trying to fly herself.

That's what I remember best about the first day of that long season. The birds and the sun and Sweetzer in the air.

Many hunters flatly declare sage grouse to be inferior table fare, some say nearly inedible—dark meated, dry, tough, and redolent of the flavor of old sagebrush. It is true that a big old rooster can be a bit gamy and stringy, and, as in the case of domestic chickens, younger birds are always more tender. I didn't say I could do it, but a competent gunner can often pick the smaller, first-year birds out of the covey rise and avoid shooting the old bombers. At the same time, sage grouse living in an area where diet comprises both alfalfa and sage buds, rather than solely the latter, tend to have a softer, more delicate flavor. Some hunters claim that if the bird's crop is removed immediately upon shooting, the meat will be less likely to be tainted by the sour taste of sagebrush; it can't hurt. As with any game bird, the major cause of toughness is overcooking. Though some people simply don't like red-meated birds, for my money, sage grouse, properly prepared (that is, rare to medium rare) is superb. The following recipe was devised by our crack Italian shooter, who cooked the birds for us that same night.

GRILLED SAGE GROUSE À LA GIORGIO

Pluck and draw birds. Make a simple baste of olive oil, soy, lemon juice, a dash of Worcestershire, a splash of Tabasco, 6–8 cloves of minced garlic, ground black pepper, a sprinkle of red pepper flakes, a bunch of fresh cilantro. Prepare a bed of hot coals—charcoal or wood. Baste frequently while grilling (back side to the fire first) until browned all over—depending on the heat of the coals and the size of the birds, about 10–12 minutes to the side, maybe less. Flesh should be rare and will taste almost like beef, only considerably more interesting. Better to undercook than overcook; if the flesh comes out gray, you've ruined it.

3

OPENING DAY
II AND III

That wildlife is merely something to shoot at or to look at is the grossest of fallacies. It often represents the difference between rich country and mere land.

Aldo Leopold

I hunted alone on opening day of blue grouse season in Colorado. Except for the fact that I have a poor sense of direction and am forever getting lost, I enjoy solitary hunting. I can move at my own pace, the dog works better without the distraction of other dogs, and I generally shoot better when there are no witnesses.

Ordinarily I avoid hunting public land on opening day, a day sometimes sneeringly referred to by serious bird hunters as "amateur hour" due to the fact that every once-a-season hunter in the state always chooses that particular day to go out. A couple of years ago, I hunted a state lease in eastern Colorado on the first day of quail season. There were so many hunters afield that I ran screaming from the field after only fifteen minutes; might as well go to the mall.

But not many people hunt blue grouse in Colorado, which is fine by me. An alpine species of which there are eight subspecies, blue grouse are considered by many bird hunters to be too "dumb" to provide sporting shooting. They got this reputation from their habit of roosting in pine trees out of which they are often reluctant to fly, even if the hunter is standing right beneath them, trying to holler them into the air. As all game birds have brains roughly the size of baby peas, I've always felt that such terms as "dumb" or "wily" are inapplicable, and that the hunter who spends too much time trying to "outwit" them is on thin ice intellectually. The fact is,

28

blue grouse tend to be so tame simply because they are hunted less intensively than most other species. A wildlife biologist for the state of Colorado told me that if blue grouse were pursued as relentlessly as their cousin, the legendary ruffed grouse of the forest, mythologized in Eastern sporting literature as almost supernaturally wild and wily, they would be every bit as challenging to hunt. And ruffed grouse in northern Canada, where there is far less hunting pressure, are reportedly just as "dumb" as blue grouse in Colorado. All of this is by way of saying that when you chase wild animals around and shoot at them, they learn eventually to avoid you. So I prefer the word "naive" to describe the blue grouse. I probably shouldn't admit to this, but when I was a boy I went to a ranch in Wyoming one summer and we killed them with rocks and roasted them over an open fire. That was my introduction to the species, and I've liked them ever since, and I don't care how they would score on the SATs.

So Sweetz and I were wandering around at timberline in Colorado looking for blue grouse. It was a gorgeous September day, clear and mild under a cloudless sky. From the top of the pass, through my binoculars I could just make out the tiny speck of my cabin below on the valley floor. I tend toward acrophobia at timberline; it gives me a lonesome, arctic, top-of-the-world feeling that makes me long for sea level.

Because it seemed that we were so alone up here, I was surprised when we dropped over the backside of the pass and walked right into another hunter's camp set in a stand of stunted, twisted lodgepole pines, eking out a marginal living in the transition zone. A fellow was sitting in an aluminum lawn chair, drinking a soda. He was dressed head to toe in camouflage, his face covered with camo greasepaint, which lent him a certain menacing quasi-military appearance. Sweetzer, who is a timid dog, terrified even of certain varieties of fruit (particularly cantaloupe, which she seems to think are small round aliens), was startled by the man and began howling at him, her hackles up, her front legs planted stiffly. All across the country, I would be apologizing for this goofy behavior of hers.

I was actually happy to run into someone up here because I was looking for a road I'd seen on the topographic map that would take me down into a creek bottom where I thought I might find some birds. I introduced myself to the man and he invited me into his camp for a soda. I had forgotten that bow hunting season for deer and elk had opened, which was what he was doing up here. I think he was glad for some company, because his partner had gone off for a couple of days to hunt another nearby mountain. They had been in the area for almost a week, and hadn't yet seen an elk or deer. I was disappointed to learn that they hadn't seen any blue grouse either—although if you're not looking up in the trees it's quite possible to walk by right under them.

I sat down and we exchanged introductions. His name was Newell and he was a hog farmer from Iowa. I don't know any hog farmers and he didn't know any writers, so we were pleased to meet each other. He wanted to know if I'd ever done any writing for the sporting magazine *Outdoor Life*, one of my favorite publications when I was a boy. Back then I used to dream of being an *Outdoor Life* writer, but now I had to admit that I had not done so. It was pretty obvious that this was Newell's favorite magazine and he seemed disappointed, but he brightened somewhat when I told him that I knew some other guys who had written for them. I pulled my map out of my game bag and asked him about the road down to the creek bottom. He smiled. The irony of the fact that I needed to ask directions in my own backyard of a hog farmer from Iowa was not lost on either of us.

Just then Newell's hunting partner, Bob, came back into camp. He, too, was dressed all in camo, his face painted a ghoulish army green. Bob's arrival started Sweetzer on another hysterical barking jag. It's embarrassing when your dog barks at people in their camp. In Wyoming, she had held a terrified elderly ranchwoman prisoner on her doorstep, which had given my friend Higgy the opportunity to remark, "That's really a good watchdog you have there. Not only won't she allow people to come in the house, but she won't let people *out* of their houses."

Bob hadn't seen any elk during his two-day hunt on the far mountain and it was clear that the bow hunters were getting a little discouraged.

Bob was also a hog farmer, and he was one of the friendliest fellows I have ever met; he chuckled and nodded amiably at everything that was said, even if it wasn't in the least bit amusing.

"Jim here's a writer," Newell told Bob.

Bob chuckled and nodded. "Have you ever written anything in *Outdoor Life*?" he asked.

"No, I'm afraid not," I said. Bob just chuckled and nodded.

We all sat around the camp drinking cream sodas, strange discount midwestern brands I'd never heard of. Newell did most of the talking and Bob chuckled and nodded. Newell told me he earned about twenty thousand dollars a year as a hog farmer and that he had a daughter in college. He got financial aid through the Farm Bureau to help pay for her education. As a young man he had wanted to go to college to become a wildlife biologist but when he had asked his father, who was also a hog farmer, about it, his father said: "There's the door, Newell. If you want to go to college you're on your own and you'll have to figure out for yourself how to pay for it. But if you stay here and help me out on the place you'll always have a roof over your head." It wasn't much of a choice. You could tell Newell had never forgiven his father for preventing him from becoming a wildlife biologist, and he was pleased that his daughter was in college because he didn't want her to have to become a hog farmer. It was a hard living, and hardly suitable work for a woman. Even though he earned only twenty thousand, which was less than some lawyers I hunted with later in my trip spent on dry cleaning in an average year, and though he had a daughter in college, he still managed to take this ten-day vacation every fall to bow-hunt in Colorado. He looked forward the entire year to getting out of the flatlands and up here into the mountains although he had yet to kill an elk or a deer with a bow and arrow. I got the feeling that he enjoyed sitting in camp sipping cream soda at timberline almost as much as he did hunting.

I thanked them for the soda and took my leave to go look for some blue grouse. Newell gave me his address and invited me pheasant hunting on his farm later in the fall if I came through Iowa. Bob chuckled and nodded. "We'll look for your name in *Outdoor Life!*" he said as Sweetz and I walked off.

With the help of Newell's directions, I found the road down to the creek and we worked our way up the bottom. Unfortunately there were too many head of cattle grazing along the creek and they had clearly been there too long; the banks were caved in and the flora trampled down or eaten to the quick. Increasingly, both publicly and privately, state wildlife and forestry managers are decrying the effects of overgrazing on public lands, as well as on game bird populations and other wildlife. "There is no lack of evidence that we've abused the habitat," Rick Hoffman, a wildlife researcher for the state of Colorado, told me. Hoffman had recently concluded a five-year study on blue grouse, a study that involved spending months at a time in the woods, in all seasons, observing and banding birds. "Some areas are worse than others," he acknowledged, "but statewide, there's no question that historically grazing has been poorly managed on public lands."

Although a number of my rancher friends will heatedly deny this, it's hard to argue with the biologists who are in the field day in and day out, even harder to argue with the evidence before one's own eyes. Even for the layman, it's not difficult to tell the difference between a vibrant, functioning habitat, with a diversity of flora capable of sustaining a variety of wildlife, and one that has been stressed, homogenized, and denuded by overgrazing. Native game birds are excellent indicator species, dependent on a diversified mix of cover and food—forbs, berry bushes, and insects—and a simple barometer in any region of the country for the general health of the ecosystem. Properly accomplished, grazing, like fire or selective logging, can serve an integral function in the processes of natural regeneration, but by admission of the state and federal agencies whose job it is to protect them, much of the public lands in the West have been seriously degraded by decades of abuse.

Sweetz and I left the main creek bottom and worked our way up one of the small feeder springs, lined with mixed aspen and pine. It was very pretty, rocky and narrower and harder going for the cows, and so less disturbed. A variety of berry bushes grew in profusion along the spring where the cattle couldn't eat or trample them, and the last of the summer wildflowers were drying on their stalks; fall seeds of all kinds stuck to Sweetzer's head—bird food and seed for next year's crop. I stopped and picked some wild raspberries to take home to my wife; I had brought a little tin along in my game bag for that purpose. I sat down on a rock by the spring to have a drink of water and to eat a few of the raspberries, which were cool, sweet, and tart. Sweetzer wallowed in a pool in the spring, drinking and watching intently for fish. I lay down on my back, a bit of warm afternoon sun filtering through the trees onto my face. Just before I closed my eyes to doze off, I looked up into the branches of a lodgepole pine directly above me where a pair of curious blue grouse watched us.

Earlier that summer, besides my pigeons and the two pheasants, I had also acquired a dozen young chukar partridges from a game bird farm to use in training Sweetzer. I used them to train her to hunt "dead" and to track cripples. This I did by planting the birds in the sagebrush out behind my cabin, letting them run around and put scent down, and then sending her for the retrieve. Because she has a soft mouth, I could use the birds over and over again this way, and though I kept meaning to shoot a few over her once they were full grown, I started to get kind of attached to my chukars and never did. This presented a problem at the end of the summer when it was time to leave. My rancher friend, Billy Cantrell, took the pigeons off my hands. He had grown fond of them in the course of the summer, and refused finally to shoot them in our dog training sessions. He built quite an elaborate pigeon coop and even named the birds, and I'm not absolutely sure I didn't catch him speaking a strange cooing baby talk to them once, though I may have only imagined that.

As neither pheasants nor chukars can survive in the wild in my region of Colorado, due to the high altitude and harsh winters, I decided to take my birds with me and release them in Idaho, where I was headed for the opening of chukar season. This was kind of silly and sentimental, I know, and must seem an odd contradiction—I was going to release my chukars and shoot others—and I probably should have just dispatched them and put them in the freezer. But I figured I'd be eating plenty of wild game birds over the course of the year.

The chukars rode in a cage in the shower of my camper, and in under two hours on the road, began to give off a distinct odor. I opened all the windows to ventilate the vehicle. A couple of hours later, at a rest stop off I-80 in Wyoming, a well-meaning retired couple pulled up beside me in an enormous motor home and helpfully explained that they'd been driving behind me on the interstate and thought from the smell that my holding tank had probably backed up.

It was a difficult day all around. After I got back on the interstate, one of the chukars somehow escaped the cage, and was suddenly flying loose inside the camper. I tried to stay on the road, while Sweetzer lunged wildly around the vehicle after the bird. She seemed to think that this was yet another training exercise I had devised for her amusement. Hadn't I been springing this sort of thing on her all summer? For one terrible moment I was certain that the lid of the cage had sprung open and that the birds were going to make a mass escape—a dozen chukars and one pheasant on the wing in the camper, with a crazed yellow Lab in hot pursuit. Buffeted by passing trucks and the infamous southern Wyoming wind, I finally managed to pull off on the shoulder about the same time that Sweetz cornered the bird on the cab-over bed and delivered it smartly to hand. Apparently our training sessions had paid off, after all.

By midafternoon, we had reached southern Idaho, where I stopped to let the pheasant out by a farm which I chose for its good cover and abundance of feed.

By evening we were in chukar country. Just at dusk I drove up into a canyon where I knew there was a resident population of wild birds. I pulled the camper alongside the tiny stream that ran down the canyon and carried the cage out. The birds scattered in all directions when I opened the lid, free at last, and then, because they are covey birds and like to be together, especially at nightfall, they began making their distinctive chuckling noise in order to locate one another. I was gratified to hear a covey of wild chukars answer their calls from higher up the canyon. I was hoping they might show these newcomers from out of state the ropes.

For the next few afternoons, Sweetzer and I went back up the canyon to check on our chukars, and also to chase them around a bit in order to make them wilder and more wary. With the season opening in a few days, I didn't want them to be too tame, although I had never seen another hunter up here. On the first afternoon we found the birds across the creek, not far from where we released them. Sweetzer got on their scent right away and flushed the covey. They seemed to be getting wilder already.

The next day when we went to check on the birds, a prairie falcon startled me by flying up out of the sage at my feet, with an angry, piercing shriek. I found one of my chukars dead on the ground, its breast meat pecked out. Well, that seemed only fair. Many of those with an anti-hunting bias have the idea that were it not for the bloodthirsty human hunter, game would live to ripe old age in a kind of idyllic Garden of Eden, all the various species frolicking gaily together and singing show tunes as in a Disney cartoon. But in the real world, game birds are prey, "born to be eaten by something," as one wildlife biologist I spoke to put it—whether by a falcon, a coyote, a fox, or an owl. Or a man. I'm quite willing to share with the other predators.

On opening day, Sweetz and I went out early to guard our chukars. We had no interest in shooting them, but I carried my gun anyway, thinking we might hunt the wild birds higher up the canyon. By "wild," I do not mean "native," as the chukar partridge was introduced to the western United States in the 1930s, imported from their native range of India and Pakistan. Easy to breed and raise in captivity, chukars have thrived and propagated in the wild in several western states, filling an interesting ecological niche. They favor steep, rocky, generally desolate mountainsides, and are one of the few game bird species actually able to benefit from the devastations of over-grazing: repeated suppression of the native grasses and forbs by cattle and sheep results in the spread of cheatgrass—poor feed for ungulates, but a fav-orite staple of the little chukar partridge. The birds in this canyon had been replanted in recent years, the original population having been decimated by a particularly severe winter; I had participated in the stocking program.

I was upset to see that there was already another vehicle parked in our spot, and after we had walked up a way we ran into another hunter working the creek bottom with his dog. It was just past dawn and the sun hadn't yet crested the canyon wall. I stopped to talk to the man. He was a beefy, jovial fellow who, by way of introduction, pulled a business card from his shirt pocket and handed it to me. The card had the man's name and the Budweiser logo on the front. Evidently, he was the local beer distributor. Indeed, he looked like he sampled a fair amount of his product. "Turn it over," he said eagerly. The back of the card read, *Hi! Today, I'm selling Budweiser. . . . Tear this card in half by the count of three, and I'd be happy to buy you a Bud on me!* "Go on," he coaxed, "tear it in half."

Though it would be impossible to imagine how many times he had played this trick, the beer distributor hadn't seemed to tire of it, and when I tried to tear the card, which was made out of some kind of untearable synthetic material, he exploded with bellicose laughter that echoed like thunder off the canyon walls. "Stop by the warehouse sometime," he said, "and I'll buy you a free Bud anyway!" This seemed to me an extremely odd encounter at dawn on the opening day of chukar season.

"Finding any birds?" I asked casually.

"Yeah," he answered. "In fact, I just killed one right here."

"Mind if I take a look at it?" I asked. He pulled the chukar out of his game bag; I could tell it was one of mine because they were younger and still a bit smaller than the resident birds. "I brought that bird here from Colorado," I said. "I just released them a few days ago. I'd appreciate it if you wouldn't shoot any more of them."

"Yeah, right," he said, smiling. "Like you own these birds!"

"No, I'm serious."

"Yeah? How can you tell this is one of your birds? I don't see a band."

I knew I was being unreasonable and though somehow I didn't mind the falcon making a meal of one of my chukars, it annoyed the hell out of me that the beer distributor had discovered them. "Did that bird even fly, or did you ground-sluice him?" I asked.

"Hey, wait a minute, buddy," he said, defensively, "the bird flew just fine. I don't shoot birds on the ground."

"I would really appreciate it if you wouldn't shoot any more."

"Well, now," said the beer distributor, "maybe you can explain to me how I'm supposed to tell which are *your* birds and which are the ones I'm *allowed* to shoot." He had a point.

I'm looking back now at the following entry I made in my journal that day:

My chukars: descended from the wild birds of the Himalayas, hatched on a game bird farm in eastern Colorado, raised in a pen in northern Colorado where, in return for room and board and all the feed they can eat, they submit to being carried around in the mouth of a yellow Lab. Driven to central Idaho and released finally back into the wild, only to turn up a few days later in a beer distributor's game bag. . . . The abbreviated saga of a species and of one short, though not uneventful, life. . . .

Later that afternoon, Sweetz and I were resting from the exertion of climbing a steep mountain slope farther up the canyon, where I shot one resident chukar, now in my own game bag, its crop full of tangy wild watercress from the stream below. Ernest Hemingway used to bird hunt around here. He makes reference in one of his later letters to hunting "along small streams in the lava rock with watercress in them." I was sitting on a flat rock, admiring the view from on high and reflecting on the fact that were it not for the act of hunting it might not occur to me to climb a mountainside like this. I was looking down on the tiny toy traffic making its way up the dirt road that wound up the canyon along the creek. An occasional car or truck followed the road up into the national forest, and even after they were out of sight, I could see the billow of dust up the canyon. A few people rode mountain bicycles down the road, and there were a number of afternoon joggers, as well.

I sat on the rock for a long time. I didn't want to go back down because it was so peaceful up here above it all. Although I was far enough away that the people passing below appeared hardly larger than ants, the canyon walls played a strange acoustical trick and I could hear every word spoken as if I were standing right next to them.

I listened in on the conversation of two women joggers running with their dogs. They were talking about real estate, a popular conversational topic around resort towns. I got the distinct feeling that they were realtors themselves because they spoke a certain unmistakable insider jargon. They were discussing the fact that this canyon had recently been sold and was scheduled to be developed into five-acre, million-dollar "ranchettes." The lots were going to be divided up evenly for sale among participating realty agencies in town, explained one of the women. I felt the weight of the plump chukar in my bag. The women had no idea that I was eavesdropping on them; they probably didn't even know of the existence of game birds in this lovely little canyon. I had a hunch they might even express their disapproval if they ran into me walking down the road with my gun in hand. Yet I knew that the chukars here had far more to fear from them than they did from this hunter's gun.

4

A MONTANA

GRAND SLAM

It is not essential to the hunt that it be successful.

Ortega y Gasset

It was the hottest September in Montana history, which seemed to lend a certain tangibility to the global warming theory. Except for the cottonwoods beginning to change colors in the river bottoms, it was hard to have any faith in fall. One tends to associate bird season with crisp mornings and wood smoke, perhaps even an early dusting of snow, and the unnaturally temperate weather seemed all wrong for hunting. Unpleasant for man and dog alike, the heat was potentially dangerous to the latter; because they don't sweat like people, dogs are especially susceptible to heat prostration, and due to the extreme exertions attendant to their line of work, hunting dogs can be quickly and fatally overcome. A few hours early in the morning and an hour or two late in the day was about all we were good for.

Even the birds weren't cooperating with the season. I managed to hunt five different species on three successive days with three separate hunting companions without once pulling the trigger. There is what bird hunters refer to as a "Montana grand slam," which is to kill on one trip (or better yet, in one day) the four major species of upland game birds resident to the state: sharptail grouse, sage grouse, Hungarian partridge, and pheasant. Since pheasant season didn't open until October, I substituted blue grouse on my own list, and I added to it ruffed grouse, so in those three days I achieved the exact reverse of the Montana Grand Slam, which, I guess, would have to be called Striking Out in Montana with the Bases Loaded.

And I went it one better with five species. The good news is I didn't have to clean my gun.

What's interesting about getting skunked, and skunked in Montana yet, the "last best place"? People buy books about bird hunting at least in part because they can go out and get skunked on their own any time they want, which is why outdoor writers frequently embellish their own experiences afield. For years it discouraged me that those lucky writers almost always had more successful hunting and fishing trips than I did, than anyone I knew personally did—they went to more exotic places, caught more and bigger fish, practically always shot their limit of birds. Then I got to know a few of them and came to understand that sometimes they stretched the truth. Sometimes they lied. Which is precisely the point: This is a true-life story. And the moral of it is: You can get skunked and still learn something, maybe even have a good time.

I hunted sage grouse my first day in Montana with an old friend, the landscape painter Russell Chatham. Chatham is a large, graceful person, his grace centered in small, almost delicate hands. Grace being a quality central to sport and art, Chatham is both a consummate sportsman and an artist of the first order. His canvases offer the viewer the kind of big, unspoiled landscape vistas that are becoming increasingly difficult to find in the real world. Though he has always maintained that his work does not make statements for or against anything, it speaks in the quiet way of all important art; beneath the obvious surface beauty of Chatham's paintings resides a deep longing, a sense of irrevocable loss, perhaps a tinge of sadness for what was and what might have been. Those paintings are heartbreakers.

Russ Chatham has seen a considerable amount of country go by in his lifetime; he has seen the countryside of northern California nibbled away by suburban development until there was little left of it; he has witnessed the virtual disappearance of California's striped bass fishery, and the destruction of the steelhead and salmon fisheries of the Pacific Northwest. Twenty-some years ago, he moved to Montana, upon which other depredations are currently being visited. Yet he is not an angry man, neither bitter nor cynical, as so many of us tend to become in the face of the sheer overwhelming force of such matters. We have not talked about this, but I know that Chatham takes solace in his art, finds peace in the pure unadulterated country of his imagination.

Chatham and I went out looking for sage grouse to a spot he had hunted several years earlier with great success. It is a common experience among hunters and fishermen to return to a favorite place after the passage of time and find it different, changed. Maybe others have discovered it and it is overrun now, or worse, it is buried beneath asphalt and concrete, and now the place where you shot a bird last time is at the exact middle of some family's living room. Sometimes the changes are much more subtle, so that you can't even identify precisely what it is about it that is different, and other times it is only you who has changed. For whichever of these reasons, many of us intentionally avoid returning to favorite old haunts, in the same way that people often avoid looking up old lovers, preferring to let them live on in our imaginations as they (and we) once were, or at least as we like to remember them. The sportsman tries to counteract these inexorable losses by searching out new places, new country. This is how we stay one step ahead of hopelessness and despair.

The farmers are plowing up a lot of sagebrush in Montana and elsewhere in the West, thousands and thousands of acres of the stuff, which, frankly, is not of much use to anything other than sage grouse. Populations of the birds are drastically down in many western states. Almost everyone you talk to has a different explanation for this decline, and the truth probably lies in some complicated combination of factors, most of which fall under the broad umbrella heading "Loss of Habitat." It takes no huge leap of imagination to know that plowing up all the sagebrush and replanting in dryland wheat doesn't do the sage grouse any good. Nor are bovine hooves a kindly influence on a nest of eggs. Sometimes natural factors alone, such as a cyclical infestation of wood ticks, can knock down a population, and when combined with unnatural factors can pack a deadly one-two punch from which a species never recovers. Others have suggested that the protection of raptors in the last twenty years has resulted in excessive predation on sage grouse, and there is probably truth in that as well. There was a time not long ago when ranchers shot every hawk and eagle they saw on principle, a predator control policy to which the narrator does not subscribe. Yet another theory has it that when the bottom fell out of fur prices, an overpopulation of coyotes reduced sage grouse numbers. My friend Billy Cantrell maintains that where we live in Colorado, sage grouse have simply been hunted into submission. State fish and game officials I have spoken to deny this. They are conducting bird counts and studies on the question and though they haven't come up with the definitive answer yet, they remain convinced that hunting pressure is not a significant factor, as do many hunters and many hunter advocacy groups. Cantrell scoffs at their counts and studies: "They can only count them because there are so few," he points out. "Can you count the blackbirds? Look at all the hunters' cars on opening day in the one place that you and I know *used to* support one flock of sage grouse and then tell me that the hunters have no effect." I think he may be right in this case, and that hunters must begin to acknowledge that in areas with a shrinking habitat base, and the resulting concentration and reduction of bird populations, hunting, too, can play a role in a complex equation. In many regions of Europe, for instance, native game birds have been virtually wiped out as a direct function of overgunning, combined with the far more deadly threat to all wildlife of an ever-swelling human population. As John P. S. Mackenzie points out in *Game Birds*, one of three volumes in his beautiful series *Birds of the World:* "The fact is, if every person in the world were to start eating wild birds, the total supply would last about one day." This is a frightening statistic from which one might deduce that hunting organizations should begin promoting Planned Parenthood and the commercial poultry industry.

A cantankerous, opinionated old Swedish American I talked to at a campground in Montana expressed yet another opinion on the subject: that the activities of man can have no impact whatsoever on anything in nature. "We're fleas on a dog's back," said the old Swede. "It's arrogant to think that we can alter nature, it's only Almighty God who can do that!" The old man grew up in this country and fondly recalled the "clouds" of sage grouse that "blackened the sky" when he was a boy. (I would eventually become inured to oldtimers' tales about the clouds of game birds that seem once to have blackened the skies all over America.) I pointed out to the old man that sometimes dogs can have severe allergic reactions to their fleas, get all kinds of nasty rashes and sores from them. He grumbled and snorted, and wagged his finger at me, one of those cranky old bastards you find in some abundance in the West. "You're writing a book, you say? About birds? Well I can tell you something about birds. And I can tell you something about writing a book, too: People don't want to read a bunch of crap!"

Chatham and I could see a farmer plowing up sagebrush as we drove by, a high cloud of dust rising behind the tractor, and we could see the miles of newly turned soil, on both sides of the highway, waiting to be planted in dryland wheat.

A recent federal farm initiative called the Conservation Reserve Program (CRP) has been a boon to wildlife and bird populations in many parts of the country. The farmers are paid to take highly erodible agricultural land out of production for ten years, and to replant it in various grasses. They are usually paid more to retire the land than they could generate by planting crops in the often exhausted soil, so this is a good deal for the farmer, and a lot less work, too. Unfortunately, subsidy programs of this nature give rise to all sorts of chicanery on the part of the American farmer. And who can blame them? Like low-income urban teenagers having unwanted babies in order to increase their welfare checks, in this case the farmer is encouraged to plow up ever more sagebrush to plant in dryland wheat in order to replace the fields taken out of production by enrollment in the CRP. In turn, due to surpluses of wheat on the world market, he is paid *not* to take much of that wheat to market. This is a peculiar arrangement, and certainly, as taxpayers footing the bill, the first question we might want to ask about such programs is, why do we have to pay the farmer to take care of his own land?

Nevertheless, in most instances, the hunter is likely to be grateful for the relatively healthy look that the retired CRP land takes on in a matter of only a year or two, and for all the new wildlife habitat created by the program, even if it is only temporary, because after the ten years has elapsed, the farmer is likely to plow up that soil and exhaust it all over again.

The first problem Russ and I faced on our hunt was to find some sagebrush. Given the thousands and thousands of square miles of the stuff in the West this shouldn't have presented much of a problem, except that Chatham's "special" spot, which he had not hunted for a few years, was one of those currently being plowed up by the aforementioned farmer, topsoil billowing behind the tractor, catching the jetstream for the Dakotas. It's the kind of thing that can dishearten the sportsman. "Hmm," remarked Chatham, whose inordinate grace prevents him from being a whiner, "there's not much sagebrush here anymore."

To save the day in situations like this, resourceful hunters come up with an alternate plan, find another spot. This is one reason it's called hunting, and one must become rather adept at this in order to stay one step ahead of the hangman. Before long we had located a patch of sagebrush nearby, but by the time we did and got out of the car, the unseasonable midmorning heat had already set in. Though later that evening over cocktails I would overhear Chatham, always the optimist, refer to our hunting efforts that day as "pounding the sage," the reality was that we covered the niggardly little piece of sagebrush in about an hour, at most a leisurely stroll and a bit of exercise for Sweetzer, who only got remotely birdy once, which at least gave us the opportunity to ready our guns, even if it was mostly make-believe. Still, we did hunt, and some days afield are just like that, quiet and bittersweet without gunfire or beating wings.

On the drive home, Russ and I discussed how he would have cooked the sage grouse that we didn't kill. It is my experience that painters are generally better cooks than writers due to their natural abilities of alchemy, and Chatham is a superb chef, his talents nowhere better displayed than with wild game. Chatham believes that most game birds don't need much help by way of fancy culinary tricks and his recipe for sage grouse is as simple as it gets, and is even better if one actually brings home a bird.

RUSSELL CHATHAM'S
GHOST SAGE GROUSE

Rub bird (plucked, never skinned) with butter or olive oil, salt and pepper to taste and roast quickly in a very hot oven, at least 450 degrees. Depending on the size of the grouse, eighteen to twenty minutes in the oven should do it (less for smaller birds). Serve rare to medium rare with a little sweet chutney on the side.

––––––––––

I met Jim Harrison at dawn the next morning in a café in Livingston. With an early start we hoped to beat the heat into the field. I will meet, over the course of the season, a hundred bird hunters in a hundred such cafés, every one of them, but for minor differences in the attire and accents of the patrons, nearly interchangeable in any region in America—the kind of place with a line of pickup trucks angled out front, and where you don't particularly want to be taking your high cholesterol count out to breakfast. At 6:00 A.M. the customers in such establishments are mostly men on the way to their jobs (as I was that morning).

Our other companion that day was a fellow named Danny Lahren, a young local guide with a reputation as the best bird hunter in southern Montana. I wouldn't hunt with many professional guides on this trip—couldn't afford to, and in any case I usually prefer to wander around on my own—but Harrison was picking up the tab. Lahren, who was accustomed to guiding swells—gentleman sportsmen attired head to toe in Orvis gear—couldn't help noting over breakfast that Harrison, a poet and novelist of some repute, was the first blue-collar client that he'd ever had. For all his travels, his movie-star and literary pals, Harrison is still at base a stalwart midwestern lad, a burly fellow (currently with sausage grease on his chin and egg yolk on his mustache), equally at home eating pig knuckles at MOM's or pâté at La Grenouille.

The heat came on fast, already in the seventies and climbing by the time we stepped from the vehicle on a gorgeous high mountain meadow. The last time I hunted with Harrison was in the rain several years ago in Michigan during the wettest fall in the state's history. Now this, the hottest September on record in Montana.

A morning mist still hung over the Yellowstone River valley below, the cottonwoods shading yellow in the bottom. The mountain slopes above us ran from tawny tans to deep fire reds, mixed aspen and pine falling away to open grasslands and the rolling breaks of the river. From on high and especially early in the morning this fine country seemed young and fresh, and looked like nothing so much as a Chatham landscape.

Lahren unloaded three high-strung English pointers from dog crates and put electronic tracking and shock collars on them. The former device, which emits a loud battery-powered beep at seven-second intervals (a noise not unlike the sound of state highway snowplows) and then beeps steadily when the dog is on point, has largely replaced the traditional collar bell as a way for hunters to know the location of their dogs when they are out of sight. And the shock collar has largely replaced a whipping as a means of disciplining and controlling the dog. Though undeniably useful tools, such high-tech gear always strikes me as somewhat out of place in the field. I have enough such equipment at home—computers and modems and fax machines, all of which make strange and irritating noises—and when I'm outdoors I like to at least pretend that life is simpler, less encumbered. For this reason I prefer old double-barreled shotguns to the new automatics, and bells to electronic collars. The clear ring of a bell on a dog's collar is a lovely, heartening sound of fall, and rather than the pulsing electronic beep, it is the *absence* of noise when the dog locks up on point and the bell stops ringing that tells of birds found. There is something to be said for the absence of noise in the field.

"You know what they say about someone who hunts upland birds in Montana behind a Lab?" asked Danny Lahren with a somewhat disdainful look at Sweetzer, as his big running pointers headed for the hills.

"What's that?"

"That he would fuck his own sister."

I thought about this for a while. "I don't get it."

"That's how dumb it is—it's as dumb as fucking your own sister. No offense intended."

Because most western bird hunting takes place in such vast open country, you really do need a dog that can cover a lot of ground and find birds and then hold them on point until you can get there. A Lab, which is a flushing dog, just sort of potters along more or less right in front of you so as hopefully to put the birds up within gun range, and you just have to hope that you bump into some birds. If the wind is wrong you might well walk right past a covey on a hillside a hundred yards or less away, a covey that any self-respecting pointing dog would certainly find for you. So, yes, I admit that it is sort of dumb.

The rancher on whose property we were hunting that day practiced rotational grazing in order to rest and rejuvenate his land and this particular section had been ungrazed this year. I've never seen country so beautiful as that country on that morning, so pristine and undisturbed we almost didn't want to walk on it; the native short grasses yellow and top-heavy with seed, the wildflowers dried on their stalks, the berry bushes full with ripe fruit— white snowberry and scarlet serviceberry, and others whose names I didn't know. The fire bush on the hillsides was a deep burnt red.

We were hunting Hungarian partridge and sharptail grouse on the breaks, and higher up in the woods possibly some ruffed grouse. I knew there must be plentiful birds in such gorgeous country, but in any case, I enjoy walking with Jim and listening to him talk.

"Pay no attention to what they say in Montana about Labs," said Harrison, who had a beloved old yellow Lab of his own at home; blind in one eye and arthritic, she would not last the winter. "You and I know that they make the best companions, and in our lonely march toward doom, writers frequently need companionship. My old Sand will sit and listen to me talk for hours, for just one biscuit. Whereas my setter is only good for about ten minutes before she gets bored with me and wanders off. I'm going to finish my life with one more Lab."

From the hillside above us Lahren cursed and smacked his electronic control box, and then lit out at a dead run for one of the dogs, which refused to come in on the whistle. His collars were malfunctioning today, neither beeping for location nor shocking for obedience. A bell, on the other hand, almost never fails.

"You know what I do when my dog won't come?" Harrison asked as we watched Lahren disappearing over the next hill, the dog maintaining a steady thirty-yard lead. "I sit down on the ground and begin to weep loudly, really wail—it's an old Cheyenne trick. The dog can't figure out what's going on, so she comes back to investigate."

We didn't need the beeper collar to locate one of the other dogs, which had just gone on point on the top of a long steep hill above us, a classic scene, the dog, no bigger than a speck, frozen in a perfect point against the blue horizon. Harrison, a serious walker to the tune of ten miles a day, cocked his head and appraised the situation with his good eye before sighing deeply, almost sadly. "We're going to have to hike up there," he said.

It was a hard forced march up the hill; I'd have to call it a mountain, actually—hills are what they have in New England—and we had to stop to rest a couple of times. When we finally reached him, the dog was still locked in a rigid point at the exact summit of the mountain, backlit by morning sun, a glistening stream of saliva running out the corner of his mouth from the long effort of concentration. Coincidentally, Harrison and I were both shooting the same make, model, gauge, and vintage shotgun—double A. H. Fox Sterlingworth 16 gauges, manufactured in the 1920s. They seemed like matching bookends as we circled in on either side of the dog, guns at the ready. That's a fine pleasure, walking in on a point with a friend, heart pounding, and trying to steady yourself for the moment to come.

But there were no birds. Maybe it had taken us too long to get up the mountain and they had run, or else it had been a false point all along, although I doubt Lahren's dogs do much false pointing. In any case, had it not been for the fact that way up here, the panorama of the valley below was even more spectacular, we might have considered the climb an exhausting waste of time and energy. As it was, we didn't mind. "The fact that I didn't die hiking up here," said Harrison, philosophically, "tells me that God is not ready for me yet."

We had one more point that morning down along a small feeder creek, but once again when we walked in there were no birds, which mystified us. Sweetzer got birdy only once, her Lablike pottering taking on a certain urgency, tail stiff and wagging furiously. The pointers were nowhere in sight. "Wouldn't it be fun," Harrison said as we followed her, "if she found some birds, and then you could say something like—'Anyone who would hunt upland birds in Montana with a Lab would fuck his gorgeous fifth cousin!'" But it was only another false alarm; whatever birds had been walking around earlier putting down scent had clearly left for parts unknown before we arrived.

And that's about it. We quit early, on account of the rising heat. Dan Lahren dunked his tongue-dragging pointers in a stock-watering tank to cool them down and Sweetzer jumped in for a little paddle herself.

But now I have this moment to remember: the pointer silhouetted against the horizon, locked in place like a statue at the top of the mountain, a gleaming tendril of drool running from his mouth. And I have that lovely upland country to recall, miles of lush, untrammeled, unspoiled range— the yellow fall grasses, the dried wildflowers and brilliant berry bushes, the aspen and pine up high, and the yellow cottonwoods along the river bottom. All this and a hike and a little conversation with a friend, as well. That's enough for one day afield. Yes, that's plenty.

I had a date to hunt the next day with the novelist Richard Ford near the tiny town of Dutton, Montana, and I drove north out of Livingston toward Great Falls. The trees were progressively further along in their colors as I drove and I had the sense of actively entering fall rather than passively waiting for its descent. Other than that it is bird season, I don't care for autumn—a strange confession for a hunter to make. Though some see fullness and ripeness in the harvest season, I see only death and the loneliness of winter coming on, and I fight a deep melancholy this time of year.

I camped for the night along a creek in the Little Belt Mountains south of Great Falls; almost no traffic on the highway, not another soul stopping for the night. It was a lovely clear evening, noticeably cooler having gained a bit of altitude. Just before sunset I rigged a fly rod and caught half a dozen small brook trout from the creek. I drank a spot of gin, fuel on the embers of melancholy, and pan-fried the trout for dinner. They were delicious. Stepping out of the camper for a walk with Sweetzer before bed, I thought I detected a change of weather in the night air. It was coming on the end of the month.

Richard Ford is a tall, erect man, with a high, broad forehead and a certain aesthetic look to him. If Jim Harrison looks something like a blue-collar laborer on his way to a job pouring cement foundations, and writes in primary colors with big, broad brushstrokes, Ford looks like a poet, and writes lean, honed prose that has somewhat the stark effect of black-and-white photography. No one is better on the dark, stripped-down side of modern life, with its edge of incipient desperation and quiet hopelessness. Ford is a writer whose work gives off a kind of autumnal chill.

Ford and his wife, Kristina, live for part of the year at the end of a dirt road, past eleven grain elevators and an old abandoned schoolhouse, in the dead middle of Montana's dryland wheat country. For miles and miles in all directions is a strange geometric pattern of rolling wheat fields—one fallow and the next in production—giving the hills a precise brown-and-yellow checkerboard appearance as far as the eye can see. The look of this land strikes me as too bizarre to be exactly monotonous; it has an unnatural quality to it, as if designed by someone who is rather too tidy for his own good.

Still, even the most soulless agricultural practices sometimes offer a niche to wildlife and to game birds, and in this instance the little gray partridge (more commonly known as Hungarian partridge) makes his living off the wheat. Originally introduced into Washington around the turn of the century from central Europe, "Huns" were released over the next several decades in a number of western states and have thrived in parts of Montana.

The Fords greeted me on the front step of their home in the middle of the wheat fields, both dressed in brush pants and hunting shirts. A native Mississippian, Richard speaks with a soft, reedy southern accent and is very much a gentleman, polite and solicitous. Kristina is a pretty, friendly, animated woman who, in her shooting attire and with her short haircut, has the look of one of those 1950s sporting wives—Mary Hemingway, or the young Jane Mason—healthy, vivacious, and outdoorsy.

We loaded the Fords' two Brittany spaniels in the car. Sweetzer stayed behind in the camper. I had the impression that Richard subscribed to Dan Lahren's feeling about the utility of Labs on upland birds in Montana. He clearly took his hunting seriously and I was afraid Sweetz might get in the way. She howled, heartbroken, as we drove off. It was the first of only a half dozen or so times that I would hunt without her over the next five months. I considered us equal partners in this venture.

We drove dirt section roads bisecting the wheat fields. Because there are no cattle in this part of Montana, there are no barbed wire fences, the fields plowed from roadbed to roadbed. There is a good deal of CRP land here as well, and we were pleased to drive by a pretty field of tall grass and to see a number of pheasants darting from it. The field was posted, unusual in this region, and Ford explained that the rancher who owned the property had leased the hunting rights to a group of doctors from Great Falls. "Paid" hunting, already firmly entrenched in most other regions of the country, is clearly the wave of the future in the West, too.

In one's imagination one might still look out over the vast, rolling, open vistas of this wheat country and see the shortgrass prairie before the arrival of the sodbusters, might imagine the buffalo herds and the Plains Indian tribes and the sheer wild immensity of country. I'd trade the partridge from eastern Europe in a second to see that, and for the native grouse that once made their home here but that have now been largely displaced by modern agriculture. Lacking that, I am glad that the Huns are here and prospering.

We parked and Richard and Kristina uncased matching 20-gauge Model 21 Winchesters. Ford is a long-legged fellow in very good condition, and he set out across the wheat field at a brisk pace, his wife and I trotting behind like Chinese rickshaw drivers, trying to keep up with his long, no-nonsense stride. You can learn a lot about people being in the field with them—how they move, cover the ground, carry their guns, work their dogs, walk in on a point, shoot, what they notice and don't notice—everyone's style and approach as distinctive and telling as fingerprints. Richard Ford is an excellent hunter, an efficient predator, distinctly not a noodler, the cool precision of his work displayed also in his hunting style. He is a disciplined man, who did not strike me as being much interested in conversation in the field, which is probably as it should be. Nor did he seem to be victim to the kind of random mental peregrinations afield that plague the narrator, whose mind tends to wander off on unrelated tangents, dreaming of buffalo and Indians and other such nonsense.

We spread out, Kristina and I dropping down into a coulee while Richard walked the edge of the stubble field above. To me the most interesting aspect of this country lies in the coulees, the old river and creek bottoms, that run like ancient, crooked fingers between the wheat fields. Most of them are dry this time of year, running water only briefly in the spring. This is the last land hereabouts that remains uncultivated, largely because it is unworkable by modern machinery, spared from the greedy reach of agribusiness because it would not be efficient to try to farm. By all definitions of "clean" farming techniques, the coulees remain messy, unruly land, in which grows the remnants of the various native grasses, forbs, wildflowers, bushes, and trees. Were it not for the coulees, game birds and other wildlife could not exist in the cold sterility of wheat country, for though there is ample food in the fields above, there is no adequate cover or water. The Huns nest down in these bottoms, and during the heat of the day loaf in the shade of the willows and elders, and they drink from the springs. In the mornings and evenings they come up to feed on the green winter wheat just poking from the ground this time of year and on the spilled grain from the recent fall harvest. I prefer to hunt the coulees; it's better walking where the soil has not been turned, the flora is a lot more engaging, and they have an older, timeless feel to them; one can imagine, if one is so inclined, that ancient spirits long since exorcised from the prairies above have taken refuge down here, and are biding their time.

One of the dogs went on point in front of Kristina and when she walked in, a hen pheasant got up. She didn't shoot because pheasant season hadn't opened yet and, in any case, it's illegal to shoot hens. Richard expressed his belief that the Huns were going to be up top this time of day, feeding in the fields, and that we were wasting our time down in the coulee. The Fords are very polite with each other, in that courtly way of southerners—she addresses him as "Baby," he calls her "Sweetheart"—and after a brief discussion about whether to hunt down below or up top, Kristina deferred to Richard and crossed the coulee and we all went up into the field. Five minutes later, the dog went on point again down in the coulee. Thinking that the dog was pointing the same pheasant, only Richard went down to investigate while Kristina and I waited up on top of the ridge. When he walked in on the point a huge covey of Huns, fifty or so, got up in front of him. Their rise is an exciting thing to watch, even for the spectator, like whirling red fireworks, and Ford shot a clean double. I enjoy watching such a scene from such a vantage point—the explosive covey rise and the superb shooting—nearly as much as the shooting myself.

Then we went back down to hunt the coulee, and the next covey that got up flushed wild at my feet. I mounted my gun and swung on the birds and just before I pulled the trigger I remembered Richard telling me when we first set out that he and Kristina shot only pointed birds and not wild flushed birds. This is a common restraint among conscientious pointing dog owners, both for sporting reasons and because they don't want to reward the dog unless he has done his job. But it can be a hard habit for owners of flushing dogs to get into because, of course, flushing is how we make game. I didn't shoot and Ford politely thanked me. It is a pleasure hunting with gentlemen, I would learn.

Kristina and I were out of position again on the next covey rise, and didn't have a shot. This time Richard missed on his first barrel but recovered on the second, and dropped a bird with an excellent long shot. I had spotted a rattlesnake moving through the grass toward him just at the moment of the covey rise, and I called out to warn him as he fired and his bird tumbled. The year before he had lost one of his Brittanies to a rattlesnake; they pose a real threat to hunting dogs—and to hunters, too—in certain parts of the country. Taking evasive action, Ford executed a lively two-step rattlesnake dance, and then we all searched somewhat gingerly for the downed bird, from whose exact point of fall the snake had distracted us. Like all true sportsmen, the Fords are extremely conscientious about finding crippled birds. Less meticulous hunters often make a cursory search before giving up to continue the hunt, but for others a lost cripple can spoil a day afield. We searched for nearly half an hour, even considering driving back to get Sweetzer (Labs are enthusiastic hunters of dead and crippled birds), before we found the bird.

We continued the hunt, climbing back up out of the coulee onto the ridge to work our way across the bare stubble field. The Fords' older dog quartered the field beautifully, saving us a lot of legwork. We all stood and admired her work.

"Beautiful dog, Baby," Kristina whispered.

"A wonder, Sweetheart," he answered softly.

The Fords also had a young, green Brittany, acquired recently as a replacement for the dog lost to the rattlesnake. Richard was concerned because the new dog hadn't yet displayed much in the way of natural hunting abilities, or even interest, and tended to ignore his whistle commands, wandering farther and farther out, until Ford, no fan of electronic collars either, finally handed his gun to his wife and took off at a long-legged run after the dog, who by then was on the far side of the wheat field. I watched him chasing his dog across the barren stubble field—head high, long legs pumping to his chest, and I thought about my hunt the day before and the story Jim Harrison told (possibly apocryphal) about his own technique to call in disobedient dogs—the "old Cheyenne trick" of sitting down on the ground and wailing.

Richard Ford caught his dog, disciplined him, and came back to us, barely breathing hard after the exertion. It was already getting late in the afternoon, and we decided to call it a day.

We drove into tiny Dutton for a glass of Tanqueray gin at the local saloon—nice to find a couple of gin fans in a region known for whiskey drinkers—a convivial end to a short afternoon hunt.

As we headed back out to the Fords' house, the sun dropped behind the big Flathead Range that muscled out of the plains to form the shimmering distant horizon to the west. The evening light shadowed the hills, high-lighting and coloring the strange geometric patterns of wheat fields, which ran west to the mountains and east seemingly forever.

"I think this is the most beautiful country I've ever seen," Ford said, looking out over the pink hills of wheat. The love of country is often an acquired taste and at first I thought he might be kidding. When I look out at the wheat fields I can't help but see the loss of the prairie, a million years usurped in one century by cold, sanitized, mechanical organization. I prefer my country a little messier. But I could see Ford's point; the stunning evening light did lend the land a certain specific, surgical beauty. All country is inherently beautiful. "The Earth is all that lasts," said Black Elk.

It was nearly dark by the time I said goodbye to the Fords, and though they invited me to share leftovers for dinner, I felt that they were being polite, that I had imposed enough on their hospitality. I have this memory of them as I drove from their driveway: standing in front of the picture window in the living room, arms around each other, bright yellow house lights on behind them, still dressed in hunting clothes, smiling and waving good-bye. A white moon was rising over darkening fields, and somehow it all reminded me of a scene in a Ford novel, made me feel a bit lonely to be driving off into the dusky emptiness of the Montana plains.

I camped for the night a few miles down the road, and Sweetz and I took a long moonlit walk through the wheat fields.

RICHARD AND KRISTINA FORD'S HUNGARIAN PARTRIDGE WITH GIN AND JUNIPER BERRIES

(Sadly, because of the heavy use of pesticides in Montana's wheat country, the county extension agency recommends skinning game birds before cooking, as toxins tend to concentrate in the fat just beneath the skin. The Fords skin all their game birds, unlike Russell Chatham, who believes this is blasphemy and is willing to take his chances with the toxins. The Fords recommend the following excellent recipe for doves and quail, too.)

Butterfly 4 Hungarian partridge breasts. Roll breasts in crushed juniper berries (about a dozen). Salt and pepper to taste. Melt a stick of butter in pan and saute breasts over medium high heat, about 4–5 minutes to the side. Remove breasts from pan, add 1/4 cup gin to drippings, light with match and flambé briefly. Pour sauce over birds. Serve with toasted bread crumbs.

5

DAWN ON THE RES

History is always made against the grain of nature.

Ortega y Gasset

JOE KIPP: *At one time the Blackfeet confederacy, which consists of three tribes, the Blackfeet, the Bloods, and the Piegans, shared a common hunting ground that went from the Yellowstone River to where the prairie meets the brush country north of Edmonton, Alberta, and from the continental divide 250 miles east to Sioux country. There were two hundred thousand souls at that time in the confederacy. The United States government did not cross the Yellowstone River until the buffalo were gone and our people were starving. Before that they did not dare. Nobody came into our country and lived.*

It was 5:30 A.M. outside Choteau, Montana. I was headed for the Blackfeet reservation and a hunting date with Joe Kipp. I came with an invitation.

In the muddy dawn light near Bynum, I almost hit a flock of Hungarian partridge that flared across the road in front of the truck; this would be an unfortunate way to make my first double on Huns. Just past Dupuyer, three cock pheasants and four hens sailed past, wings set, soundless as apparitions in the rising mist.

The evening before, the owners of a gas station in Choteau, a very pleasant older couple, had warned me against spending the night on the reservation—the "res" as it is called by Indians and non-Indians alike.

They told a story about a traveling salesman who had recently been beaten to death outside one of the bars in Browning. A few years ago when liquor sales were legalized on the reservation, said the woman, twenty-six bars opened in town, and now all the Indians are drunk and murderous. The couple in the gas station also told me how the Indian kids spit on the white spectators from the balcony during high school basketball games. I had seen a busload of Browning high school students a couple of days earlier at a rest stop off the highway. Their team is called the Browning Indians, one of the few in America with a true right to use that name, and they looked like nice enough kids to me. Honestly, if I were an American Indian I might have an overwhelming urge to spit on white people.

Defending the homeland and hunting buffalo was very difficult and it weeded out the weak and the sickly. So genetically this was a very strong culture. That's not the case, anymore. However, in the last fifteen to twenty years there's been an incredible resurgence of Blackfeet culture—a growing interest in our language and traditional religion. I think our tribe is going to be healthy again. The hardest part is resisting assimilation, taking pride in being an Indian. Later I will tell you a few stories about my grandfather. . . .

I met Joe Kipp for our hunt just after daylight at his trailer house near the tiny town of Blackfoot where he lives with his wife and three sons. A handsome, black-haired thirty-year-old, Kipp is a hospitable man, talkative and inquisitive, with a deadpan sense of humor. He had a new, slightly squirrelly year-old Lab pup that he was just starting on birds. She crawled around in a submissive posture on her belly trying to lick Sweetzer's mouth.

We loaded guns, dogs, and lunch in Kipp's pickup truck and headed out across the plains. I liked the looks of the country. Some of it is in dryland wheat, most of that leased out to white farmers. Historically, the Blackfeet have never been much interested in farming. "Farming was something for the women of other tribes to do," Kipp explained with his sly smile. "Personally, I could not tolerate driving around in a circle all day." Much of the rest of the reservation is grassland prairie—grazed by horses and cattle, and for the most part the land looks healthy. The Blackfeet are conscientious about their land use, and tribal management quite conservative when it comes to grazing policy. A white man is likely to notice that the fencing is not nearly as tidy as on the average ranch off the res. Many of the fences are makeshift and patched, crooked or falling down, horses and stock loose along the road or in the wrong pastures. This is the kind of thing whites tend to interpret as an example of laziness, although fences, like saloons, are a white man invention, of which Indians clearly have not altogether gotten the hang.

The old Indians would burn off the prairies to make better grazing for the buffalo, and then they would walk through it, so the other tribes called us Blackfeet. But the Crows and the Crees to the north, all our old enemies still refer to us as Piegans. My grandfather always told me that we were the last of the true Piegans. We're better looking, we're more intelligent . . . and we're better endowed!

"I've just gotten interested in this bird hunting during the last couple of years," Kipp was saying as we drove. "Traditionally in our culture we didn't hunt birds, because we wouldn't eat them. We ate only split-hooved animals. Birds were considered dirty because they're bug eaters. Fish, too, were dirty for that reason."

We arrived at a piece of ground belonging to Kipp's father-in-law along the Cutbank River, parked, uncased our guns, and set out down a rutted two-track. An old Indian drove by in a pickup, grinning a toothless smile. We appeared to be objects of great mirth to him.

"What's so funny?" I asked Kipp.

"Because we're on foot, instead of riding a horse or driving a truck," he explained. "It's not cool for an Indian to be seen walking. If I went up to the store this afternoon, they would tease me about it."

"Why?"

"Because you're not a cowboy if you're walking."

I could see that I had a lot to learn about Blackfeet.

A thin wind with a decidedly wintry edge had come up, pointing out how close I was to Canada. We were hunting Hungarian partridge. Though there are sharptail grouse on the reservation, too, Kipp had carefully explained to me that non–tribal members are not allowed to shoot these native birds. The Blackfeet are a proud, possessive, historically fearsome people. Enemies in the old days with virtually every other Indian tribe in the country—north, south, east, and west of them—they have never tolerated trespass by anyone, including the white tribe. There is no mistaking the fact that one is an invited guest on their land and I had the odd sensation of not being in the United States any longer, but of having a temporary visa in a foreign country with which I was still unfamiliar.

We came upon a dead red-tailed hawk on the ground on the side of the road; it looked like it might have flown into the power line overhead. I picked up one of the primary wing feathers and was about to put it in my game bag as a souvenir. "You may *have* that feather," said Kipp pointedly, and I realized that, of course, I should have asked first. This was his land, his hawk, his feather. So like a white man to take without asking.

"Thank you," I said.

"You're welcome."

Lewis came up the Cutbank River to find out how far north the rivers went. He was hoping they went beyond the 49th parallel because in those days the Republican Party wanted to establish the U.S.-Canadian border at the 54th parallel. He only had a small group with him and they were trying to get celestial readings, but it was cloudy. They were very apprehensive because they noticed that the game was skittish and so they knew that Indians had been hunting in the area. On the third night it finally cleared up enough for them to take readings. The next morning two Blackfeet youths showed up at their camp and demanded trespass fees. Someone in Lewis's party grabbed a gun and shot and killed one of the Indian boys. The other got away and ran back to tell the camp. A war party chased Lewis back to the Missouri, a close pursuit the whole way. That was our first contact with the American government and since then we've never really trusted them.

We hunted along the top and then dropped down into the Cutbank creek bottom, a lovely meandering stream, thick with cover. Sweetzer was working well, quartering in close, and paying attention. Joe had taken his pup back to the truck after only an hour because it was clear that she was too green to be of any use. It would be a rare occasion, indeed, that Sweetz got to be the oldest, most experienced dog in the field.

We worked our way up a draw, Kipp an observant and careful hunter, a master at reading sign. He showed me a place where the Huns had been dusting, the delicate pattern of their wing feathers distinct in the dirt. He pointed out a coyote scat, composed almost entirely of grasshoppers, and the tiny frail skeleton of a baby coyote—seemingly unimportant things that only a good hunter would bother to notice, or care to know, but that make a day afield infinitely richer.

Besides being a rancher, Kipp is a fishing guide on the reservation. The lakes here have gained some notoriety in the angling world over the past few years for producing ten-pound rainbow trout, and Joe is an accomplished fly fisherman in his own right. More recently he had started offering a "cast and blast" combination for paying guests—fishing part of the day and hunting the rest. He was beginning to recognize the economic potential of the recreational resources on the reservation, as was the tribal council. "We're learning," he said. "We're finally learning the importance of *nippiosy.*"

"Nippiosy?"

He smiled and rubbed his fingers together in the universal gesture for money. "Nippiosy," he repeated.

"I had a dream recently," Joe said. "In the dream I owned a couple of big-running pointing dogs. And I was hunting on horseback. The dogs would go on point way off in the distance and I'd ride over, dismount, and shoot the covey rise. Then I'd get back on my horse and the boy I had with me . . . a white boy . . . would run out and pick up the dead birds and carry them for me."

I had to look very closely at Kipp, to see if he was pulling my leg or not, and even then I wasn't sure.

Sweetzer began to get birdy, moving faster, tail wagging. We broke into a trot in order to keep up with her, and then suddenly fifty Huns were in the air all around us, coming off the ground like a swarm of bees. Kipp dropped to one knee, in the classic style of the deer hunter, and one I had not seen in a bird hunter before, and promptly unloaded all five shells from his 12-gauge pump shotgun. I fired both my barrels. We watched the birds disperse, most of the covey sailing down the draw, following the contour of the land around the corner, Sweetz in hot pursuit, certain, I think, that with all that gunfire, surely at least one would fall from the air for her to pick up. It did not. Kipp and I looked at each other. We laughed. I think we were both somewhat relieved that the other was not a crack wing shot. The only thing that brings hunters together faster than both shooting doubles on the first covey rise of the day is both whiffing. Now we could relax and not worry about embarrassing ourselves. "O for seven, Joe."

The Sioux sent a runner up to invite us down to the Little Bighorn but we said we would stay on our side of the Yellowstone River and if the soldiers crossed the river we would take care of them. And Custer sent a party of one hundred troopers as far as the Yellowstone. Some of their scouts crossed the river and they saw this one Blackfeet warrior on the hill. They identified him by his headgear. And they were leery of an ambush so they sent ten soldiers over to investigate. And a little later, the soldiers came running back, screaming, "Run for your lives! Every man for himself! It's a trap! There's three of them over there!"

We walked back down the draw to see if we could hunt up the birds again and just at the base where it widened out, Sweetzer flushed a bird from the grass. It got up right in front of me, I mounted my gun, swung through it, and just as I touched off the trigger it occurred to me that this bird was not a Hun at all but a sharptail, off limits to non–tribal members.

Too late. I like to think that I instinctively checked my swing, thus missing the bird intentionally, for it flew on unruffled. More likely I missed simply because I'm not a very good shot. But miss or not, by pulling the trigger on a sharptail, I had violated if not the letter of tribal law, certainly the spirit of it, and the etiquette. A bonehead white boy move, if ever there was one. My single shot rang out against the bluff, seemed to hang indefinitely on the air like an accusation. "Shit," I murmured, lowering my gun, wishing I could somehow draw the shot back into the barrel. "I forgot I'm not allowed to shoot sharptail," I added lamely. Joe looked at me with a glint in his dark eyes. I think there exists a kind of residual genetic fierceness in his character. In another time he might have been a great warrior. He looked at me with that glint in his eyes and the same small, fierce smile that I noticed when he related tales of his ancestors' exploits. He did not say a word.

In 1873 Eugene M. Baker's troops destroyed a village of 316 souls on the Marias River near Shelby. They waited until they had starved us out, until only a few remnant herds of buffalo were left and our people were sick and hungry. After that we never fought the whites again. My grandfather watched his whole family being massacred. Joe Kipp was a scout for that army and he adopted two orphaned teenage Indian boys. One of them was my grandfather. He took those boys back east and sent them to school in St. Louis where they learned to read and write.

We got into one more covey of Huns before breaking for lunch. Joe shot a double. As if being tested, I kicked up two more sharptail, and each time I mounted my gun but I did not shoot. We ate sandwiches and apples by the truck, and muffins that Joe had baked himself.

"Did you know that today is National Native American Day?" Joe asked. "National Injun Day!"

"No, I didn't know that. What are you supposed to do in honor of it?"

"I don't know. Spend the day with your favorite native American, I guess."

"Well good, I guess that's what I'm doing. And I guess that makes you my token Injun."

"Token Injun my ass!" Joe said, reaching for his gun.

"Only kidding, Joe."

After his education my grandfather came back here. This was about the time the Texans were stealing Mexican cattle and driving them up to Wyoming and Montana. My grandfather always said that he had a contract with those folks and he would ride down to southern Montana or northern Wyoming. Because it was a long trip he always arrived late at night. He would select the cattle he liked, and being a good-mannered man, and not wanting to wake the Texans so late at night to pay them, he would just leave very quietly with their cattle so as not to disturb anyone.

After lunch we left the truck and resumed our hunt. A steady wind blew out of the north, the day seasonably cool, and clouds beginning to mass on the horizon. Joe was a wonderful hunting companion. I liked his pace, which was neither overly fast nor dawdling, but steady and deliberate. I liked his alertness and attention to the earth, his knowledge of flora and fauna. He was clearly at home on this land, and he seemed neither bitter about the past nor discouraged for the future—and utterly content with the present. We worked our way down either side of a long, deep coulee and then went up on the ridge to hunt the high meadow sweetgrass.

Let me tell you what it means to me to be an Indian. This was the center of our ancestral land, right here, this reservation—the very heart of it. A few years ago the Canadian government brought some archaeologists in to study an old buffalo jump near here. It had been mined for minerals during the first and second world wars. The archaeologists started excavating and they determined that that buffalo jump had been used for between 7,800 and 8,000 years, and by the tool points and the other objects they found, they were able to identify that it had been used by Blackfeet people for that long. What it means to me to be an Indian is that every step I take, one of my ancestors has stepped there. There is not one inch of ground that they have not touched, have not shit upon, have not pissed on . . . their bones are all over here, their bones are the dirt. I have a relationship with that dirt. I can drive a four-wheel-drive truck and live in a trailer home and have all the modern conveniences, but as long as my sons can go outside and pat the dirt lovingly, I know that they are Indians.

Working the edge of a stubble field, Sweetzer lifted her nose to the air and winded a strong scent. She started running across the field, and I could tell that she did not have in mind to wait for us. I blew my whistle but a nose full of bird overrode the command. It was her worst hunting habit and I had not yet learned how to break her of it. It would plague me periodically across the country. Kipp and I broke into a run to keep up with her. Running and blowing my whistle until I was red in the face, I felt like a frustrated, overweight city cop trying to apprehend a fleet-footed teenage offender. It can be a disheartening thing to hunt hard all day and not see many birds and then watch your dog bust a covey out of range. However, we stayed close enough to her and when the covey got up it cooperated by swinging our way. They got up in staggered groups of two, three, and four at a time, one great advantage in having five shots rather than only two. Joe shot another double and Sweetzer retrieved them to me. He had forgotten his game vest and so I carried his birds in mine. "You know," he said, smiling wickedly, "I think you must be that white boy I dreamed about."

We hunted hard all afternoon, covering miles of upland pasture and wheat fields, up and down draws and coulees and river bottoms. It was a lovely day, punctuated by just enough birds to keep us interested. We found the last covey at sunset feeding in a stubble field.

Driving back to Joe's in the dusky light, I watched a black horse with a long mane and tail running a fence line just for the fun of it.

> *We would go out and steal horses from the Crows. We made the men cry and the pretty young women would follow us home. Our ancestors raided and pillaged as far south as Mexico. Sometimes they would be gone for three or four years at a time, huge war parties of two to three hundred men, sometimes as many as five hundred to a thousand. Kit Carson would always meet the Piegan bands ten miles out from his trading post and give them all kinds of gifts to keep them from coming to visit. Everyone wet their pants when they heard the name Blackfeet.*

I camped for the night behind Joe's barn, drank a beer, and roasted a pair of Huns in the oven for dinner. After dinner I was working in my notebook when Kipp knocked on the door of the camper.

"You wouldn't have an extra beer in there, would you?" he asked when I opened the door.

"Sure I do," I said.

"Don't worry," Kipp said with his sly smile, "I won't get drunk and murder and scalp you."

"I'm glad to hear that, Joe."

He came in and sat down at my small dinette table. "I like to drink a beer or two sometimes after supper," he said.

"So do I."

"Alcoholism is a very large problem on the reservation, but we're handling it. Our biggest enemy is stereotyping. The noble savage/mystical warrior? Bullshit. Wino? Bullshit. I take everyone at face value, white and Indian alike. Everyone is welcome at our services. We have guards there and they ask everyone that arrives the same question: 'Do you come to watch us pray, or do you come to pray with us?' We don't care what color they are, or what they look like. If they have the right answer to that question, they're welcome."

The thunder started in the middle of the night, a distant throaty growl rolling off the prairie. The temperature dropped and rain began to tick against the camper. Sweetz crawled under the down comforter with me. I like the warmth of dogs in bed and over the next months we would sleep many cold nights curled together like this.

It rained steadily all night, turning to a messy half-sleet by morning. I cracked the curtain and peered out the window over the bed. The sky was murky, streaked with dawn light on the eastern horizon. A train rumbled by, blowing its horn at the crossing in town. Most of the buildings out here were trailer houses, shacks, or low-income row housing. The day before on my way in, I had driven through Browning, the largest town on the reservation. By any standards I know, it is an ugly place. Until a few years ago many of its residents used to live in shacks on their own ancestral land, but the United States government, for reasons known only to itself, built a number of substandard housing projects in town and moved the people off the land, thus creating a bonafide urban-style ghetto in the middle of the Montana plains.

I got up and put the coffee on, fed Sweetz, and dressed quickly in the morning chill. We had said our good-byes the night before, and so I drove out of Joe Kipp's yard, across the railroad tracks, and back onto the highway. As in many Latin countries, white crosses, some adorned with faded plastic flowers, marked the places where people had died in traffic accidents, the great majority of them alcohol related. They are a sobering sight at dawn on the res and though the sky was lightening and I had the heater on high, I couldn't get the chill out of my bones.

There were four things that a Blackfeet could obtain that signified great bravery and daring: a jaguar hide from Mexico, a sea otter hide from the Pacific coast, a polar bear hide from the Hudson Bay, and a wild turkey feather (at that time turkeys were not native west of the Mississippi). If you could obtain one of those four things it was a mark of great honor for all time.

So much for the white man's puny version of the Montana grand slam. Sweetz and I headed east across the plains, one step ahead of winter.

OCTOBER

South Dakota

Minnesota

Wisconsin

Michigan

Ohio

West Virginia

Pennsylvania

6

TWO-BIT ADVICE

We are not separate from our environment; each species we destroy and each habitat we ravage, whether by bulldozer or pesticides, represents one more bridge that we have burned in our own ultimate battle for survival.

Paul A. Johnsgard, GROUSE AND QUAILS OF NORTH AMERICA

I was next in line to pay for my gas at a truck stop outside Gillette, Wyoming, when a family of tourists came bustling excitedly through the door. There was a mother and a father, a boy and a girl. They looked like they had been carefully chosen by central casting to play a family of American tourists. They wore T-shirts and sweatshirts from some of the places they had visited on their vacation, sneakers, and shorts. The kids had braces on their teeth and were eating ice cream cones. The father had pale, hairless, strangely muscleless legs beneath his Bermudas. He clearly had a desk job. He approached the cashier. "What are those animals that we see along the interstate," he asked, "the ones that look like deer?"

"Antelope," said the cashier.

"Antelope!" said the father, turning to his family.

"Antelope!" they all said, smiling and nodding eagerly.

"Do they raise them around here, or are they just wild?" the father asked the cashier.

"They're just wild," said the cashier. The family bustled back out the door, discussing this new information excitedly. "Antelope!" they were saying.

I stepped up to pay for my gas. "Aliens," the cashier explained with a knowing look. "We get 'em through here all the time. They come down to spy on us."

The front that had chased me across Wyoming finally caught me in

Deadwood, South Dakota, bringing with it the first real snow of the season. I spent the night parked in the driveway of an old bird hunting friend from Colorado. Stephen and I hadn't seen each other in several years, but I'd heard that he had had troubles. He'd been fired from his job as a high school English teacher for insubordination, and had gone to work as a night watchman in a lumber mill. It wasn't a bad job for him because all he really liked to do was read, but then his wife ran off with the owner of the mill, and the drugs and the drinking began to get the upper hand. One night he was in a bar in Denver and two days later he woke up in a hotel room in Waikiki with a lei around his neck and a woman named Dolores from Duluth, Minnesota, in his bed. He did not remember how he got to Waikiki, or who Dolores was, although she claimed to be his new bride and told him that they'd been married in Reno the night before. "We're in love," he remembers Dolores explaining to him that morning in Hawaii.

Stephen took the next plane back to the mainland and when he walked into his house he discovered that he had been robbed while he was away, probably by some of his unsavory drug connections. They killed his cat and took everything in his house—television, stereo, every stick of furniture, all his books, his clothes, his dishes and cookware. They even cleaned out the refrigerator. Professional movers do not empty a house as thoroughly, and, of course, they generally don't kill your cat. The robbers also stole his car, which had been parked in the driveway.

Recognizing bottom when he saw it, Stephen decided that this might be a good time to start over. He checked himself into a rehab clinic, joined AA, quit drinking and taking drugs, fell off the wagon, twice—hard—and finally went home to Deadwood to live with his mother. For obvious reasons, Stephen avoided contact with his old friends. He quit hunting, too, sobriety being a kind of full-time vocation. I admired him for the way he had pulled himself out of the hole, but our relationship seemed to have taken on a new cautious tone, a certain stiff, arm's-length formality. I'm sure that I, too, reminded him of times that he would rather forget, and though I understood, it made me sad just the same. I hadn't given him much notice of my arrival in Deadwood, and he was unable to have dinner with me because it happened that that same night he was attending an AA convention at a local motel.

Before I left at daybreak the next morning, Stephen came out to the camper and presented me with a beautiful little 20-gauge Parker shotgun that had belonged to his father. "I'm finished with hunting," he said simply, "and I want you to have this."

"I couldn't possibly take that gun," I protested. "Anyway, you may change your mind one day."

But Stephen insisted; it seemed terribly important to him that I have that gun and I finally agreed on the condition that he could have it back if he ever changed his mind. I certainly would never sell it. At the same time, we both tacitly understood that we were not going to see each other again, and that the Parker was a parting gift, closing that particular door. A fine snow was falling as I drove out the driveway.

Later that day I stopped at the Two-Bit Saloon near the little town of Fort Pierre, South Dakota. I didn't know anyone to hunt with around here and needed some information. Bars are notoriously bad places to obtain reliable hunting and fishing information, and there was only one customer in the Two-Bit at this early hour, a local farmer drinking screwdrivers. "If there was any chickens around here," the farmer said, referring to the native prairie chicken (pinnated grouse), "I'd be out hunting them right now." He tilted his glass toward the bartender as a signal for a refill. The bartender was a dark-haired, sinewy woman, strikingly pale, with a distinct shadow of black moustache. "I ain't seen a chicken or a sharptail in this country in four, maybe five years," the farmer said. "Used to be some, but we had a bad winter in eighty-four and they never came back. Also, when the bottom fell out of the fur business people around here stopped shooting coyotes and now we got too goddamn many of them. They don't give the birds a chance to come back."

I decided to ignore the farmer's advice; I had a suspicion that one reason he hadn't seen a game bird in five years was because he'd been sitting on a bar stool most of that time. I drove out to the Fort Pierre National Grassland where I found a place to make camp for the night and some nice-looking cover along a dry river bottom. It was pretty in the bottom, a clean fall breeze rustling the cottonwoods and Russian olives that grew along the banks. The snow had melted, the air was washed with a pure, cool scent. The prairie above was tawny with soft autumn light, and notable for having boot-top-high grass growing on it. The agricultural community has tremendous political clout in South Dakota, as in most western states, and the designation "national grassland" does not make land off-limits to grazing, or, indeed, even ensure that there is sufficient grass left standing for use by the native species that depend on it.

I knew very little about this area, but sometimes it's lovely to explore new country alone, to hunt unfamiliar terrain without benefit of a local guide. Besides the miles of healthy-looking prairie grasses, there seemed to be plenty of good cover and feed, both native and cultivated— chokecherry bushes and wild rosehips, as well as small plots of sorghum, sunflower, and corn. To see familiar trees, plants, bushes, and crops can make a hunter feel at home in any country, like running into old friends.

Two whitetail deer bounded out of a willow thicket, startling us, and we watched them, tails flagging up and down until they were out of sight.

We followed the winding ribbon of trees along the dried riverbed, cracked in endless mosaic patterns. I wondered if this river ran year-round in better rain years, or before it had been diverted for irrigation purposes when the Sioux still inhabited the land; it would be a fine place to set camp, and I wondered if young Indian boys hunted birds in this same bottom that I now walked. Unlike their enemies to the west, the fearsome Blackfeet, the Sioux ate game birds—grouse, ducks, and geese—though they were hardly considered suitable game for grown men to pursue, left largely to the boys.

We didn't put up any sharptail and I decided to leave the river bottom and look for prairie chickens in the tall grass above. At one time, prairie chickens (of which there are three subspecies: greater, lesser, and Attwater) inhabited the Midwest by the millions, from Ohio to Minnesota to New Mexico—wherever there were large, undisturbed tracts of prairie grasslands. In his classic, *A Sand County Almanac*, the great conservationist and father of game management (and avid bird hunter) Aldo Leopold writes of the year 1873 when food brokers in Chicago purchased 600,000 prairie chickens from market gunners. No misprint there—600,000. The species was driven to near extinction by the early 1900s, both as a result of this relentless market hunting pressure and by the even more devastating loss of its traditional range as more and more miles of virgin prairie were plowed for grain cultivation or grazed by cattle. Though the prairie chicken thrives near croplands, it also requires large, relatively pristine blocks of tallgrass prairie for nesting and roosting, a sensible balance increasingly hard to maintain in a world of single-crop agribusiness and overgrazed federal lands.

Today the prairie chicken exists in small, isolated populations in a handful of western plains states, only four of which maintain huntable numbers of the bird. Nor will it be sport hunting, finally, that finishes off the species; were it not for the efforts of various sportsmen's organizations in concert with state game departments, even less prairie chicken habitat would remain. American sportsmen, in turn, have been compensated and placated for the demise of this wonderful, once prolific grouse by the introduction of the ring-necked pheasant from Europe, a fine game bird in its own right and one considerably more adaptable to modern agricultural practices, but in this hunter's opinion a shoddy substitute for the extirpated natives.

Even unluckier than its western cousins, a fourth species of prairie chicken, the eastern pinnated grouse, or heath hen, became extinct in 1931. In his monumental work *Grouse and Quails of North America*, Paul

Johnsgard tells the bitter tale of the lonely mating dance of the last heath hen: "It is a melancholy thought that, after its compatriots had disappeared, the last surviving male heath hen in North America faithfully returned each spring to its traditional mating ground on Martha's Vineyard, Massachusetts, where it displayed alone to an unhearing and unseeing world."

Sweetz got birdy on the edge of a low grassy swale, from which the prairie climbed to unbroken horizon; I hurried to keep up with her and heard the heavy rustle of wings in the grass, followed by the heart-stopping whir of liftoff, the blurred, mottled brown-and-white vision of bird against late afternoon sky. The prairie chicken has graced the savannahs and prairies of North America since the ice retreated; its ancestors evolved on this continent somewhere around twenty-five million years ago. *Twenty-five million years.* Can there be any doubt that we owe them a place to live? I mounted my gun, swung, and fired as the bird leveled off and set its wings to glide for an instant before the perfect parabola of flight was interrupted—a limp form, already dead, tumbling back to earth.

I gathered dead wood in the river bottom and built a fire as the sun set over the prairie. I roasted the chicken over red-hot coals.

7

HOUSTON LAW

In all revolutions the first thing that the "people" have done was to jump over the fences of the preserves or tear them down, and in the name of social justice pursue the hare and the partridge.

Ortega y Gasset

"Frank runs a first-class operation here," said Charlie, a twangy Texas tax attorney, with a mouth full of roast beef.

"They really know how to take care of you," agreed medical malpractice specialist Mike, nodding.

"They *really* know how to take care of you," concurred personal injury litigator Lance.

"We come without the wives," explained Peter, a divorce lawyer. "Gives the partners a chance to get to know each other one-on-one, outside the office and away from the cocktail party circuit. Lets us compare notes and touch base with the different departments of the firm. It's very valuable, not only from a 'people' point of view but in terms of overall operations."

I was visiting Stukel's Birds and Bucks, a family farm and game bird preserve in Gregory, South Dakota, run by the brothers Stukel—Ray, Frank, and Cal. At the time of my visit, a group of attorneys—a baker's dozen—the senior partners of a prominent law firm in Houston, Texas, were spending the weekend at Stukel's. The lawyers were on one of those corporate retreats that involve brainstorming and bonding with one another in the great outdoors. Personally, I'm sorry to see the outdoor pursuits of fishing and hunting increasingly used as management "tools" by corporate America. This kind of thing strikes me as altogether counter to the real point of fishing and hunting, which, as the Spanish philosopher Ortega y

Gasset put it, is to provide us with a "vacation from the human condition."
And I'm pretty sure he didn't mean a working vacation.

By all appearances, private preserve shooting represents the future of
bird hunting in America. For centuries in Europe, the sport has been
exclusively the domain of the ruling classes, a holdover from the days of
feudalism, as well as a result of overpopulation and an exponentially shrinking land base. In a very real sense our ancestors left the Old World so that
they might hunt and fish freely in the wide open, game-rich spaces of
America. Sadly, the same process of privatization is underway in many parts
of the United States—perhaps less so in the West due to the extensive
public lands, but certainly in the Midwest, the East, and the South—and
for the same reasons that it occurred in Europe: too many people, not
enough available land.

Such renowned pheasant hunting states as South Dakota and Iowa are
becoming increasingly locked up by hunting leases, private preserves, and
pay-to-hunt operations. There was a time, not so long ago, when farmers
and ranchers in these parts freely gave permission to hunt their property, at
no charge, expecting in return only that the hunter perform the basic
courtesies of closing gates, treating the land with respect, and perhaps
sharing a bird or two from his bag. This democratic and amiable relationship between hunter and landowner was intact for many years and indeed,
there are isolated pockets where it still exists, but they are more and more
difficult to find. Now it is possible to drive for several hours in South
Dakota, past vast posted acreage, to stop at a dozen farmhouses in a row
and be denied permission to hunt because the hunting rights are leased,
either to individuals or to sportsmen's groups. You can't blame the farmer,
who has discovered hunting as yet another cash crop, and a profitable one at
that. At the same time, too many hunters over the years have abused the
landowner's generosity—leaving gates open, knocking down crops, pushing over fences, even peppering the farmer's house with shot or accidentally
shooting his stock. All too often hunters don't ask permission at all, but
simply trespass at will. Not without justification is the modifier "slob" so
frequently attached to the noun "hunter."

If the future of bird hunting in America appears to lie squarely in the
hands of private ownership, the good news is twofold: Due to economic
incentive, in many cases private landowners, rather than state or federal
agencies, have taken the lead in protecting wildlife and enhancing habitat,
while, with the gluttonous "rabble" no longer able to hunt many areas,
pressure on game bird populations may actually be reduced. As a member
of that rabble, I can tell you that the bad news, of course, is that the
"people" are being locked off the land, while hunting pressure on remaining public lands is actually increased. But that's the way it is at the tail end

of the twentieth century, and my suggestion to those who can't afford to pay to hunt is to cultivate the friendship of someone who can.

Sometimes aptly referred to as "whorehouse" shooting, stocked preserve shooting is to real bird hunting what whorehouses are to sexual love— sometimes a pretty good substitute, even an uncanny imitation, but always an illusion and never quite the same thing. I would visit three preserves in three different regions of the country during the course of my trip, but Stukel's would be the only one I would actually hunt. I prefer hunting wild birds in wild country; to me that's the primary joy of the sport, and I've never been able to get beyond the artificiality of most stocked preserves. In Georgia, for instance, I visited a silly little place that billed itself grandly as a "plantation," but in reality consisted of a mere forty acres on which pen-raised birds were released just prior to the shoot. There I was greeted by the proprietor, a bandy-legged southern gentleman, dressed in the English style—plus fours and tweed shooting cap—who carried the illusion to the limit by affecting an English accent in order to provide a more "authentic" experience for his guests.

As preserves go, Stukel's is as good as they get, and the Stukel brothers don't pretend to be anything other than exactly what they are. Ray, the oldest, is the rancher in the family, a taciturn man who manages Stukel's Angus Ranch, a separate working cattle ranch on the Missouri Breaks where I would hunt sharptail grouse the following day. Frank, the youngest, is the farmer; more gregarious and outgoing, he handles the pheasant hunting operation and deals with the guests. Cal, the middle brother, is the chef and baker of the operation—a cheerful, roly-poly fellow, perpetually coated with a light dusting of flour, who runs Stukel's Cafe in town, a family business which he took over from his father. The boys all grew up in the hotel above the café, three out of a raucous family of ten kids, their parents hardworking, thrifty immigrants from Eastern Europe.

That morning one group of attorneys had been hunting sharptail grouse on the ranch, while the other hunted pheasants on the farm. The actual hunting day at Stukel's is a leisurely affair for the sports, an hour and a half or so in the morning, about that long in the afternoon. In between, Cal puts on an enormous country-style feed and at night a similarly sumptuous dinner feast for the guests.

The sharptail hunt hadn't been too successful, only one bird, but the attorneys came back with an anecdote to tell on one of their group. "You can put this in your book!" said corporate lawyer Jack. So here it is: Frustrated by the slow hunting and hoping to double the day's bag, Donald, a probate attorney, shot a grouse off a power line at the end of the morning, but he only crippled the bird so that it flew strangely along the ground with its tail tilted down at an odd angle [laughter here]. The shooter chased after the crippled grouse, like a Keystone Cop, trying to grab it [more laughter], but the bird, though clearly mortally wounded, escaped, and the hunters didn't bother trying to search for it because they were afraid they'd miss lunch.

After lunch, while the attorneys retired to their rooms for reading and nap time, I rode around the farm with Frank, admiring the ongoing habitat improvement work he was doing on the place. "It's nice talking to someone who has an interest in the land," he was saying. "That seems to me such an important part of hunting that it always surprises me when we have guests here who have no interest in anything other than pulling the trigger. They don't care where the birds come from, whether they're wild or planted, what they eat or where they live, so long as they have something to shoot at, and so long as they shoot their limit."

"You're speaking of the present guests?" I inferred.

But Frank, a fit, easygoing man, a fine host and extremely diplomatic, was not taking the bait. He just smiled and said, enigmatically, "We get some really great people here."

The Stukel brothers have done a spectacular job of enhancing habitat on their farm and implementing farming practices that are beneficient, not only to pheasants but to wildlife in general. Though they raise and release some 1,500 birds in an average year, the habitat work they have done has also resulted in a large increase in wild pheasant populations, as well as in many other kinds of wildlife. Their property is a lovely anachronism, a throwback to the days when farmers grew more than one crop, without pesticides, and before they mowed down or doused with herbicides every other living thing that wasn't part of that crop. "We let our fields get dirtier than other farmers," Frank explained. By "dirtier," he meant simply that they don't discourage border cover from growing between the fields and along fence rows and are not so intolerant of the grasses, weeds, bushes, and trees that make a farm a natural part of the landscape. It's a gorgeous place, the kind of farm that makes a hunter's heart glad. Besides a wonderful vegetable garden and squash patch, the Stukels raise corn, milo, cane, wheat, alfalfa, and oats. Cottonwoods, cedars, plum brush, Russian olives, ash, honey locust, black walnut, wild rose, cattails, and cotoneasters grow profusely around the place, some naturally, others strategically planted in rows and contours as cover and winter protection for the pheasants. Frank plants several thousand trees and bushes every year, and has dug out ponds and catch basins all around the farm to provide water. "I love to do all this," he says proudly. Around the ponds more cover has seeded in and grown up. In twenty-four hours on the farm, I saw a family of foxes crossing the road, heard coyotes yipping at night and the somber tones of a great horned owl before dawn, watched deer in the fields in the evening and red-tailed hawks circling the thermals by day. A raccoon woke me in the middle of the night, nosing curiously around the camper. The presence of all these animals suggests a living ecosystem, a habitat where wildlife and human beings, predator and prey alike, can coexist and prosper.

That afternoon I went out in the field with the senior partners. I didn't carry a gun, both because I wasn't a paying guest and because I'm not much of a fan of group pheasant hunting, which always strikes me as too regimented and militaristic. I prefer my own peregrinations afield to be less formal—working the edge cover and fence rows, alone with the dog or with one or two companions.

Modeled after the European style of driven shoots, one group, the blockers, is dropped off and positioned at the end of a cornfield, while the other, the beaters, walk toward them through the field with the dogs quartering ahead. The pheasants tend to run in front of the dogs, until reaching the blockers at the end of the field, when they are forced to fly and the shooting begins.

Watching Frank organizing his guests in the first field that afternoon, I was reminded of the last time I was involved in a group pheasant hunting situation, several years ago in Kansas, where, somehow, I hooked up with a party of detectives from the Kansas City Police Department. We rode out to the cornfield in the back of a pickup truck, the cops, serious, somewhat humorless fellows, as silent and stony-faced as if on the way to an undercover drug bust rather than a pheasant hunt. They had several enormous, blocky-headed black Labs with them and, trying to make conversation, I asked the detectives what their dogs' names were. They answered in clipped professional tones.

"Rocky," said one.

"Rambo," said another.

"Cobra," said a third.

"First Blood," said a fourth.

First Blood? "Boy, you guys must really like Sylvester Stallone," I said lamely. They just looked at me with flat, inscrutable expressions. In retrospect, I'm grateful that this was before I had my own little Lab. "My dog's name is Sweetzer," I'd have had to say, and they probably would have slapped the cuffs on me right there.

That day I was stationed as a blocker in a line of several officers at the end of the cornfield. As the other group marched toward us through the field, one lone pheasant got up between us. As if on signal, the KCPD detective squad raised their automatic shotguns and opened fire, a volley of gunfire that put me in mind of the climactic scene at the end of the film *Bonnie and Clyde*, when Faye Dunaway and Warren Beatty are ambushed in their car. It stands to reason that the detectives were more than competent shots and in the face of their considerable firepower, the hapless pheasant didn't stand a chance. It was a bloodbath—the bird cut to ribbons in the air, feathers flying. When the guns fell silent and the smoke cleared, one of the dogs retrieved the mutilated carcass of the victim, which looked like it had hit the grille of an eighteen-wheeler doing 90 mph on the interstate— to my way of thinking a clear-cut case of police brutality.

The only thing that made the afternoon pheasant hunt with the attorneys slightly more enjoyable was the fact they were not nearly as good shots as the detectives, and any pheasant flying the gauntlet between beaters and blockers had better than even odds of escape. Frank told the attorneys exactly where to stand and how to work the fields but for some reason they tended to ignore his instructions and do it however they pleased. I have some of the shooting that afternoon on tape. You can hear the beaters coming through the field, swishing the corn, yodeling and calling out, much like cowboys on a cattle drive, urging the herd on. Then you can hear the pandemonium erupt when the pheasants begin to fly, the excited cries of the attorneys, as if addressing the bench, "Hen!" they yell, as female pheasants, protected by law from shooting, get up (though that doesn't necessarily keep the lawyers from shooting at them). Or, "Cock! Cock! Cock! Over there, coming toward you, Jack! Get 'em. Coming your way, Harold! Cock! Cock! Shoot the son of a bitch!" And the sound of shotguns, puny little pops on the tape, but reminiscent of the moment all the same. *Pop-pop, pop-pop-pop, pop-pop, pop, pop.* A volley of shots, shouts, and laughter as the attorneys cut loose, caught up in the hunt, and with no judge or jury to censor their behavior.

I rooted hard for the birds, and I still remember one particularly extraordinary rooster dodging lead from six separate shooters as he made his courageous flight across the cornfield to the safety of the field behind them, not a feather disturbed, though I counted 17 shells discharged at him, an average of 2.83 shots per shooter. It was not that bird's day to die.

Much of the action I watched from behind one of the trucks, like a cowardly soldier avoiding combat. Frank had already identified for me the two or three least experienced shooters in the field, among them an environmental lawyer named Harold, whose job it was to defend industrial clients against pollution raps. Harold wore a brand-new, full-length Australian-style drover coat and carried his gun at his waist, pointed straight ahead, the way a gangster carries a machine gun. If he happened to turn around to address you he would swing the gun barrel right across your midsection—a real heart-stopper.

The attorneys hunted four fields before limiting out for the day. It was that collective body count that most seemed to interest them, and when all the pheasants were lined up on the tailgate and the figures tallied and the hunt declared over, everyone went home happy. It was conversely clear that had the attorneys not shot their limit every day, the weekend might be considered far less successful, tips perhaps even withheld from staff. Indeed, ensuring that the attorneys filled their limit was a large part of Frank's responsibility, and came under the heading of "taking care" of his guests. I'd have liked to take some of the counselors chukar hunting in the high lonesome of Nevada, say a forced march up a mountain slope of loose scree at nine thousand feet, with a stiff wind at the summit and a sheer cliff falling away on the backside.

"How can you stand baby-sitting these assholes?" I finally baldly inquired of Frank after the hunt. But sly Frank was not going on record as being anything other than a gracious host. "This is the first time we've ever had a whole group of lawyers!" was all he would say, with a smile.

That afternoon, Frank let me take Sweetzer out alone for a short hunt. We walked the edge cover by a cane stubble field and jumped a pheasant right away. My nerves still jangled from the earlier shoot (at least that's my excuse), I shot and missed. We hunted around the tall grass surrounding a pumpkin patch. Next to the pumpkin patch, in what must have been the original farm dump, and nearly obscured by grass growing up through it, lay the old neon Stukel's Cafe sign, relegated to the dump during a remodeling some years ago. Frank had told me that as a boy he used to lie in bed at night in his room in the hotel and watch the bulbs flash around that sign outside his window. "I *hated* that sign," he had said, laughing. I was just about to sit down by the sign and try to imagine what it must have been like growing up in a family of ten kids in a hotel above a café in Gregory, South Dakota (compared to my own relatively solitary childhood in the Chicago suburbs it struck me as terribly romantic), when suddenly a cock pheasant rocketed up out of the grass right in front of me, seemed to fly right out of the neon sign like an idea. I recovered my composure just in time to squeeze off a shot, and the pheasant folded. It was Sweetzer's first pheasant and after she brought it to me I sat down on the sign and indulged my reverie. I didn't care to kill any more pheasants.

Later over a poker game in the lodge, I was inquiring of Bob, a tall bankruptcy attorney dressed in lizard-skin cowboy boots, if the firm's business had suffered in the past few years because of the downturn in the Texas oil industry. "Quite the contrary, Jim," said Bob, whose overly earnest demeanor put one in mind of a particularly oily used car salesman, "our company has actually grown in the last few years, directly as a result of the oil bust. You see there's been a tremendous amount of oil litigation and many companies seeking protection under Chapter Eleven. This has resulted in a corresponding boom in the legal field. It's been very good to us, Jim."

"Have you ever likened your firm to a pack of jackals, picking the bones clean, Bob?"

"A dirty job, Jim," said Bob, exposing jackal-like incisors, "but somebody's got to do it."

"Now I have a question for you, Jim," Bob said.

"Shoot, Counselor."

"Are you going to defend us against the antihunters in your book?"

"We'll need a friendly jury, Bob, but I'll sure do my best."

More weather came in overnight, and I woke in the camper to a dense fog and several inches of heavy wet snow on the ground. I was headed out to Ray's ranch to hunt sharptail, and I stopped first in town for a dawn breakfast at Stukel's Cafe, which may be one of the best small-town cafés in America. (I offer as proof of my qualifications as Middle American café critic a stunning 100-point rise in my cholesterol level in five months on the road.) Cal Stukel is a considerable cut above the average short-order cook, and especially adept in the baked goods department.

Wet snow turned to wetter rain by the time I arrived at the ranch, but the fog was lifting. Ray met me at the house and drove me around in his truck to give me the lay of the land before leaving me to my own devices. He was a quiet, soft-spoken man who had only recently recovered from a heart attack and, as is often the case, was profoundly moved and changed by the experience. "I never really knew how Ray felt about the land," Frank had told me the day before, "until after his heart attack when he suddenly started talking about it." Ray was responsible for much of the enlightened land management and beneficent land-use practices implemented on the farm and the ranch, and from the look and condition of both, his efforts had been a resounding success. It's not hard to identify land that is loved by its stewards as opposed to that which is simply used.

The rain had slowed to a light misting drizzle and I set out down the muddy ranch road, dressed in rubber hunting boots and hooded raingear. The soil was of a heavy, slick clay composition and clung to my boots and to Sweetzer's paws; soon we both owned ponderous feet of clay. We left the road, trying to shake off the mud, and worked our way up across the grassy slopes of the Missouri Breaks overlooking the river in the distance. It was easier walking here but still strenuous—up and down the rolling hills and across the ridge tops, classic upland country that perhaps due to the chilly mist under a dark, moody sky reminded me of the Scottish moors, although I've seen them only in photographs and paintings. The range was in excellent condition, the grass sparingly grazed and heavy with brown seed, the hills sparsely studded with rock and junipers, the deep reds, yellows, and browns of fall intensified by the wetness. Small oases of cover were tucked into the swales and saddles—clusters of sage green Russian olives and thickets of bright red rosehips. We watched a red-tailed hawk try to set down on the branch of a large perfectly formed juniper tree at the top of a hill above us. The branch was not sturdy enough to support his weight and he had to keep his wings parted for balance; finally he gave it up as too precarious and lifted off again.

We climbed the hill to the juniper tree, which seemed almost super-naturally beautiful—deep green in the rain, shining with brilliant purple berries, a delicate lace of wet spider webs glistening between the branches. In the distance beyond and below, the river snaked wide and huge, the breaks going off as far as I could see. I watched a mule deer disappear over a distant ridge top, and three tiny white-tailed deer bound from a thicket below. I looked up to see the redtail, circling high again, like us, hunting. In the face of such splendor, I had long since forgotten my litigious company of the day before. I picked a sprig of berries and needles from the juniper tree and put it in my bag as a totem.

We worked over the top of the hill and down the other side, and Sweetzer began to get birdy on the edge of a dense stand of Russian olives that grew along the slope. She dove in, tail wagging stiffly, and flushed a sharptail. It came out heavy-winged and lumbering, reluctant, I think, to give up its cover in the nasty weather. I brought my gun up and swung on it, but for some reason I didn't shoot. I watched over the barrels as the bird set its wings and sailed toward the Missouri.

8

HOPE

We must immerse ourselves wholly and heroically in an occupation in order to dominate it, to be it!

Ortega y Gasset

I woke late the next morning parked on the edge of a cornfield along a two-track dirt road outside Hope, Minnesota. After a splendid hunt on the Missouri Breaks, which is distinctly western country, I had driven until nearly midnight and I was now in the flat Minnesota farmland—back in the Middle West, no mistaking it.

A lovely, cold fall morning, clear outside, the first sunshine I'd seen in days. The camper windows were beaded with dew and neither Sweetz nor I seemed able to get out of bed. We burrowed deeper under the down comforter and I pressed my face into her fur; she still smelled of the breaks—the clay, the wet and verdant hills. In Wyoming she smelled of sage and on the Blackfeet reservation, swampy, from wallowing in an alkali pond; all across the country she would carry the scents of the land in her fur.

This seemed a good time to take stock. It takes time to settle into the rhythms of the land and of the hunt, but if you love country, you will never really be lonely, and if you love to hunt, you will certainly never be bored. Yet I felt still distinctly clumsy, as if only halfway through the metamorphosis, shedding the layers of dead skin that need to be sloughed off before one can truly enter the landscape. It had begun to occur to me that it is virtually impossible to be a real hunter in this culture, in this era; the closest one can hope for is a kind of make-believe that mimics the illusion of the game preserve, and requires a certain conscious effort at that. I had not opened a piece of junk mail in over a month, nor paid a bill; I had no telephone where I could be reached. Though I had an answering machine at home, I had stopped calling it. Except for periodically checking in with my wife, the hunter was now officially incommunicado. (When she told me on the phone that so-and-so had been trying to get ahold of me, I would answer, portentously: "Tell him I can't be reached.") No television, and I'd barely looked at a newspaper in the past month. Momentous events shook the world, America geared up for war, and my interest was entirely taken up by the pursuit of game birds, by where and with whom I would hunt next. Surely this was escapism of the most frivolous sort. There would be sufficient bills and oceans of junk mail awaiting on the back end of the trip to bring me jarringly back into the "real" world, but for now the hunter and his dog were at large in the countryside. We had shotguns and shells, a larder full of game birds to eat, and plenty more to hunt.

9

THE PRIMEVAL
FOREST

Considering the prodigious achievements of the profit motive in wrecking land, one hesitates to reject it as a vehicle for restoring land.

Aldo Leopold

If you ever walk in a large mature aspen forest, and pay attention, you will notice several things: One, the tall, slender, white-barked trees that are still alive are quite lovely, they sway seductively to the slightest breeze, their high leafy tops straining for the sunlight above. Two, many of the trees are beginning to die, some standing dead, others already fallen to decay on the forest floor. Three, very little else grows on that forest floor. It is a kind of biological desert without enough sunlight penetrating the leafy canopy to allow other, low-growing species of flora to exist. There is, for the most part, no species diversity—no bushes, grasses, weeds, wildflowers, or berries. Without these things, it stands to reason that there is also very little in the way of wildlife. Which is not to suggest that the old forest is a "bad" thing, only that it has passed its prime. In a healthy, functioning, natural forest, there would be stands of trees of all ages in all stages of growth and regrowth—much as in a healthy human society—young, middle-aged, and old. In the primeval forest, the tall, standing dead timber would eventually be struck by lightning and ignite; the fire would spread to the deadfall on the forest floor and the ensuing conflagration would destroy the old forest. Inside of a year the suckers from the aspen roots would break ground; wildflower and grass seeds would blow into the new opening or be carried in by birds and animals, which also love sunlight and clearings. In the primeval forest, all would thrive in the fire-enriched soil and the process of regeneration would begin anew. And the grouse would take up habitation.

Recently while I was living in Idaho, protestors in our valley chained themselves to a couple of old cottonwood trees that were scheduled to be cut down to make room for a new lane on the highway. I admired the conviction of the protestors, though given that the environmental quality of the valley had already been seriously compromised by over a decade of rampant, no-holds-barred development, the gesture struck me as quite a bit too little, too late. The time to protect those trees was long gone; now the highway department had no choice but to make the road wider to accommodate the traffic from all the new residents—the builders, developers, realtors, workers, and the thousands of incoming lifestyle seekers. I mention this only by way of pointing out that cutting down trees, any trees, has become an extremely sensitive issue of late, symbolic of far deeper troubles, both locally and globally, and inextricably linked in the minds of the public to the decimation of old-growth forest in the Pacific Northwest and to the continuing destruction of the rain forest in the Southern Hemisphere (different issues in different ecosystems, altogether). These days, earnest, if often badly informed, celebrities are forever popping up on television suggesting that everyone do their part to "save a tree," a real public relations nightmare for the beleaguered timber industry, which is already under fire for better than a century of over-harvesting and bad timber management.

The logging practice of clear-cutting is particularly vulnerable, and, like dead baby seals, makes a convenient and compelling poster child to point up the horrors of our environmental insensitivity. Badly accomplished in many parts of the West, where timbering of steep slopes causes severe topsoil erosion and stream siltation, clear-cuts are ugly to look at in the early stages and encourage the public perception that *all* logging is a messy, destructive business, undertaken by beer-swilling, low-class cretins who leave in their wake a wasteland of stumps, dead land, and extinct species. Yet there is also such a thing as sustainable logging—sensible, sensitive, rotational cutting programs designed by competent, conscientious professional foresters, often working in conjunction with wildlife experts. We have two choices if we want a living forest: Let the fires burn, when and where they will; or manage through sustainable logging practices. Just as we're unlikely to have the buffalo herds, the free-roaming Plains Indian tribes, and the clouds of prairie chickens back on the prairie, I'm afraid it's too late to recover the primeval forest.

"It is no coincidence that grouse and aspen trees get along so well together," wildlife biologist Gordon Gullion explained, "because indications are that in the primeval forest we experienced significant fires every thirty or forty years across northern Minnesota and probably across most of the range of aspen. Aspens recover quickly from these so-called disastrous fires, which are actually essential to maintaining the health of the forest. Grouse find their niche in the aspens, and they need the trees in all their growth stages. The ten- to twenty-five-year-old trees offer prime habitat as cover, and the birds feed on the buds of the thirty-year-old and older trees. Throughout the spring and summer they eat the leaves of all age trees but in the fall the leaves on the young suckers stay green and fleshy longer and are an important late-season food resource."

I sat in Gullion's small, cluttered log cabin office, an isolated, monklike enclave set deep in the pines at the Cloquet Forestry Center in northern Minnesota. An electric desk light was no match for the afternoon darkness of the northwoods in the fall. When you've just come from the open spaces of the West, the midwestern forest can take some getting used to.

Gordon Gullion is widely acknowledged as the world's foremost authority on the habits and habitat of the ruffed grouse, his book *The Ruffed Grouse* the standard reference work on the species. A friendly man with a deep, easy laugh, Gullion has passed the seasons of his lifetime in the forest pursuing grouse—observing, trapping, banding, and tracking them. For my part, this was a kind of pilgrimage on the hunter's road, undertaken with the same reverence with which one might approach a Zen master— partly in the hope of absorbing some modicum of his knowledge, and also to pay respect.

"It's taken me twenty or thirty years of work in the field to learn what makes good grouse habitat," Gullion said. "Now with the cooperation of the lumber companies and the foresters in this area we're beginning to understand how to manage the forest to the best advantage of the birds. And the modifications and improvements we're implementing in terms of timber practices not only benefit grouse but other species of birds and animals as well."

Much of Gullion's work has been underwritten by an organization of sportsmen called the Ruffed Grouse Society, and he credits the bird hunters with having provided not only many of the funds to improve habitat and increase grouse populations but also with providing the economic incentives to the lumber and paper companies to institute specialized clear-cutting procedures that are more expensive than traditional methods. "It's the hunters who put a value on the birds that otherwise wouldn't be there," explained Gullion, who has been a researcher long enough to understand the modern realities of wildlife management. "Without their interest and the resulting economic value, there would be no reason for concessions to be made in forest management. I hope the antihunting forces don't prevail, because if they do I guarantee you there will be a marked decline in wildlife of all kinds. It's important that people understand that."

Gullion might laugh at the notion, but it struck me that beyond his fundamental practical, scientific nature, there was a spiritual quality to his devotion to this single species of game bird. "I've never been much of a hunter, myself," he said. "Personally, I'd rather handle them than kill them. I probably handle between sixty and seventy birds in an average year, which is a lot more than most hunters see in a season. I band them or put tracking collars on them and turn them loose. Then I retrap them and handle them again."

"Catch-and-release hunting."

Gullion laughed. "Well, yes . . . I guess it is!"

It also occurred to me while we talked that if I had another life to live, I might wish to live it as a wildlife biologist or a naturalist, the best of whom, like Gordon Gullion or the late Aldo Leopold, acquire a more intimate knowledge of the processes of life and nature, based on thousands upon thousands of hours of observation in the field. The wonder of such a familial understanding of the land (which we might wish upon our politicians) lies in the simple notion that the seemingly esoteric concerns of a single species suggest a whole world, an entire biota, the survival and well-being of one species ensuring that of another. Nearly all native cultures took this rather obvious fact for granted, and hunters, assuming that they care about something other than just killing, also know it, as do some poets, artists, shamans, and philosophers. How sinister that we have systematically destroyed every other civilization in history in which this fundamental knowledge was held in high esteem.

Recently, Gullion upset some of his benefactors in the Ruffed Grouse Society when he offered the findings of a thirty-plus-year study that provided incontrovertible evidence that hunting pressure could also have a negative impact on grouse populations. This information is anathema to many hunters and to almost all pro-hunting organizations, which, like other special interest groups, are sometimes less interested in the truth than they are in promoting their cause. "It was a bit of a bombshell," Gullion said, "with real political fallout." The RGS, which had made Gullion its professional spokesman and the darling of its banquet circuit, now largely ignored the results of his study. "It's got them pretty disturbed," he added with a philosophical chuckle. "I don't think they really want to hear it."

It was late in the afternoon, and I had some miles to travel yet. Gullion walked me to the door of his cabin.

"You must be going over to the National Grouse and Woodcock Hunt this weekend?" he asked.

"No, I don't know anything about that," I said.

"It's an annual affair held in Grand Rapids, which is just a few hours north and west of here. It's pretty exclusive, only important contributors to the Ruffed Grouse Society are invited."

"That would disqualify me."

"I helped get the hunt started," Gullion said. "We have a team of biologists there who collect data on the birds harvested—each bird is aged and sexed and its crop contents examined, where it was killed, etc. This provides us with valuable information about population cycles, diet, and habitat. You really should go up there. I think you'd find it very interesting. You tell them I sent you."

"Aren't you going?" I asked.

Gullion smiled sadly. "This is the first year I'll miss it," he said. "I have cancer in both lungs. Tomorrow I begin another round of chemotherapy. I'm afraid my days are numbered."

"I'm very sorry." I shook Gullion's hand. "Good luck to you, sir."

"Same to you, Jim. Listen, if you go up to the hunt, please tell everyone hello for me, would you?" I think Gordon Gullion had tears in his eyes.

"Sure I will."

Driving away just at dusk down the long winding dirt drive of the Forestry Center, I saw my first ruffed grouse; it sailed across the road and disappeared in the dark timber on the other side. I thought it must be some sort of sign, although of what I had no idea.

10

MY BIOLOGIST

Well, I did not shoot to murder, I shot to live. I might need one grouse today, so I did not shoot two, but would shoot the other one tomorrow. Why should I shoot more? I lived in the forest, I was a son of the forest.

Knut Hamsun, PAN

I crashed the opening night barbecue of the National Grouse and Wood-cock Hunt in Grand Rapids, Minnesota (a town best known as the birth-place of the late Judy Garland, although town fathers prefer not to call attention to that fact because in later years the singer made unkind remarks about the city and then, of course, there was the matter of her suicide: "It's not the way a girl from Minnesota is supposed to end her life," said a censorious local spokesman in an interview).

I'd been driving all day and I was hungry—thirsty, too—so I stepped up to the buffet table at the local gun club, which was hosting dinner, and helped myself to some quite passable barbecued beef and sausage, and then I filled a large plastic cup at the beer keg and sat down alone at a table to enjoy my meal.

The RGS puts on quite a wingding for their invited guests, an exclu-sive group of contributors to the cause. In an ideal world, wildlife would be protected and preserved for its own sake, no strings attached, simply because it deserves protection on fundamental moral grounds. In this world, it is sportsmen's organizations like the Ruffed Grouse Society, the Izaak Walton League, Trout Unlimited, Ducks Unlimited, Pheasants Forever, Quail Unlimited, *et al.*, that provide the economic incentive and the vast majority of the funds to protect and improve habitat and ensure continuing game populations. Ironically, as Gordon Gullion pointed out, the efforts of antihunting groups, ostensibly formed to save wildlife from

84

the hunter's gun, actually encourage its decline. If polled, surely every garden-variety environmentalist, conservationist, or animal rights activist would vote to protect the ruffed grouse, the prairie chicken, or the duck. But the sportsman puts his money where his mouth is. He buys wetlands; funds the work of such dedicated professionals as Gullion; cajoles, woos, threatens, and pays off lumber companies to initiate better timbering methods; bankrolls subsidies for farmers and ranchers to maintain and improve wildlife habitat degraded by poor agricultural practices.

For all that, some of us are not joiners of groups, and would prefer to be sons of the forest; we would prefer the natural world to be still wild and free, and for mankind to cultivate a reverence for nature that extends beyond economic interests and remains independent of them—although this seems an increasingly farfetched and romantic notion these days. As Aldo Leopold pointed out over forty years ago in *A Sand County Almanac,* without an ethic of this kind, we are doomed to deplete everything for our own purposes, and the best efforts of any organization or government become mere fingers in the dike. For all the thousands of acres of wetlands saved by Ducks Unlimited, how many more have been lost? For all its dedicated work in the field, millions of dollars poured into the cause, and hundreds of paper-miles of conservation legislation initiated, who can honestly say that waterfowl habitat and populations are not still in precipitous decline? National Wildlife Federation statistics suggest that half of the original wetlands in the continental United States have already been destroyed and that we continue to lose an additional 300,000 or so acres per year. The Audubon Society has the figure even higher—400,000 acres per year. Scare tactics, the developers and boosters will tell you; so what? ask the growth junkies, who needs swamps and marshes when you can have parking lots and shopping malls? In any kind of economic footrace, the natural world always loses and too often the same people who are backfilling wetlands to build the shopping mall with one hand are bidding on bad sporting art at a Ducks Unlimited banquet with the other.

I considered these grand ethical, moral, and economic arguments as I, uninvited guest, stuffed my face with Ruffed Grouse Society barbecue and swilled their draft beer. I felt a bit conspicuous among the invited guests, a little nervous at being such a shameless party crasher, though no one appeared to notice me. Maybe they just assumed I was one of them and that I had forgotten my name tag. Halfway through my second plateful of barbecue and another draft beer, someone "made" me.

"Gordy sent me," I hastened to explain to the fellow who came over to my table, and whose tag identified him as Dan Dessecker, a biologist with the Ruffed Grouse Society. He was a ramrod-straight young man, with a quick, efficient stride, eyeglasses, a clipboard, and a clipped professional manner. He looked kind of like Clark Kent in khakis.

"Gordy sent you?"

"Yeah, I saw him yesterday down in Cloquet. He said to say hello to everyone. He said to tell you that he was sorry that he couldn't make it this year."

"How's he look?"

"He looks pretty good. But today he started another round of chemo. He hated to miss this hunt."

"I know."

I explained to the biologist that I was researching a book about upland bird hunting, and that at Gullion's suggestion, I'd come up here to have a look around. He excused himself, crossed the room purposefully, and relayed this information to a couple of large, beefy fellows in close conference over cocktails by the bar—one, I later learned, the executive director of the Ruffed Grouse Society, and the other the local host of the event who owned the motel in town where the participants were being lodged. They eyed me suspiciously. I ate like a dog whose bowl is about to be taken from him, and drained the last of my beer.

I was just getting up to leave when Dan strode back over to my table. He didn't ask me to leave, after all; instead, he told me that he had been assigned to look after me, show me around, answer my questions, and even take me out hunting tomorrow if I so desired. "First we'll have to get you a name tag," he said. Evidently Gordy's name opened doors. Also, as I was beginning to learn, if you want to get invited on a lot of interesting hunts with interesting hunting companions, it doesn't hurt to tell people that you're writing a book about bird hunting. You see? One minute I'm a party crasher with barbecue sauce on my chin and beer foam on my upper lip, and the next I have my own biologist and I'm getting an official name tag.

I drove back to the motel, found a spot to camp in the lot, and arrived at the meeting room in time for the prehunt briefing and an inspirational film about ruffed grouse. My biologist stayed right at my elbow. I got the feeling that he had been charged with keeping an eye on me.

The hunters enter the event in teams of two and almost all of them bring their own dogs. Each team is assigned a "huntsman," usually a local familiar with the country, who serves both as guide and scorekeeper. The competition is scored on a point basis—with points awarded for dog work (birds pointed, flushed, retrieved) as well as for total number of birds killed. (The legal limits are five grouse and ten woodcock per day per hunter.) I believe that any such competition runs against the grain of a true hunting ethic, and there's no point in trying to obscure the fact that the points awarded for dog work are largely a matter of ceremony, as the winners are invariably the team that kills the most birds in the course of the three-day hunt.

Grouse hunters tend to be a solitary lot; aficionados of other kinds of hunting might even accuse them of a certain elitism. Heir to the grand tradition of such American sportsmen as William Harnden Foster, Dr. Charles Norris, and George Bird Evans, they admire elegant pointing dog work and double-barreled shotguns and are notoriously closemouthed about their favorite coverts. Many of them are more than willing to hunt hard all day, busting for hours through dense, briar-tangled undergrowth in order to flush one grouse, to hear the deep sound of wingbeats in the forest, and perhaps catch a glimpse of the bird through the trees. These are hunters who pursue their game more for the intense esthetic value of the sport than for the killing.

I will not bore the reader with further tales of the cocktail and dinner parties of the next few evenings; no more descriptions of well-appointed buffet tables, or tiresome auctions and raffles. Suffice it to say that nearly all the hunters I spoke to salved their consciences with the rationalization that they were participating in important scientific studies, collecting invaluable data for the team of working biologists who at the end of each hunting day sexed, aged, and examined the crop contents of all the birds killed. For the biologists, this is a strange kind of symbiotic relationship; conscientious professionals, generally underpaid and overworked, they enjoyed the hoopla attendant to the hunt, schmoozing with the wealthy sportsmen, and grazing at the lavishly laid buffet table. Who wouldn't? I liked it, myself. It becomes harder and harder to be a son of the forest.

"Gordon was an eloquent defender of the hunt," explained Dan over beers in the bar that first evening after the briefing. "He understood that you have to put a dollar value on something before people are going to support it."

"But don't you ever worry that by overpromoting the sport, you might also do harm to the resource, to the very thing you're trying to protect?"

"No, I'm not concerned at all with that. Hunting is not a factor. We know that."

"Gordon told me that he had the results of a study that clearly indicated that hunting pressure can suppress grouse populations."

"That study was done in a relatively small refuge near a large urban center [Minneapolis/St. Paul]. Up here we have over a million acres to hunt. Fifty teams of two hunters hunting for three days can make no significant impact on bird populations."

"He said that the Ruffed Grouse Society didn't want to hear the results of his study. That it was too hot politically."

"Gordon said that?"

"Yes."

"Well, we can ask Sam about it [Sam Pursglove, the executive director of the Ruffed Grouse Society] but I certainly don't think we would ever ignore Gordon's findings. He was instrumental in getting the hunt up here started."

"Let's put it this way then: Do you think that a competition like this is somehow counter to the spirit of grouse hunting?"

"How do you mean?"

"I mean esthetically. That you're turning the essentially solitary and esoteric tradition of the sport into a kind of grand 'promo' affair."

"You mean, does the means justify the end?"

"Something like that."

"Well, you tell me: We've proven to the lumber companies via the community and the chamber of commerce that there is a real economic value attached to grouse. Without that there would be no reason for them to spend the extra time and money clear-cutting in a way that is beneficial to the birds, and to other wildlife, as well. It isn't just a question of esthetics."

"It so rarely is."

"Look, one of the biggest myths in this country is that of the American wilderness. There is no wilderness left in North America. Period. As soon as fire suppression became official federal policy back in the 1930s we altered the natural balance. We became land managers. That's our responsibility now."

"Not a very romantic notion, is it?"

"I'm a scientist."

Touché.

The dogs woke me the next morning before daylight. The camper was surrounded by trailer and pickup truck kennels, whose occupants began to fidget, whine, and bark, anxious to get on with the day's hunt. When their masters came out of the motel rooms to feed and walk them at daylight, Sweetz and I peeked through a crack in the curtain to watch the activity. It was another gray, overcast, drizzly fall day in the northwoods. Hunting weather.

Nearly every hunting breed was represented at the affair—English setters, Gordon setters, English pointers, German shorthairs, German wirehairs, vizslas, Brittanys, weimaraners, griffons, springer spaniels, Labs, you name it. It was great fun watching them all mill about excitedly, their owners talking to them, hollering at them, chasing them, scolding them. Small harmless turf skirmishes broke out among some of the more aggressive dogs, while the rest went about their business—lifting legs, squatting, dragging their owners along at the end of their leashes. Dozens of dog poops steamed on the motel grass in the misty dawn.

I was feeling a bit logy and disheveled from several too many beers with my biologist, and I got up, put the coffee on, and quickly got back under the comforter while it perked. I'd almost forgotten our hunting date when Dan rapped smartly on the door. Where at first I had thought him to be rather humorless, as I had gotten to know him over beers, I found that he just had one of those senses of humor so dry that it sometimes passes nearly undetected. This morning, dressed in hunting clothes and orange cap, with clipboard in hand and dog whistle on a lanyard around his neck, he looked as crisp and efficient as the evening before, almost annoyingly so.

"Morning, Jim," he said, chipperly, as I peered around the door of the camper. "I thought you'd be ready to go by now. I thought you'd want to get into the woods before the hunt participants shot every grouse and woodcock in northern Minnesota."

My father used to take me on fishing trips to the northwoods when I was a boy. He died a quarter of a century ago and I hadn't been back much since. Now the midwestern trees seemed all new to me and yet vaguely familiar, like running into old acquaintances whose names you have forgotten. The forests here are lush, dense, and close, particularly to one accustomed to the open, Spartan aridity of the West. Though there are no vistas here, no "views" to speak of, and the closeness can seem claustrophobic at first, I was beginning to lose my prejudices about country, to give up the chauvinism that so many westerners, native and adopted, feel about the big open. This was good country, too, only different—impossibly damp, verdant, and rich, with a remarkable diversity of flora. The trees—aspen, white birch, red maple, sugar maple, black ash, white ash, green ash, all in different stages of their poignant fall dance—had begun to shed their leaves, opening up the canopy and leaving a carpet of color on the forest floor—reds, yellows, golds and greens—a kind of hunter's autumn cliché.

My biologist lined me out on the flora as we hunted, identifying plant species and explaining good grouse cover, food sources, and general habitat requirements. Sweetz worked the dense cover well for a rookie, though sometimes ranging a bit too far out. This was an entirely new game for us, and when I saw the first grouse flush wild out of range through the trees, it occurred to me that there was an excellent chance that I would never actually hit one. How can you shoot them with all those trees in the way?

Dan had his German shorthair, Jute, hunting out ahead. A slightly hardheaded dog, he was giving the biologist fits by busting grouse out of range; we could hear their wingbeats reverberate through the forest, even if we couldn't see the birds. Then Dan would chase the dog down and punish him. He would pick him up off the ground by the ears and shake him, until Jute made piteous howling noises, terrible sounds as if he were being murdered. All the while, Dan would be patiently lecturing the dog, explaining to him with the calm, articulate, precise diction of the scientist all the things he had done wrong, and all the things he must not do again lest they have to repeat this unpleasant business. Sweetz and I would wait out these disciplinary sessions, like listening in on a domestic dispute, looking at each other with faintly embarrassed expressions. We're afraid we had been through a bit of it ourselves, our looks seemed to say, and it isn't very pretty, is it?

Now we walked leaf-covered roadsides, and paths through the forests, and worked the edges of clearings and clear-cuts. As you can never get up high enough to find out where you are in this country and as I was born with a poor sense of direction, I'd have been hopelessly lost in under five minutes if I hadn't had Dan along as my guide. We came upon an old abandoned farm site, slightly elevated on a rise where finally I could have a look around. I breathed a sigh of relief, and didn't want to leave it right away. If I had a farm in this country a hundred years ago, this is just where I'd have put it, too.

Jute pointed a woodcock in a wet alder thicket and Dan killed it. Woodcock are easier to shoot than grouse; they hold well for a point and when flushed tend to fly straight up in the air, pausing at the apex above the cover before leveling off and flying away, making a startled, plaintive cry. All game birds may have roughly the same level of intelligence, but some species clearly have better personalities than others, and woodcock are nice little birds with their chubby bodies, long beaks, and large soulful eyes. I know a number of hunters who have difficulty killing them. It has something to do with their portly carriage and those big prescient eyes looking up at you, a certain feeling of wrongdoing to shoot something so sweet and trusting who will sometimes hold so tight to a point that the dog and bird will be facing each other, inches apart, nose to nose. Dog handlers prize the "timberdoodle," as they are sometimes called, for their quality of holding for the point, but if I ever see the bird on the ground first I simply can't shoot it when it flies. This is one advantage in using a flushing dog, where the flight comes as a surprise, the shot as a reflex. And I do love to eat the woodcock—a large-hearted, rich, red-meated migratory bird.

So we killed a couple of woodcock and later Dan killed one grouse. I had an opportunity to shoot a double on a grouse and a woodcock that flushed milliseconds apart out of the same thicket, but I fell apart and missed them both. We decided to call it a day.

As we were driving back down a dirt road in the national forest, we happened upon a car of road hunters. A favorite method of the locals, road hunting is usually pursued on weekends or in the evenings after a hard day's work. Frequently it involves beer drinking, and can be an outing for the whole family, as well as a good way to obtain dinner. In the mornings and evenings the grouse often come out onto the road to gravel or to dust themselves, or just to loaf and feed along the edges; road hunting can be an effective technique to find birds and easy on the legs, too, and it infuriates and disgusts traditional grouse hunters.

As we approached the road hunters, we watched the driver lever his gun out the car window. "I can't believe it," Dan said. "He's going to dust that bird right in front of us! He's breaking at least three laws: carrying a loaded firearm in a vehicle, discharging a firearm from a vehicle, and discharging a firearm from within twenty yards of a public road."

The driver squeezed off a shot, jumped out of the car, and picked up his dead grouse on the side of the road. A small child tumbled into the front seat from the back, and an enormously fat man in the passenger seat took a long swallow from a tallboy can of Old Style beer.

"And his partner's drinking beer," I pointed out.

"Four laws."

"Why don't we make a citizen's arrest?"

"No, you don't want to mess with these people. But I'm going to get his license plate number and turn him in to the game warden."

As we passed the road hunters, the driver beamed and proudly held the bird up for us to see, the passenger tilted his beer can toward us hospitably, and the child, a little girl, waved. They didn't look so dangerous to me.

"Let's stop," I said. "I'd like to talk to them."

Dan was stony-faced and tight-lipped. "Absolutely not," he said, angrily. "I'm afraid I'll lose my temper if we stop."

So I just waved back to the happy road hunters as we passed.

The next morning, I went out early by myself, and parked along the road until I spotted a car of road hunters. You can't miss them because they drive so slowly, no more than five miles per hour, scanning the roadside. I got out of my car and flagged them down.

I explained to the driver, a stocky, bearded man who introduced himself as Merlin, that I was writing a book about bird hunting and I asked if I could ride along with them for a while, see how they went about this. Merlin, an auto mechanic in town, and a very friendly fellow, said sure, and he seemed pleased at the opportunity to hold forth about his sport; he clearly fancied himself to be something of an expert. He told his passenger, a big man in coveralls named Carl, to get in the backseat and let me ride up front. We all got situated.

"You want a beer, Jim?" Merlin offered. It was nine o'clock in the morning.

"Only if you're going to have one, Merlin."

"Why not? It's Saturday, isn't it?"

"Sure is."

"Carl, hand us a couple of beers there."

"Merlin, let me ask you something," I began. "You know they've got that group of Ruffed Grouse Society people staying in town this weekend. Some of them would say that the way you hunt here, ground-sluicing birds from the car, besides being illegal is also unsportsmanlike—that it violates the traditions of grouse hunting."

Merlin smiled a wicked smile. He had small, twinkling eyes. "The *traditions of grouse hunting?*" he said, mimicking me disdainfully. I could see that Merlin had a sense of humor.

"That's right."

"You want to know something, Jim? *This* is my tradition of grouse hunting. This is how we've always hunted partridge—by the way, *we* don't call them grouse, *we* call them partridge. This is how my father hunted partridge, and this is how his father hunted partridge—Hey, lookit there, there's a partridge!" Merlin stopped the car and slid a single-shot .410 shotgun with a short sawed-off barrel (the gun of choice for road hunting) from the floorboards between his legs. The bird was poking around in the brush at the side of the road. Slowly, Merlin maneuvered the gun out the window.

"Aren't you going to get out of the car?" I asked. I was certain we were going to get arrested and that I'd have to go to jail with Merlin and Carl, as an accessory to a crime, even though I was just an innocent spectator.

Merlin sighed and looked at me with a tolerant expression, and addressed me as if talking to a child. "Jim, if I get out of the car," he explained patiently, "the partridge will fly away."

"Oh, yeah, of course."

Merlin took careful aim and dusted the partridge.

"All right!" Carl said from the backseat.

Merlin retrieved his grouse and we went on creeping down the road.

"Doesn't it bother you that this is illegal?" I asked.

"They haven't caught me yet." Merlin smiled. "Getting back to those grouse people, Jim? You know they all come here from out of state. They bring their fancy dogs—did you know that some of those dogs cost five thousand dollars? Yeah, that's right, *five thousand dollars!* You think I can afford a five-thousand-dollar dog? Well, Jim, I sure as hell can't. I can't afford a five-thousand-dollar car! And anyway, I don't have time to train a dog. Then they got their fancy ten-thousand-dollar shotguns. You know how much this shotgun cost me, Jim? Forty dollars. So these rich assholes come out here every year; they run all over the woods with their five-thousand-dollar dogs shooting *my* partridge with their ten-thousand-dollar shotguns; they shoot hundreds of them, and then they complain that they don't like the way *I* hunt? Hell, I admit it, I'm a meat hunter. I like to eat partridge. So maybe I kill twenty birds in a whole season this way. Is that so terrible? Mostly we come out here just to drive around, get out of town, have a few beers. What's so wrong with that? And it really *pisses me off* that these rich guys from out of town turn their noses up at me when they see us out here. This is *my* home, not theirs, and I'll hunt however I goddamn well please. Hey, Jim, up ahead on your side of the road! There's a partridge. See him? I'll pull up a little farther. You get the gun ready. When I get in position, blast him."

"Oh, gee, I don't know, Merlin." I'd read all the sporting literature about the mythical ruffed grouse, and this was not precisely the way I wanted to shoot my first one.

Merlin looked at me with his thin, wicked smile, his hooded, twinkling eyes. "You one of them, Jim?"

"Does it come down to that, Merlin?"

11

MAKING GAME

But what was lovely was the fall to go hunting through the chestnut woods. The birds were all good because they fed on grapes and you never took a lunch because the peasants were always honored if you would eat with them at their houses.

Ernest Hemingway, A FAREWELL TO ARMS

"What's the most important tree for the ruffed grouse?" a Ruffed Grouse Society banquet guest asked Bill Hunyadi.

"One that's on the back of a lumber truck," answered Hunyadi.

I had met Hunyadi, a regional biologist for the RGS, the evening before, the last day of the National Grouse and Woodcock Hunt. I was helping collate scorecards and record data on birds harvested—age, sex, crop contents, color phase, etc.—working at a table under the tent where the hunters dropped off their day's bag before retiring to the banquet room for cocktail hour. After examination by the team of biologists, the birds were cleaned and packaged for the sports to take home.

Hunyadi was an enthusiastic supporter of the hunt for the opportunity it provided to collect this extensive data, although when pressed he admitted that from a practical management point of view such information was of limited value, and simply "added to the body of knowledge about the species." ("How many dead birds do they need to look at?" the crusty writer/sportsman George Bird Evans, a critic of the RGS and of grouse biologists in general, would ask me when I visited him later in my trip.)

This morning Bill and I had the woods to ourselves, the competition over. The sun had finally come out a bit, and the forest was wet, pungent, and alive, a fine day to be afield with gun and dog and a new hunting companion. Bill had his beloved old deaf setter, Hogan, hunting with him. I had Sweetz.

"Grouse are an excellent ecological indicator species," Hunyadi was explaining. "They thrive with diversity and they utilize a wide variety of food resources, everything from bugs and berries to leaves to aspen buds to mushrooms. Nothing in nature is static; things change, it's an incredibly complex interaction of events and species, in which man now plays a central role. Look around here, at the variety of cover and plant life. This has all been logged at different times and is now regrown in different stages. This is a rich, viable, full-of-life place. And I guarantee you that there are grouse here."

We split up and moved in parallel through the forest. An obvious advantage in hunting with a grouse biologist is the fact that they generally know where to look for grouse, even in areas they have never hunted before.

Suddenly Sweetzer came bounding out of a thicket with a live grouse in her mouth; she delivered it proudly to hand. Given that I had not shot the bird, nor had Bill, this was an interesting retrieve, her first, in fact, of the species. I called Bill over and we examined the grouse. It had one broken wing and one broken leg, and must have been shot the day before during the competition, without the hunter's realizing that he'd hit it. No points are awarded hunt competitors for diligently searching for cripples, and sometimes it's easier and more expedient to find another bird to shoot than to waste valuable time looking for one already down.

Though unable to fly or run, and totally at the mercy of predators, the grouse had continued to feed on the ground and later, when I cleaned it, I found that its crop was packed with fresh green clover. Bill plucked a primary feather from one of the bird's wings and slipped the sharp quill up the back of its neck into its brain, neatly dispatching it.

We continued our hunt until the sky darkened and the rain began again and it was time to leave the forest. I was headed one direction and Bill another: hunters off on separate roads. We had only spent a few hours together, but there is no faster way to get to know a person than by being afield with them. We exchanged addresses on scraps of paper and said our good-byes, promising another hunt, another day in other country.

I drove until dusk and pulled off the road onto a tree-lined lane in the woods. A soft steady rain fell on the camper. I roasted a freshly killed grouse and ate it with Minnesota wild rice and a sliced sautéed patty-pan squash that I had bought at a farm market along the road. Fall is a wonderful time to travel around the country, harvest time for hunters and vegetarians alike. I drank a good Chardonnay with my dinner and wrote for a while in my notebook. Sweetzer was having REM dreams in the bunk after her day's work, eyes rolling back in her head, legs twitching, nose working, muscles rippling beneath her sleek coat. She was probably still hunting, running down a scent trail, flushing a bird from a thicket. I hoped that in her dreams I made the shot.

*   *   *

The next morning I stopped in at the office of the Department of Natural Resources (DNR) in a small town in eastern Minnesota. There the game warden showed me an extraordinary videotape of a hidden camera "sting" operation whereby DNR officers entice road hunters by placing a stuffed grouse on the side of the road. In the video in question, a car pulls over and a man and teenage boy get out. The man extracts a shotgun from the backseat of the car and offers it to the boy. The boy refuses the gun, telling his father that it's against the law to shoot the bird this way. (The boy had recently completed a hunter education course, the game warden explained as we watched the video on a television in his darkened office). The father begins viciously berating his son, humiliating him with a variety of derogatory names that call the boy's manliness into question. He orders his son to shoot the bird. Finally, and obviously reluctantly, the boy accepts the gun and shoots at the grouse. But being a stuffed bird, it does not, of course, fall over dead, and the father, believing that the boy has intentionally missed, tears the shotgun from his son's hands, saying, "Gimme that you little faggot, I'll shoot the goddamn partridge myself." He aims and shoots the grouse; still it does not fall over. An unmistakable flicker of a smirk crosses the boy's face. Now Dad's really mad. He shoots a second time, which is about when three DNR officers step out of the bushes and arrest the man, who is later prosecuted to the full extent of the law. No charges are brought against the boy as the evidence clearly indicates that he was coerced into shooting at the decoy.

By next afternoon I was in Wisconsin, near the town of Hayward ("Home of the World Record Muskie") for a brief visit with a young graduate student named Dave Lauten, who was doing a two-year grouse study in a wildlife management area here. I liked the country, a little more open and hilly than Minnesota, a land in which the ubiquitous northwoods are dotted by thousands of lakes and interspersed by farms and cleared agricultural land. The kaleidoscope effect of all this subtly changing country rushing by was beginning to have a strange vertiginous effect on me, a kind of overwhelming sensual bombardment of sight, smell, and motion. I had a sharp pang of homesickness for my own land when some big, muscly storm clouds gathering on the horizon put me in mind of the mountains. But it didn't last long.

   Native roots betrayed by New Jersey accents, Lauten and his girlfriend, Kathy, recalled the old hippie activists of my college days. They had a peace symbol prominently displayed in the rear window of their car, which was plastered with Greenpeace and Nature Conservancy stickers. ("I don't want to work for corporate America," Dave said, "and I don't want to work for the government.") Dave was an audiophile, a skate boarder, a diehard Giants fan, a gregarious, hospitable, hyperactive, talkative man who asked me if I "needed a place to crash." A few years ago he and Kathy had gotten "turned on to birding" (bird watching) and they had recently driven all over the United States visiting wildlife refuges, camping out at night, and keeping a life list of the birds they saw. "Why shoot them, when you can look at them?" Dave wondered. In Colorado, they told of climbing for hours, way above timberline, just to catch a glimpse of a single white-tailed ptarmigan. I admired the dedication of these young students, their enthusiasm, and clear love of the natural world. And their knowledge. As John Madson—writer, conservationist, naturalist, and hunter—once put it: "I'll listen to any antihunter who wears out two pairs of field boots in a season."

"I don't object to the good hunters," Dave was saying. "But when we first moved up here I was pretty surprised at how little some of the hunters knew about grouse. Like, they don't know the first thing about what makes good habitat, or where to look for birds. I don't mind the guys who've done their homework and who are willing to bushwhack and bust through thickets and get back into the country. And they always find birds. But I hate the slobs and I don't like the guys who can't be bothered to learn anything about the species they hunt."

That afternoon I rode around on the back of Dave's four-wheeler, checking his grouse traps with him. I hung on to the bar across the seat, while he drove very fast—too fast for me—down the paths and lanes through the forest. He kept up a running commentary, a nonstop monologue, and seemed to have an inexhaustible repertoire of bird stories. Much of the time, due to the whining engine noise of the four-wheeler, the racing wind, and the trees whooshing by, I couldn't make out his words; they spilled in an indistinct jumble over his shoulder. When we stopped to check the next trap in line, he would still be talking. "Oh!" he would exclaim. "Here's another funny great horned owl story!" and off we would go.

I parked for the night in the yard of Dave and Kathy's farm cottage. Strict vegetarians who snack on granola and don't drink alcoholic beverages, they invited me to join them for a dinner of soyburgers and Kool-Aid. I begged off, pretending to have work to do, and secretly roasted another grouse in the camper. I felt mildly guilty about it, as if I were eating one of their pets. Still, with a good Chardonnay and some tiny new potatoes and a fresh farm market salad, my dinner, when held up against soyburgers and Kool-Aid, seemed particularly exquisite that night. The next morning I left a note for my young friends and slipped off before dawn. I wanted to spend a few days hunting alone in the woods and I was anxious to be on my way. Fall was deepening in the air, nipping at my heels and propelling me across the country.

*   *   *

I camped for a number of days on Sailor Lake in the Chequamegon National Forest outside Park Falls, Wisconsin. "The Ruffed Grouse Capital of the World" read enormous signs recently installed by the chamber of commerce on either end of town—nearly impossible these days to avoid the business of the hunt. The summer tourists had long gone home and I had the campground to myself.

Sweetz and I hunted for an hour our first afternoon and we flushed four grouse and three woodcock. That evening I barbecued a pair of woodcock I'd brought with me from Minnesota; they had been aging in the refrigerator for a few days. I basted them with olive oil, garlic, lemon, soy, and a dash of Worcestershire. Excellent!

I was beginning to feel at home here in the northwoods, learning where to find the grouse and woodcock. My initial claustrophobia had given way before the lush beauty of this wet, rich ecosystem, which made the West seem so stony and austere by comparison. The trees had become familiar old friends by now—the white birch and yellow hemlock, the red oak, spruce, and maple. Most of the leaves were down, thick on the forest floor, and floating on the still, black water of the creeks and swamps. I had never seen such black water before, black and still. The earth was spongy and mossy, cushioning and silencing the hunter's step. Those were quiet days in Wisconsin; we did not see or talk to another human being for nearly a week. Just Sweetz and me in the woods with the grouse and the woodcock; we weren't a bit lonely.

One afternoon, I had all the game I needed and I decided to go into a nearby town to drink a beer or two at the tavern. It was time for some conversation. Like bakeries, there is no shortage of taverns in the north country, and one never has to drive far to find one. I drove into the hamlet of Fifield, where I located a fine corner bar called the Ram's Head. I ordered an Old Style draft beer, which came in a small six-ounce glass and cost a quarter—a real inflation buster. I drank it down and ordered a second beer—it tasted wonderful—and went over to the pay phone to call my wife, whom I hadn't spoken to in a week.

"Where are you?" she always began the conversation.

"Somewhere in Wisconsin," I answered.

"Let me get my map," she said. "By the way, so-and-so is trying to get ahold of you."

"Tell him I can't be reached."

"Are you having fun? How's Sweetzie? Do you miss me?"

"Yes. She's fine. And, yes, very much." Being a hunter would be a lot less fun if I didn't know that I had my wife to come home to afterward.

"Don't get lost up there. You know what a terrible sense of direction you have."

"Ah, but I'm a son of the forest now!"

"Yeah, right! You just be careful."

I went back in the bar and had a third beer. I was now down a full seventy-five cents and, feeling extravagant, I gave the bartender a quarter tip to make it an even dollar. This was like living in the 1950s. I considered moving here. I could probably rent a nice little place above the bar for a hundred dollars a month. I wondered how my wife would like it.

While I was enjoying my beer and chatting with the bartender, a tall taciturn Norwegian fellow named Lunther, a group of a half-dozen grouse hunters came in, easily identifiable by their attire. Several of them were extremely drunk, although it was barely four o'clock in the afternoon. Lunther seemed to know them and took their orders.

"You fellas grouse hunting?" I asked hunter number one, the man nearest me, by way of initiating a conversation. He happened to be one of the drunkest of the group, and he looked at me with one of those overly long, slack-jawed, rheumy regards.

"No," he finally said, "we came here on our vacation all the way from Pennsylvania so we could have a circle jerk in the woods."

"Oh? Having any luck?"

"You a smartass?"

"There no goddamn birds here," said hunter number two, leaning around his friend. "It's a big fuckin' rip-off to get out-of-staters to come here and spend their money. Ruffed Grouse Capital of the World my ass! We got more birds than this in Pennsylvania and we don't have shit there."

"You know how many birds we killed so far in four days of hunting?" asked hunter number three. He looked at me expectantly, leading me to believe that this was more than a rhetorical question.

"You want me to guess?"

"He's a fuckin' smartass," grumbled hunter number one.

Hunter number three held up his hand and made a zero with thumb and forefinger. "That's how many," he said.

"We seen a couple fuckin' woodcock," said hunter number four. "My dog won't retrieve 'em. I won't even shoot 'em."

"Ah, bullshit!" said hunter number three, "you'll shoot anything."

"I got four hundred dollars into this trip so far," said hunter number two. "And I promise you this, this goddamn rip-off state will never see my money again. Wisconsin better watch out," he predicted darkly.

Hunter number five, a quiet man seated at the end of the bar, who seemed less drunk than his compatriots, and embarrassed by them, spoke up. "The reason we haven't seen any birds," he explained to me, "is because these guys don't get out of bed until ten o'clock in the morning, and we're not in the woods until eleven. Then we hunt for an hour before we break for lunch and they start drinking beer. After lunch they hunt for another hour and then they want to go to the bar. *That's* why we're not finding birds."

The hunters from Pennsylvania were bar-hopping and they paid their tab and moved on to the next stop. Lunther watched them out the door, shaking his head. "How'd you like to run into those guys with loaded guns in the woods?" he asked as he picked up their glasses and wiped down the bar.

"Not much." The image of this group of drunken louts crashing through the forest, flushing every bird within miles, was enough to make a hunter hang up his gun.

Lunther paused in mid-wipe and smiled. "You know what the best part is, though, don't you?" he asked.

"That they're never coming back to Wisconsin again?"

"You got it!"

As I was headed back to my campsite that evening, I ran into yet another hunter, a very nice gentleman from Georgia named Art. He was walking a good-looking German wirehaired pointer and we got talking about this and that—dogs and guns—as hunters do. Art was semiretired from the whole-sale furniture business and he and his wife spent a lot of time traveling around the country in an Airstream trailer while Art fished and hunted. He was a curious, open, forthcoming sort of man and wanted to know all about my travels. He asked right off if writers made much money, and I admitted that, no, most of us did not. Art had a friend flying up from Atlanta the next morning and they had hired a local guide for the next few days. He invited me to join them for dinner the following evening in their Airstream, which was parked at a nearby campground. Hunters are for the most part a hospitable lot and I gladly accepted Art's invitation. He said his wife was an excellent game cook and would prepare a wonderful grouse dish. I told him that I was grilling woodcock on the barbecue tonight. Art made a face: "Oh, no, you have to eat the poor timberdoodle?" he asked sympathetically, implying that only an impoverished writer would be forced to stoop so low.

"I think they're delicious."

But I could tell that Art didn't believe me; he thought I was being proud. "How do you cook them?" he asked.

"Rare," I said and I described my standard baste.

"And then you throw the bird away and drink the baste!" Art joked. For some reason many hunters disdain the woodcock as table fare; to me they're superb when not overcooked.

We set a time for dinner and promised respective hunting reports.

Some weather moved in overnight, beginning with black, ominous storm clouds massing just at dusk, a distant rumbling and a fast drop in temperature. Heavy raindrops were splattering the camper by the time I crawled into bed. Around 1:00 A.M., Sweetz and I were jolted awake, both literally levitated off the bunk by a deafening *boom* of thunder that seemed to originate directly overhead and had roughly the effect of both barrels of a shotgun being discharged next to your ear. I peered out the window to see the campground strobe-lit by intense prolonged lightning, and noticed that another camper had come in during the night, and pitched a tent down by the lake. I pulled the comforter around me and hugged Sweetzer close.

There were six inches of fresh wet snow on the ground by morning, the sky gray and close. I went over to meet my new neighbor and invite him in for coffee. Relative to his tent, my camper seemed like a snug condo. I assumed he must be a bird hunter, as no one else in their right mind would be in a campground here this time of year. His name was Pete, a house painter from Chicago, and he looked a little unkempt and worse for wear after the storm. He drove an old beat-up, paint-splattered Toyota truck with a Fiberglass shell over the bed. It was packed tight with groceries and gear and a dog crate with a young springer spaniel inside.

Pete was one of those seat-of-the-pants sportsmen of the old school—a thoroughly ungentrified, unmarried working stiff who spent all his free time, and then some, pursuing game of one sort or another. "I hunt and fish all the time . . . too much," he said over coffee. He spoke with a trace of sad resignation in his voice, suggesting that this addiction was altogether out of his hands. "Even when I shouldn't be. I'm right in the middle of a big wallpapering job right now. I'm not even supposed to be up here but I told the owner that I was sick and I drove up a couple days ago."

"Are you finding some birds?" I asked.

"Oh, sure, I shot my limit yesterday in an hour and a half." He shrugged apologetically. "My dog eats a whole bird a day himself."

"You feed grouse to your dog?"

"Yeah, he loves them, and that way I don't take up space packing along a bunch of dog food."

Then Pete told me his secret for finding late-season grouse. I hadn't heard it from any of my biologist friends, not one of the innumerable "experts" whom I had hunted with or spoken to, nor any of the wealthy sportsmen with their own personal dog trainers and string of thousand-dollar bird dogs. I certainly hadn't heard it from the Pennsylvania bar hunters the evening before. No, this secret I had to learn from a down-at-the-heel housepainter from Chicago with duct tape on his shotgun stock and an unpapered springer spaniel that he told me he had picked up at the city pound for twenty bucks. It is such an obvious, sensible, and yet clever deduction that I will not share the secret with the reader. Find your own housepainter; my lips are sealed.

I had never before—and have not since—shot a limit of ruffed grouse. I think that in matters of limit the sportsman should follow his conscience, never shooting more than he needs. But this day, I took Pete's advice into the field and in two hours, irrespective of my own distinctly spotty shooting abilities, I had a bag heavy with five grouse. Two of the birds went in the refrigerator, two went out Federal Express as a gift to my wife, whom I missed. And Sweetzer got to eat the fifth. I was back in the camper by noon where I spent the rest of the day reading, writing, and napping, which was fine by me as it rained steadily all afternoon.

I arrived at Art's trailer at the appointed time for our dinner engagement, but that evening Art and his friend, Ron, were late getting back in from hunting. Art's charming wife, Robbie, and I had already had a couple of cocktails and were beginning to worry about them when the hunters finally pulled up after dark. They were soaking wet and exhausted and though they were good sports about it, I could tell they were discouraged with the day's hunt. They peeled off their raingear and collapsed on the couch for much-needed drinks and they related how they had spent the whole day hunting the river bottom, very tough going, marshy and dense with undergrowth. Their guide hunted with vizslas (ratlike little dogs in my opinion), and asked that Art leave his wirehaired pointer in the car. The vizslas really covered the ground, but just couldn't find the birds. The reason they had been so long getting back, the hunters explained, was because late in the day Art had finally shot a grouse and it had fallen in the river and the vizslas, who are not much in the retrieving department, refused to go in the water after it. Being a conscientious hunter, and abhorring that a downed bird be lost, Art, though in his sixties, ran all the way back to the car to get his wirehair, who was an eager, strong swimmer and an excellent retriever. But by the time he returned with his dog, the grouse had drifted downriver and they never did find it. Thus, after having paid a cool $250 in guiding fees to slog for eight hours up a swampy, densely overgrown river bottom, they had, in effect, been skunked.

Art took a long, weary, hard-earned swallow of his bourbon. "So, Jim, tell me, how was your day hunting?"

12

DIANA

Happiness is intoxicating. I fire my gun and an unforgettable echo answers from hill to hill, drifts out over the sea and beats against some sleepy helmsman's ear. What am I happy about? A thought that comes to me, a memory, a sound in the forest, a person. I think of her, I close my eyes and stand still on the path and think of her; I count the minutes.

Knut Hamsun

The next evening I was scheduled to meet a poet friend, who goes by the single nom de plume of Swanson, over in the Upper Peninsula of Michigan. I was reluctant to leave Wisconsin just yet and though the weather had turned even fouler by morning, with intermittent snow, rain, and sleet, I decided to hunt for a few more hours before I left. I dressed in raingear, the hood pulled tight, and high rubber hunting boots. Sweetz and I set out.

The DNR (Department of Natural Resources) maintains mowed "hunter's trails" in the national forest here and gives out a free map showing their location to all inquiring hunters. Overseeded with clover, which attracts the grouse, who also like to loaf in the openings, the trails are of various distances and generally loop back so that the hunter ends up where he began—near his car. They make for pleasant, leisurely walking and virtually ensure that the hunter won't get lost, but they are also somewhat artificial, and one is always liable to run into other hunters on the trails. So after my first couple of days, after I had familiarized myself with the country, I had taken to bushwhacking farther and farther back into the woods. This is much harder work but the farther away one gets from the road and the mowed trails, the more birds and fewer hunters one is likely to find, and it is altogether wilder and more interesting. Of course, it's also easier to get lost.

On this last morning, Sweetz and I were hunting a new area, composed of large blocks of clear-cuts in different stages of regrowth. The blocks were laid out in seemingly random patterns, and I made a plan to work my way in a large semicircle which would eventually bring me back to the road. I took a compass reading.

It was hard walking in the clear-cuts, which were littered underfoot with slash, obscured by regrowth. I stumbled and tripped and periodically stepped into invisible tree stump holes—like jungle booby traps—filled with rainwater. I was soaking wet inside of fifteen minutes, my rubber boots sloshing. A light steady rain, turning periodically to snow, fell and the sky was dark and ominous; a low ground mist further cut visibility. It was a lousy day for hunting and I wondered why I wasn't back in the camper drinking coffee. Negotiating the slash was no fun for Sweetz, either, and it didn't take long for her to deduce that the best place to walk was directly behind me because then I'd fall in the stump holes and she could avoid them. She quit hunting altogether and took up this position at my heels. We exchanged words about it. "Go on," I said, "get out there and find some birds." Of course, if she was in front and falling in the holes first then *I* could avoid them. But she just looked at me stubbornly and refused. I tried reasoning with her. "You're the dog," I explained, "you're supposed to be in front. Get out there and hunt." No dice. We seemed to have reached an impasse. Finally, I decided to take a different route, trying to get to the edge of the clear-cut where the walking would be easier. In my haste and discomfort, I forgot to take a new compass reading for my change of direction.

We gained slightly higher ground, a bit easier going, and Sweetz deigned to resume hunting. I emptied the water from my boots, and we continued on. It was another half-hour before it occurred to me that I wasn't absolutely certain where I was. I took a compass reading: Impossible! I decided that I must have made an error on my original reading.

I am of the belief that a good sense of direction is like a talent for numbers, or a facility with language—far more a natural genetic quality than a learned one. My poor sense of direction has always been a source of great mirth to my wife; I can, and, in fact, have, gotten lost mere blocks from home on the way to buy a newspaper. I almost always get lost in shopping malls, loathsome things that they are.

Out west it's harder to get lost in the field than in the northwoods, as you can usually climb up high enough to have a look around and the openness makes it easy to find your bearings. And in the mountains, when worst comes to worst, you can always head downhill until you strike a road. This is not the case in the northwoods, where there is no chance of gaining altitude, no hope of having a look around, very little in the way of visual landmarks, and where downhill generally means below sea level and puts you in the bottom of a bog. What you've got here is flatness—acre after acre, mile after mile of forest, all of which looks pretty much the same.

Being "not absolutely certain" is the euphemism the newly lost use to describe their situation. Panic does not kick in all at once at such times, rather it is titrated gradually into the system, and it's only a matter of time until a fatal dose of the stuff is coursing through the veins. First, I looked around, tried to get my bearings. Nothing looked even remotely familiar. I had been concentrating so hard on my immediate surroundings—specifically, trying to avoid falling in stump holes, and tripping over hidden slash, that I had simply not been paying attention to where I was going. And if you're not paying attention to where you're going, how are you to know where you are, and where you've come from? Only later was I able to consider this question in its broader metaphorical sense.

Slowly the panic was reaching toxic levels. I remembered a film I had seen years before during a state hunter safety class. The film was a reenactment of several "real-life" experiences in which hunters or fishermen became lost in the wilds. In the sequence I recalled most vividly, a deer hunter (in Wisconsin, as a matter of fact) got separated from his companions, became disoriented, wandered around aimlessly for a while before finally panicking, at which point he began to blubber hysterically, threw his gun down, stripped off his coat, and ran blindly through the woods. His friends found him the next day, kneeling on the ground with his arms wrapped around a tree trunk. He was alive, but in a state of severe shock and suffering from hypothermia. Rescuers had to pry his arms loose from the tree; he must have considered that tree his last friend in the world.

I remembered the snickers from the hunter safety class as the macho deer hunter's composure disintegrated. I remembered that I had snickered myself, but now suddenly I was feeling much more sympathetic to the poor fool's plight. For some reason, the memory of the film calmed me, kept my own panic at bay, and I resolved that under no circumstances would I behave like the deer hunter, because in the unlikely event that I wasn't lost forever and didn't die out here in the middle of the Wisconsin woods, I didn't want to be ashamed of myself. If it came to that, I resolved right then and there to "take it like a man." This resolution had far less to do with courage or with Hemingway's famous "grace under pressure" than it did with the fact that as a young man I had watched my father die a difficult death, and now I had the odd sense that he might be watching me. I refused to humiliate myself under his strict, unforgiving gaze.

I sat down on a tree stump in the woods to think things over. Sweetzer, who didn't seem to know, or care, that we were lost, quit hunting and came back to see what was up. "Do you have any idea where we are?" I asked her, but unlike Lassie in the television series of my childhood, it was clear that she was not going to lead me to safety. I decided to make a plan. I took another compass reading. It was equally meaningless. I tried to decide if I was fuzzy-headed, as one reportedly becomes with hypothermia. I did know that I was wet and cold and lost, but I didn't think I was fuzzy-headed yet. I took stock: In my hunting bag I had a space blanket, waterproof matches, high-energy chocolate bars, a plastic bottle of drinking water. Even with waterproof matches I didn't know how I could possibly start a fire with everything so wet; it had been raining off and on for days. Suddenly my waterproof matches seemed like a preposterous, cruel hoax. "What the hell good are they if everything else is wet?" I demanded out loud. It occurred to me that being annoyed with one's matches might be the first stage of fuzzy-headed thinking. I decided that I should keep moving. One thing that did seem to be to my advantage was that it was morning rather than afternoon. If you're going to get lost, this narrator's advice is to do it in the morning because then at least you have the whole day to find your way out before dark.

The immediate question that presented itself once I decided to keep moving was: in which direction do I keep moving? I consulted my compass again. I was secretly annoyed with it, too, as if somehow it had betrayed me. I might as well have been trying to decipher Mandarin Chinese for all the sense it made. Nor was it simply a question of choosing one of four directions and heading that way; rather there seemed to be a paralyzing array of choices, limitless tangents on the compass like spokes on a wheel. Like panic, disorientation is its own fodder: Absolutely nothing made sense, no choice was right. I picked a direction almost at random and started walking.

Sweetzer, who still hadn't seemed to grasp the gravity of our situation, continued to hunt, and she flushed a grouse that offered me an easy crossing shot. I shouldered my gun, swung, and fired. How I would love to be able to report that although hopelessly lost, and possibly hypothermic, my finely tuned hunter's instincts prevailed and I cleanly killed the bird. But no better shot under the influence of incipient panic than on any other day (though probably no worse, either), I missed with both barrels and the grouse sailed on.

We walked and walked, we stumbled back through a clear-cut, Sweetzer taking up her former position at my heels. Whether or not it was the *same* clear-cut that we had come through earlier I had no way of knowing. One clear-cut looks much like the next, particularly when you're lost. For one extremely fleeting moment, I considered abandoning my gun and my bag to lighten my load, and then I remembered that one of the really stupid things that the deer hunter had done in the hunter safety film was to throw away his gun and strip off his coat in panic. *What a bonehead!* I had thought at the time. Besides, I liked my gun, and in case I didn't die, I was going to need it for the rest of the trip.

We walked and walked, we stumbled over slash and deadfall, we fell into stump holes. We cursed. (Well, I cursed.) I kept consulting my compass and readjusting my direction. *It's got to be this way, no, no, it must be this way.* I remembered an essay my friend Swanson had once written entitled "On Being Lost" and it seemed cruelly ironic that I was supposed to be meeting him tonight in the U.P., a six-hour drive from here, but that I was never going to make it because, of course, *I was lost.* I was mildly heartened to know that I hadn't altogether lost my sense of irony, and then I decided that irony has no place in the outdoors, anyway. With that thought, I was pretty sure I was becoming hypothermic. I remembered a line from Swanson's essay, something about the "enormous fresh feeling of being really lost." Sure, easy for a poet to say, and then I was suddenly annoyed with Swanson, as if this whole business was somehow his fault. But the more I thought about that line the more solace I began to take from it. I tried to look at this cavalierly, as a great adventure, not a matter of life and death. *I'll find my way out and I'll laugh when I remember this day!*

But mostly, I thought about my wife. She was going to be really mad at me for getting lost; she was forever warning me about that and I was going to be in terrible trouble at home if I died out here in the northwoods. Usually when I hunt alone, I arrange to have someone to check in with at the end of the day, and I had promised her that I would always do so on this trip. But I had broken that promise today, all week in fact, and she would never forgive me for it.

Wet and exhausted, I had one particularly despairing moment when I considered sitting down and having myself a good cry over my predicament. But then I felt my father's stern gaze from on high and decided against it.

I altered my direction incrementally and walked on. I began looking around for a friendly tree to hug. I had been lost now for over four hours, and I convinced myself that all this time I had been walking in exactly the wrong direction. I turned around and started back the way I had come. I walked a hundred steps before I realized that Sweetzer was no longer at my heels, she was still standing where I had turned, watching me. I trudged back to her, hoping that maybe she was like Lassie after all. Less than fifty feet beyond where I had turned around the first time, I stumbled out of the woods onto one of the mowed hunter's trails. Standing before me on the trail and rather startled by my sudden, and what must have been my wet, wild, bedraggled appearance, was a beautiful young blonde woman in a yellow rain slicker. You think I'm making this up? I am not.

At first I thought she might be an angel come to lead me to heaven, in which case death by exposure in the northwoods was looking up; she was so stunningly beautiful, the purest blonde hair, flawless milky skin, rosy red cheeks—the most beautiful woman I'd ever seen in my life. Sweetzer started barking at her and I realized from the insignia on her slicker that she wasn't angel at all, but an employee of the U.S. Forest Service, and that we had been saved. I wanted to tackle her, wrestle her to the ground, and smother her with grateful kisses. Lucky for me, and for her, I restrained myself. Instead, I tried to maintain my composure, tried to appear nonchalant.

"Hello there!" I said, a bit overly hearty. "What are you doing out here on a day like this? Quiet, Sweetzer."

"I'm with the cultural research department," she explained. "I'm looking for old cabin foundations, or anything else that might need to be saved."

Me! I wanted to shout, but I did not. "Well, I think I'm going to call it a day," I said casually. "Lousy hunting weather." I didn't want to admit that I had no idea which direction to take on the trail to get back to the main road. "Are you headed back to your vehicle?" I asked.

"Yeah," she said, "too wet out here today for me, too."

"What's your name?"

"Diana."

"Ah, Diana! Goddess of Chastity, of the Moon, and of the Hunt!"

Diana looked at me strangely. "Really?" she said, nervously. "I've never heard *that*."

"You mind if I walk along with you, Diana?"

"No, I don't mind," she said. "What's your dog's name?" And Diana led us out of the woods.

13

SWANSON

Few of my readers have probably had an opportunity of getting a good view of a village tavern, but we hunters go everywhere.

Ivan Turgenev

I was giddy and lightheaded after my narrow escape from the dark clutches of the northwoods, and back at the camper I changed into dry clothes and brewed a fresh pot of coffee. Certainly the best part of being lost is being found (and not found dead); suddenly life seems inutterably more precious; I was filled with an inexpressible joy, a love of all things and all people. And I had an uncontrollable urge to stuff myself with midwestern pastries. I stopped at the first bakery in the first town I came to and bought a huge box of assorted baked goods—glazed donuts, jelly rolls, apple fritters, sticky buns. I remembered a similar incident years ago when I was a young man and had gone off to Paris where I hoped to become an expatriate artiste. I was crossing the street in the Rue St. Denis—where I hung around at all hours of the day and night with the prostitutes, just like Toulouse-Lautrec—and I was very nearly run over by a car; it missed me by inches, and I had the same sense of delivery, of having cheated the Grim Reaper. I went immediately into a *patisserie* and bought half a dozen chocolate eclairs, which I ate right there on the spot. The same kind of gluttony consumed me now and I drove with my box of pastries in my lap, alternately stuffing them in my face and feeding them to Sweetzer. Later, we both threw up, our stomachs unaccustomed to such riches.

It was dark by the time I drove down the rutted lane to Swanson's isolated log cabin in the U.P. Light from the fireplace glowed through the windows. Swanson met me at the door, barefoot, a cigarette dangling from his mouth, his ample belly hanging out of his bathrobe, his head cocked back in that distinctive way of his. "What took you so long, Jimmy?" he asked in his nasal midwestern accent. "I expected you hours ago."

I had made it just in time for dinner; having purged myself of my pastry binge, I was starving again, and Swanson had prepared a wonderful *puttanesca*, the raw Italian whore's tomato sauce, his signature dish, with plenty of rough-chopped garlic, capers, black olives, anchovies, and large chunks of skillet-browned Italian sausage. Served with fresh grated romano cheese, french bread, and a bottle of red wine; eaten by flickering firelight. Over dinner, I told Swanson of my ordeal in the woods and of being rescued by the goddess of the hunt, and I thanked him for the bit of help that the line from his poem had given me.

After dinner, promptly at ten o'clock we drove into town for a nightcap at the village tavern, then we returned to the cabin and retired.

The Wisconsin weather had tracked me eastward, and the next morning dawned cold and blustery. A howling gale-force wind drove sheets of rain across Lake Superior, which looked like the sea in a Winslow Homer painting—frothed with whitecaps, huge breakers dashing on the jetty.

We decided to hunt anyway and drove up into the upland country above the lake, into stands of mixed aspen, pine, and alder, the open, rolling moorlike hills, studded by rocks and covered with ferns and a delicate sage green moss. I picked a clump of the moss and put it in my bag. I had taken to collecting these small mementos of my trip, a kind of tactile mnemonic device to recall the country and my companions: a hawk's feather from the Blackfeet reservation in Montana; a sprig of soft needles and berries from a cedar tree on the Missouri Breaks; a curled cylinder of white birch bark from Minnesota; a chunk of marble from a crumbled eighteenth-century grave marker in West Virginia; a pure white shorebird feather from the delta of Mobile Bay; a rabbit's foot from New Mexico; a shard of prehistoric pottery from Arizona; assorted mosses, ground covers, feathers, stones, and the crop contents of various game birds—all these I would put in a clear plastic bag that sits now on my desk, many of the items disintegrated and melded together in the bottom of the bag but others, like the clump of moss from the U.P., still intact, still retaining its lovely sage green color, still redolent of the wild, blustery day on the moors with Swanson.

We didn't hunt long that first day, and only put up one woodcock, on which Swanson made a brilliant long shot in the trees. It was a late bird, a plump hen, most of the migratory woodcock already having passed through this far north land. Swanson held the dead bird in his hand. She had probably been laid up by the weather and would have been headed south at the first sign of clearing, he hypothesized. "Better not to think about that," he said sadly, "or I'll get all teary-eyed." There is something wonderful about a big, burly one-eyed poet who gets teary over a dead woodcock.

At the cabin, we warmed ourselves before the fire, happy to be out of the wind and rain. We had wisely prepared lunch before we went out and it was waiting in the oven—a hearty bean stew with oxtails and pork neck bones, followed by a leisurely afternoon spent reading and napping before the fire. Sweetz crawled up into bed with Swanson, to sleep with her head resting on his leg, both of them snoring in concert. Later we took a drive down to look at the lake, still as wild as any sea.

The norther had intensified by night, knocking the power out in town. We went to the tavern, anyway, as did many other townfolks, seeking refuge from the storm and company in the darkness. We hurried from the car through wind and rain toward the faint light glowing from the windows of the tavern. Inside, flashlight beams described strange arcs across the ceiling while candles flickered on the bar. "Hey, everybody, the power's out!" Swanson announced by way of entrance. The owner set drinks up for us. He was an old friend of Swanson's, a quiet, steady guy named Jack, who had just beaten the storm home earlier that day, returning from a trip to the city, where he went to buy his son a new pair of hockey skates. Last winter Jack's wife had gone insane and had to be committed to a mental institution. The winters were long up here.

Early in the evening, a large man named Mace brought a freshly smoked lake trout in and laid it on the bar for everyone to sample. A local fisherman and artisan, Mace had hands the size of baseball mitts with which he somehow carved exquisite miniature wood figures—trout decoys and turtles with tiny, delicate moving parts. Swanson had showed me one in his cabin.

A bit later, the Lutheran minister came in, sat beside me at the bar, and ordered orange juice on the rocks. He needed Swanson's advice about his brother-in-law, an auto dealer in Detroit who had just been indicted by the DEA on money-laundering charges. Swanson is the kind of person who knows about such things, and after he had advised the minister, he went in the back room to make a few phone calls on his behalf. The minister ordered another orange juice and leaned toward me. "Satan is here," he whispered.

This information sent a chill up my spine, what with the storm raging outside and the native strangeness of the candlelit tavern. "What?" I asked.

"Satan," the minister said. "Satan has found an opening in this town. He's infiltrated our lifeblood."

"How do you mean by that, exactly?"

"Five divorces so far this year, a higher than usual incidence of family violence, child and spouse abuse, alcoholism, suicide, murder, insanity. . . ." The minister was right; these are boom times for the forces of evil in small-town America.

"How do you think he got in?" I asked.

"Beamed in on satellite television, I would guess," said the minister.

"Makes sense to me."

As we were talking, and as if sent to illustrate the minister's point, a very drunk young woman came in and took a stool on the other side of me. She had been crying. The minister ignored her. "Is there something I can do for you?" I asked.

"Yeah, you can order me a bourbon and Coke." She pulled a handkerchief from her purse and blew her nose. I ordered her the drink. The minister glanced over disapprovingly, and went to sit alone at a table in the shadows against the wall. I admired the way he came right into Satan's lair, to stand guard over his wayward parishioners.

"I have to whisper," said the young woman, nodding toward him. "That's my minister."

"Why do you have to whisper?"

"Would you mind if I asked you something?"

"No."

"Do you think I'm unattractive?"

"Not at all. Why do you ask?"

"Well, tonight I fixed a special dinner for my husband," she said, "his favorite dish. I served wine and we ate by candlelight. . . . I don't know why I'm telling you this, I don't even know you . . . what did you say your name was anyway?"

"Jim."

"Anyway, Jim, my husband gets in these terrible depressions and he doesn't pay any attention to me for weeks, sometimes months at a time. He hasn't made love to me in three months . . . so I fixed him this special dinner tonight, with wine and music, and candlelight. After dinner, I changed into . . . Jesus!" she said, covering her eyes with her hand, "why am I telling you this? I don't even know you. You're a friend of Swanson's right? Have we ever even met? I'm sorry, what did you say your name was?"

"Jim," I repeated. I don't know why it is but total strangers are always cornering me like this and spilling their guts. I must have a sympathetic demeanor.

"Yeah, right, Jim, I'm sorry. Okay, Jim, so I changed into my night-gown, actually it's kind of a negligee, you know? But when I got back into the living room my husband had already fallen asleep on the couch."

"Why didn't you wake him up?"

"I did. I woke him up and he got off the couch and went to bed. He hardly even looked at me. Said he was too tired."

"I see. Gee, I'm sorry."

"Yeah, you and me both. So I started drinking and then I got dressed and came down here. What do you think's the matter with me?"

"What do you mean?"

"I mean, why won't he make love to me? Am I unattractive or what?"

"No, not at all. You're very pretty."

"Yeah? Thanks. That's really nice of you to say. You're a friend of Swanson's right? I'm sorry to keep asking you this, but I'm kind of drunk. What did you say your name was?"

The storm had abated somewhat by morning. It was still cloudy but the wind had layed down, and the rain—which had turned to a fine snow overnight—had stopped. After a breakfast of leftover *puttanesca* mixed with leftover bean stew and reheated, Swanson and I went hunting again. The green moss on the hills was lightly dusted with snow and the ferns had turned brown. Swanson had his lovely English setter, Joy, a fine, stylish hunting dog. She and Sweetz made a good team; Joy would go on point in a thicket and Sweetz would go in to make the flush. At one point, Joy trailed a running grouse, pointing, moving, pointing, moving; she worked the bird beautifully. Finally Sweetz went in and put the bird up, and Swanson killed it cleanly. Swanson was the most gracious of hosts, always trying to put me in the position for the best shot. But I was shooting badly, as was usual on my first day or two in new country, when I tended to be more attentive to the landscape than to the business of hunting.

I finally grew disgusted with myself. "You go ahead in on this point, Swanson," I said, "I'm hopeless today. I couldn't hit my ass with both barrels."

Fortunately Swanson shot beautifully, never missing and going four for four—three grouse and one woodcock. That evening for our dinner he prepared a pair of grouse that I had brought with me from Wisconsin—using a recipe that he had come up with in a dream a few years earlier. Anyone who is familiar with Swanson's work will know that he leads a rich dream life.

SWANSON'S DREAM GROUSE

Cut grouse into pieces and soak overnight in a mixture of $^2/_3$ cream to $^1/_3$ Tabasco sauce. Dust pieces with cornstarch and brown in butter. Set aside in warm oven. Sauté diced shallots in pan drippings, add finely chopped fresh sage, Italian parsley, thyme, and white wine. Add several tablespoons of the cream/Tabasco mixture to sauce (or gravy, as Swanson, a stalwart midwesterner, insists) and pour over grouse pieces. This dish is excellent served with garlic mashed potatoes, which involve mashing potatoes with a dozen or so garlic cloves that have been poached in butter until tender.

14

MILAKOKIA

You good forest, my home, God's peace, shall I tell you from my heart . . .

Knut Hamsun

Somewhere down around Escanaba, Michigan, I met a beautiful young Chippewa woman who worked in a bakery. No, I was not back on the sweets; in fact, I went in for a cup of coffee and to see if I could find a nice nutritious bran muffin. Unfortunately, the highly touted health benefits of bran have not altogether infiltrated the north country yet; they had no bran muffins and I had to settle for a glazed donut.

Having just come in from the woods, I was dressed in my hunting clothes, and the woman, who's name tag read Milakokia, asked me where I had been hunting. I told her.

"I know a much better place for grouse hunting," she said.

"Really, where would that be?" I asked. Hunters get their information where they can.

"You'd have to take me out with you," she said slyly. "I could show you. I love to grouse hunt. I'm a very good shot."

I hesitated. She looked at me directly with large oval brown eyes. She had long straight black hair that fell all the way to her waist and was incredibly shiny. She was really very pretty.

"Are you married?" she asked.

"Happily," I said.

"Is that what you're worried about?"

"No," I lied.

"Because I just want to go hunting. I love grouse hunting and I never

115

have anyone to take me out. My boyfriend doesn't like to hunt and he won't let me go."

"If your boyfriend won't let you go, how can I take you?"

"I won't tell him," she said simply.

"What if he finds out?"

"Then he'll probably beat me up. And he'd probably kill you. He's Sioux and he has a terrible bad temper. Especially when he drinks, which is most of the time. He killed a man with a bottle one time, but they said it was self-defense."

"Doesn't sound like a good idea to me," answered your cowardly narrator.

"He won't find out. You can pick me up right here. I have tomorrow afternoon off. Please? I just love grouse hunting. I know the best place. You've never seen so many birds. I promise. I'll show you."

I don't know if it was the idea of all the birds or simply because she had such a pleasant, direct manner, but I agreed to take her out hunting the next day. We set a time.

"Ah, one thing is I don't have a gun," she added. "Do you have an extra one I could borrow?"

"I suppose so. Do you have a hunting license?" For my part I was working on my seventh nonresident hunting license of the trip.

"Yes, that I have."

I picked Milakokia up the next day in front of the bakery. I confess that I kept a nervous lookout for an angry, possibly drunk Sioux boyfriend, but he didn't seem to be around. She was still wearing her white bakery uniform and carrying a bundle of clothes. She seemed to be in a fine mood, excited and talkative.

"What a great camper!" she said. "If I had one of these, I would leave here and never come back. He'd never find me then. Look at all the gear you have! You must be rich. Is that all you do, travel around hunting? Can I change my clothes back there while you drive? Pretty dog! What's her name? Sweetzer? Boy, that's really a silly name! Where did you get such a silly name? Which is the gun I'll be using? I brought a few twelve-gauge shells, they're all I had. You don't have a twelve-gauge? Well, I could pay you for some of your shells, or we could stop at the sporting goods store."

We drove into the Hiawatha National Forest. Mila, as she liked to be called, directed me down a complicated network of logging access roads. I was happy to have a guide because the roads—through the kind of flat, undifferentiated aspen and pine forest that had me a bit spooked since my Wisconsin misadventure—all looked the same to me. Mila led me to a small clearing where I pulled off and parked. I readied our gear. I let her use my Belgium 20-gauge, while I carried my Fox 16-gauge. I could tell right away from the sure way she handled the gun that she'd had experience with firearms, and judging from the look of the woods around here she seemed to be familiar with good grouse habitat as well. Dressed in jeans and hiking boots, she was all business.

It was a crisp fall afternoon, dry and clear, nearly all the leaves off the trees, which makes the shooting so much easier. We got into birds almost immediately, flushing one just on the edge of the clearing. Mila neatly dropped it with her first shot. She was very pleased. "This is a good gun," she said, "I can't miss with a gun like this!" Sweetzer retrieved the bird to me, a young cock, and we admired it. Mila smoothed the feathers with a soft, thoughtful touch. She had long, brown, slender fingers.

I would not hunt with many women on this trip, and though this will probably be roundly attacked as a sexist remark, it strikes me that often they have difficulty with the killing part of hunting. Mila seemed to have no such reservations, though I noticed that she took particular care with each of the three birds she shot that afternoon, regarding them and handling them with some reverence as if they were each quite special and precious. I don't know if this is a feminine characteristic or not, but it's the way it should be for men and women alike. I would hunt with some men in the course of my trip who simply stuffed dead birds in their game bags, with hardly a glance at them, in the same offhanded way that they might toss a pack of chicken parts into the grocery cart. This seems to me to diminish the sport, to reduce hunting to a cold, mechanistic meat-gathering exercise. I think that we owe the game we take some measure of respect and thanks—each animal we kill a kind of silent prayer. I was reminded of my friend Swanson mourning the dead woodcock in hand.

Mila shot three birds in just over an hour, and I, two, and we decided that that was enough hunting. I left three of the birds in feathers, undrawn, to age for a few days in the refrigerator. I had wanted Mila to take them home with her, but she said that because of her boyfriend she could not. We had drawn the other two in the field immediately upon killing them and we plucked them now for an early dinner before dark, which came on fast in these shortening northern days. Freshly killed and immediately drawn birds, eaten *au bout du fusil* as the French say, meaning literally "at the end of the gun," have a special flavor and texture. I grilled them over hot coals, seasoned simply and brushed with olive oil, and served them with fresh eggplant, also brushed with olive oil and grilled on the small barbecue I carried with me.

"You're a pretty good cook," said Mila, who ate her grouse with relish, with her fingers, as game birds really should be eaten. "I don't exactly eat like this at home." She had talked nonstop through the bird plucking and the cooking and even the eating, excited with her day's shooting; she was an

excellent shot, using only three shells for three birds, whereas I had discharged a full half-dozen for my two. Now in the growing dusk she grew
silent and pensive, and we went through that period of specific awkward-
ness that occurs sometimes between men and women, in this case a bridge
not to be crossed.

"I hope you can find the road back in the dark," I said.

"I could find my way back blindfolded," she answered, and she
laughed, her dark eyes bright. She gathered a handful of heavy gleaming
black hair and tossed it over her shoulder.

We drove back out of the woods and at Mila's direction I dropped her off
under a streetlight on a corner in town. She held her bakery uniform
bunched up in her hand. "Thank you," she said in her simple, direct
fashion. "I had a wonderful day."

"Are you going to be in trouble at home?" I asked.

"Sure," Mila answered. "I'm always in trouble at home." She smiled.
"I think that's what I like best about grouse hunting."

15

PRIMEVAL MAN

Only in the contemporary period and, within that, only in the most demoralized regions of Europe has an affinity for hunting been held in disesteem.

Ortega y Gasset

I hunted one day in Michigan's Lower Peninsula with a fellow by the name of Nick Reens—a man who lives to hunt, who hunts to live. I would hunt with perhaps a half-dozen such total devotees over my 17,000-mile journey—sporting maniacs for whom hunting is no casual recreational pursuit, but a way of life, complete and self-contained. These are hunters who seem to be throwbacks to another time, who represent a kind of genetic aberration in which the hunting instinct, so dulled and recessive in most of us happy shoppers these days, is still quite dominant in their makeup. If you were a prehistoric woman, these would be the fellows you'd have wanted to marry in a hunter/gatherer society—efficient, dedicated predators who really knew how to bring home the bacon. Your husband would be much esteemed by his peers, your larder full with all manner of game, you and your children dressed in the finest hides. You'd never have to worry about being cold or hungry. Now, of course, such pure venatic prowess has fallen into some disfavor; now, a prized husband is more likely to be one with a six-figure income and a couple of dozen "power suits"; at dinner and cocktail parties these days, especially in urban areas, but also in many upscale rural locales, the hunter must be cautious about recounting tales of his sporting triumphs, lest he be viciously berated by all manner of what the writer Jim Harrison has dubbed "lifestyle Nazis"—those who would have everyone live as they do: cleanly, bloodlessly, politically correctly.

A fine fiction writer named Joy Williams recently took on hunters and the hunting establishment in a much-discussed essay in a popular men's magazine. Williams made the case that hunters were criminals and should be prosecuted for their crimes against animals; this is the kind of stance that really gets the dander up in the nimrod community. The fact is, she scored many legitimate points against sport hunting, citing numerous despicable acts committed by the sadly vast legion of "slob hunters" in America—an easy target, indeed. She concluded her attack by calling for the abolition of hunting in this country—supporting her position with the statistic that as only 7 percent of the American populace are hunters, the other 93 percent majority should (and could) do the right thing by banning the evil business altogether. Of course, this is the worst kind of majority thuggery, and might well be applied to ban any number of minority activities—say, bowling, gardening, farming, ranching; even the reading of fiction might be outlawed simply because not enough people do it.

To this hunter's mind, a far more useful statistic is that 98.5 percent of all Americans are not capable of basic survival—that is, they rely on others to provide food, shelter, and clothing for themselves and their families. This group, which grows each century, each decade, suggests an increasingly urbanized, antlike culture, estranged from the natural processes of hunting, gathering, food growing, and animal husbandry, and commensurately top-heavy with a lot of extremely unresourceful and useless citizenry. It might occur to that majority of dead wood, commonly known as the "Public" (of which the narrator is one), that it would behoove us all to be somewhat more tolerant of the tiny 7 percent among us who enjoy the hands-on activity of procuring their own dinner from field or forest, even if that activity, no longer strictly necessary for survival, has been ritualized into sport. As John G. Mitchell points out in his excellent book *The Hunt* (by far the most evenhanded and thorough examination of the pro/anti-hunting controversy), by all estimates man has been hunting for meat from one-half to two million years. Taking the long view, someday we might need those largely forgotten skills again, might need to press the old recessive hunting gene back into action. Maybe we ought to keep a few hunters around as brood stock.

Given the lopsided nature of the aforementioned statistics, it goes without saying that antihunting pressure comes from all quarters these days, and not just from the traditional animal rights organizations. Increasingly, the hunter finds himself in the unpleasant, defensive posture of apologizing, rationalizing, explaining, or even hiding his predilection—as if it were some sort of dark, secret perversion.

On the back cover of Datus Proper's fine book *Pheasants of the Mind,* I was surprised to read a jacket blurb by the renowned food writer M. F. K. Fisher, who wrote: "I am surprised to admit that I like this book, although I deplore hunting and eating anything beautiful and wild and living." What does Ms. Fisher mean exactly—that she will eat only ugly, domestic, dead things? Does she mean that it's morally wrong to kill a pheasant (a fancy member of the chicken family, which, in any case, has been domesticated for milleniums) but not wrong to kill a barnyard chicken, simply because the pheasant has handsomer plumage? Does the pheasant care whether it dies from a well-placed load of birdshot, or in the jaws of a coyote or fox, or in the talons of a hawk or owl? These are not difficult questions. Of his beloved ruffed grouse, biologist Gordon Gullion, who spent his life in the forest studying the species, cut right to the heart of the matter: "Grouse are born to be eaten by something," he said simply. And why not by a man?

But, of course, I do know what M. F. K. Fisher means, and no hunter worth his salt kills another animal without silently voicing some variation of the same question: How can I kill something so beautiful? or, Why do I take pleasure in killing a wild creature? (Let's not make any bones about it—hunting, among other things, is *fun*.) These are more difficult questions, impossible to answer to anyone's, including the hunter's, satisfaction. We may be predators, like the raptor and the coyote, but we are also, for better or worse, human beings with brains rather too large for our own good. Personally, it is no easier for me to kill a domestic chicken (I tried raising some once but got too attached to them to be able to whack their heads off), and I am very grateful that I don't have to dispatch my own cow every time I want to eat beef.

So before we throw the baby out with the bathwater by legislating against hunting, we might do well to consider whether or not our motives for such a ban have less to do with modern man's sense of benevolent enlightenment toward all living creatures (which given the way we continue to treat the Earth and its species is the worst kind of hypocrisy) than it does with our increasing ignorance of the natural world.

I seem to have digressed! One minute your narrator is about to go out on a hunt with Nick Reens in Michigan, and the next he has launched into a lengthy apologia for something that really requires no such thing. Hunters must make their own peace.

Reens put all five of his lovely setters down on the ground for the hunt that day, poor Sweetz a bit out of place in the company of these stylish bird dogs, all of whom were also blood relatives. On the drive out to the grouse coverts, she had to ride in the back of the truck under the shell with the setters; they kept her backed up in the corner of the truck bed where they watched her vigilantly. She was still a young, timid dog (we had only just celebrated her second birthday), and had not yet learned her immense Lab strength, and the fact that she didn't have to take shit from any gangly English setters.

Let us say that Nick Reens might be considered a bit of an eccentric (like most good hunters and nearly all of the best). His hunting attire consists of a corduroy sportscoat, which he buys secondhand at thrift shops, and English "Wellies" worn outside his jeans. With his slender, straight-backed carriage and brisk long-legged stride, this outfit gives him somewhat of a natty continental look afield. He hunts with an elegant little Spanish side-by-side .410, the smallest gauge, hardly more than a peashooter in the world of shotguns, a tiny thing with pencil-thin barrels, that made my 20-gauge look like an ungainly blunderbuss.

Not a man short on opinions, Reens is no joiner of organizations and no fan of the Ruffed Grouse Society. "When you have a good thing going like grouse hunting," he was saying in the car, putting an index finger to his lips, "what you do is keep your mouth shut about it. The last thing in the world you want to do is blab to everyone else about how great it is. Basically, what the Ruffed Grouse Society does is encourage more people to hunt. I would argue that their efforts have never created *one* single grouse, yet they have been responsible for the shooting of countless thousands of them through overpromotion. There are already enough people in the field—too many in my opinion. Why would we want to promote the sport?"

Reens hunts fast and confidently, covering the ground with a steady, no-nonsense step. He is intimately familiar with his coverts, hunting nearly every day of the season and spending the off-season months "prospecting"—driving around the region, hiking new country and potential new coverts with his dogs, while obtaining the necessary hunting permission from landowners. In short, he does his homework and knows his stuff; he knows good grouse and woodcock habitat and the habits of the birds as well as any biologist or field researcher.

That morning we hunted along a black, slow-moving, gently winding river. I kept to the ridge top while Reens dropped down to work the bottom. The cover was thick and thorny, like all good grouse cover, but somehow he seemed to move fluidly and effortlessly in it, an innate talent I had noticed in the best hunters—an almost animallike ability to walk through the densest undergrowth without ever appearing to be hung up or slowed down by it. As one who spends a fair amount of time stumbling about in thickets, wrapped in underbrush, tearing clothes and flesh on briars and thorns, I have always envied this natural grace, the sign of a hunter at home in his environment.

Two of the setters went on point on the slope above the riverbank, a third honoring the point—a beautiful sight. Reens went in and flushed the grouse; it came out his side of the thicket, flying low for the cover along the river. He dropped it cleanly. The bird had been feeding on wintergreen, its crop full of dark red berries, its breast flesh stained purple by the fruit.

Though we hunted the river for another hour, we didn't move any more birds, and worked our way in a broad circle back to the truck. Then we drove to one of Reens's favorite woodcock coverts in the trees on the edge of a farm meadow, where we flushed half a dozen birds in under half an hour. Reens is an excellent shot, the kind who makes the average shooter (or in my case, the below average shooter) feel particularly clumsy and inept. He is lightning fast and aggressive, yet another quality I had identified as essential to the successful hunter. If you've ever watched another animal hunting, you will have learned that there is no room for tentativeness. The tentative predator is a contradiction in terms. In nature, the tentative hunter starves.

I was shooting poorly, the beginning of a long, discouraging slump that would carry on over into New England and, in fact, plague me on and off across the country. Perhaps it's more accurate to say that my shooting abilities are such that they could be described as being in a permanent slump with occasional tiny upturns. I have this entry in my journal of that day:

> Reens shot a fine double on a pair of woodcock with his ludicrous little .410 which looks to me like a BB gun, the shells for it not as big around as a woman's pinkie.
>
> Right after, Sweetz flushed another pair of woodcock directly in front of me, an easy double. I missed. Both barrels. How hopeless I am! Too vague, I'm thinking about other things—admiring the country, examining the cover, trying to identify a tree, or shrub, or a songbird, daydreaming over the blackness of the river, the large hearts of woodcock. And when the birds fly I am rarely ready. Or I get flustered. I notice that I shoot better when hunting alone. Perhaps I am anxious in front of these experts.

As expert as he is in the field, Nick Reens is equally masterful at the grill. It goes without saying that hunters also tend to have a better-laid table than the other 93 percent of the citizenry. Dinner that evening at Reens's house after the day's hunt would be one of the most memorable of my entire trip (and I ate some spectacular game dinners along the hunter's road), a superb mixed bag—pheasants, woodcock, grouse, and a venison tenderloin, with several sauces, sautéed wild mushrooms, a spinach salad with pine nuts and prosciutto, roast new potatoes, and several excellent wines. I can't find it in my heart, or in my palate, to deplore or apologize for the fact that everything on our plates and in our glasses that night in Michigan was "beautiful and wild and living." I only wish that M. F. K. Fisher could have been there. I think she'd have enjoyed herself.

NICK REENS'S WOODCOCK SIMPLY PREPARED

Allow 1–2 birds each as an appetizer. The birds can be prepared immediately upon shooting but are best if refrigerated in the feathers, undrawn, for up to 6 days. When plucked and drawn, rub cavities with freshly ground black pepper and small amounts of lemon juice and Worcestershire or soy sauce. Let sit until room temperature while preparing coals. Grill over medium-hot coals (or on stovetop grill), basting with mixture of melted butter and Worcestershire or soy sauce, turning occasionally. Birds will be ready (medium rare) in approximately 8–12 minutes. Check by poking with a toothpick—the birds are done when juices run clear. Present the birds whole, with game sauce either poured over them or served on the side for dipping. Woodcock should be eaten with fingers, as utensils have been known to taint the delicate flesh. The legs should be pulled off and eaten first. Then bite into both lobes of breast simultaneously and eat with abandon. Snipe and dove may also be prepared this way with excellent results.

(Additional notes: Late-season birds are best, as fat buildup renders them virtually self-basting. Woodcock do not freeze well so limit freezer time to a maximum of 3 weeks. Save hearts, livers, and carcasses to add to the saucepot.)

16

LOOKING FOR MR. GROUSE

Now it is a question of extreme and rapidly advancing scarcity. Now it is a matter of fewer animals each day. Now it is a matter of a dramatic reality: that the game is disappearing, that hunting is dying, that soon man will have to stop being a hunter, and that this outstanding form of his happiness is on the verge of vanishing.

Ortega y Gasset

I spent some days toward the end of October in the Ohio River Valley, that part of the country where the states of Ohio, Pennsylvania, and a thin finger of West Virginia come together. You can drive across the three borders here in a matter of minutes, and I would do so a number of times, back and forth, some days not even sure which state I was hunting in, and some days hunting in all three. In this once renowned grouse country, especially Green County, Pennsylvania, bird numbers began to decline precipitously over the past decade and have never recovered. As in other parts of the country where this phenomenon has occurred, nobody seems to know for sure what caused the drastic reduction in the grouse population, although if there is a shortage of birds, there is no shortage of theories to explain their decline. Game management is still largely an empirical science and during my visit to the region I would speak to biologists, state game officials, and hunters, and would leave more confused about the matter than when I arrived.

Among the favored theories (in no particular order) for the regional decline of the ruffed grouse:

A. Hunting pressure (more hunters hunting an extended season);
B. A natural cyclical phenomenon (grouse populations are believed by biologists to fluctuate on seven- and ten-year cycles);
C. Loss of habitat (due to overmature forests and lack of managed clear-cutting);

D. Change in weather patterns (this is the southern end of the ruffed grouse range and milder winters in the last decade with less snow pack and wetter springs may be adversely affecting breeding success);

E. Parasites (grouse are known to host a number of parasites, some especially devastating to young and breeding birds);

F. Predation (protection of raptors and less hunting and trapping of other predators due to the collapse of the fur industry);

G. An act of God (remember, this is the heart of the Bible Belt);

H. Some, or all of the above.

As such a list would indicate, it's a hard world for game birds; threats to their existence are rife, and never more so than in this age. As the ruffed grouse is the official state bird of Pennsylvania, so designated back in the days of plenty, and as Pennsylvania is also home of the Ruffed Grouse Society, there is some cheap irony to be had from the fact that these days Pennsylvania hunters are apt to travel to the more virgin reaches of Minnesota, Wisconsin, and Michigan in search of grouse. To an unamused RGS spokesman in Pittsburg I suggested this idea for a organizational bumper sticker: Remember the Heath Hen.

I spent my first night in the region in Dallas Pike, West Virginia, in a campground set in the "hollows" of a dark, old-growth forest along the Ohio River. It was a vaguely unsettling place, a strange depressed corner of the nation. If the northwoods seemed at first claustrophobic for being so flat and monotonous, the hills, mountains, and hollows of this part of the country seem mighty tight in their own way, as confining and close together as the boxy mining and steel mill row houses that line the banks of the Ohio.

The next morning, I phoned a fellow named Harold Pickens, an optometrist in nearby Bellaire, Ohio, and a friend of the biologist Bill Hunyadi, with whom I had hunted in Minnesota. I was beginning to amass a shoe box full of scrap paper with names, phone numbers, addresses, and directions scribbled on them, leading the diligent, if somewhat disorganized, narrator on a convoluted trail of bird hunters across the country. Below Pickens's name and phone number appeared the notation "reputed to be *Mr. Grouse* in these parts."

It was Friday and Harold was confined to the clinic, but he invited me to go hunting with him the following day. "If you're looking for something to do today," he told me, "you really should go over to Washington, Pennsylvania, and talk to Les Zimmerman. He's a sporting art dealer, owns a gallery there. He's also actively involved with the state in a grouse study program they're doing down on his farm in Waynesburg. Les is *Mr. Grouse*, around here."

"Wait a minute, I thought you were Mr. Grouse," I said.

"Oh, no, I'm just your basic grouse hunter. Les knows a lot more about grouse than I do. Let me just warn you though, watch out for his wife. She doesn't care much for grouse hunters and she can be a little bit of a . . . how can I put this politely . . ."

"Bitch?"

"Well, I didn't say that."

"You mean to say she's married to Mr. Grouse, they're sporting art dealers, and she doesn't like bird hunters?"

"I'm afraid that's right," Harold said.

Harold gave me Mr. Grouse's phone number, and I called him as soon as we hung up. Unfortunately, Mrs. Grouse answered the phone. "Mr. Zimmerman is with a customer," she said coolly. "Perhaps I could help you?"

I briefly explained my mission.

Mrs. Grouse was a tough audience; she was not buying. A stony silence ensued on the line. "Hello?" I finally said.

"Mr. Zimmerman is very busy today," she answered.

"Perhaps I could just come by and say hello."

"I'm afraid he wouldn't have time to see you."

"Well, I have plenty of time," I said, not to be deterred. "I'd like to come by anyway and take a look at your artwork. I'm interested in acquiring some sporting prints."

"That is arranged by appointment only," said Mrs. Grouse.

"Then I'd like to make an appointment to come by and look at your artwork. I'm quite a collector."

"We have nothing available today."

"How about tomorrow?"

"Nor tomorrow."

"I see." Clearly, Mrs. Grouse was not going to fall for that one, either.

I drove to Washington, Pennsylvania, anyway. I must say I was still having trouble warming up to the country. Everything was so *steep*. The streets in Washington were all straight uphill and down, narrow and nearly impassable in the camper, which suddenly seemed completely out of scale, a great wallowing behemoth in these tight spaces. I found the Zimmermans' gallery; it was on a tiny, steep, one-way street and it took me a number of passes around a maze of other one-way streets that made me feel as though I was trapped in Sartre's *No Exit* before I was finally able to pull up in front. I parked partway down the slope of the hill, as if suspended on the crest of a roller coaster. I had the odd sensation that if I

undid my shoulder strap I would fall right through the windshield. I set
the emergency brake. Then I waited, my partner, Sweetzer, sitting up in
the passenger seat beside me, staring straight ahead. All we needed now
to complete our stakeout was rumpled suits, coffee in Styrofoam cups,
and cigarettes—although the camper was not exactly an unobtrusive un-
marked car.

I watched as people walked in and out of the gallery. At one point, I
thought I spotted Mrs. Grouse at the door eyeing me suspiciously. A few
minutes later, I saw a man I was certain was Mr. Grouse walking out the
door, chatting with two customers. He accompanied them to their car,
which was parked directly behind mine. He was a small, wiry, energetic
man with a quick, jaunty step and a friendly smile. Now was my chance; I
jumped out of the camper like a process server. "Excuse me, sir, are you
Mr. Zimmerman?"

"Why, yes indeed, I am," he said, as pleasant as can be. I introduced
myself and gave a quick abbreviated version of my purpose; I could see
Mrs. Grouse watching us from the doorway.

Mr. Grouse looked nervously up toward her. "Could you come back
tonight?" he asked. "I could meet you back here at seven. There might be
some other grouse hunters here, too. Sometimes they come by in the
evening to visit. I'd love to talk to you."

Suddenly Mrs. Grouse was marching down the steps to the sidewalk.
Everything had steps in this country, nothing on the level, everything
straight up and down.

"Excuse me," said Mr. Grouse, "I'd better go now. I'll see you
tonight."

She was headed right for me. I jumped in the camper, yanked the
emergency brake, and took off at a wild, breakneck coast down the hill,
jumpstarting the engine halfway down. In the rearview mirror I saw Mrs.
Grouse standing on the sidewalk watching me drive away.

That night I returned under cover of the dark. It was exactly 7:00 P.M. when
I met Mr. Grouse under a street lamp in front of the gallery. He let me in.
There were no other grouse hunters present, after all. We sat in straight-
backed wooden chairs in a back room of the dimly lit gallery.

"Now, tell me, what can I do for you?" he asked pleasantly.

"I was told that you were Mr. Grouse and that I really ought to talk to
you about grouse hunting in this area."

"Oh, no, I'm not Mr. Grouse. If you really want to speak to Mr. Grouse,
you need to go down and see Professor Michaels at the University of West
Virginia. Now *he's* Mr. Grouse."

I found this information mildly irritating. How many Mr. Grouse did they have around here, anyway? "But I was told that you were Mr. Grouse."

"Oh, no, Professor Michaels has been working with grouse much longer than I. Who told you I was Mr. Grouse?"

"Harold Pickens over in Ohio."

"Well, that's very kind of Harold. But I'm not really."

"Maybe we could just say that Professor Michaels is Mr. Grouse, Senior, and you're Mr. Grouse, Junior?" I coaxed.

"Well, yes, I suppose we could say that," Les agreed. "Although I've also heard George Evans referred to as Mr. Grouse."

"Really? I'm visiting Evans on Sunday."

"Just between you and me, Dr. Michaels knows a hundred times more about grouse than George Evans. George is just higher profile. Actually, George is very opinionated, he's really a bit of a grouse demagogue."

"A grouse demagogue?"

"Don't misunderstand me, George is a wonderful writer, but I don't think he knows as much about grouse as he would like to believe."

"In the Midwest people refer to Gordon Gullion as Mr. Grouse," I pointed out.

"That's mainly because of all the exposure Gullion's gotten through the Ruffed Grouse Society. Actually, Dr. Michaels knows as much about grouse as Gordon Gullion, and in fact, in this area, which is completely different habitat, he knows far more. Gullion doesn't know the first thing about Pennsylvania grouse."

"So maybe we could say that Gordon Gullion is Mr. Grouse of the north country, while Dr. Michaels is Mr. Grouse, Senior, of the Ohio River Valley, and you're still Mr. Grouse, Junior."

"Yes, you could probably say that if you wanted, except that I have heard some people refer to Sam Pursglove [Executive Director of the Ruffed Grouse Society] up in Pittsburgh as Mr. Grouse, too."

As Zimmerman and I were chatting, another grouse hunter came in. He wanted to take a look at a new shotgun Les had recently acquired. Les went to get it and the grouse hunter and I fell to talking. "You're a long way from home," he said. "I noticed your license plate. What brings you here?"

I told him.

"That's wonderful!" he said enthusiastically. "Boy, I've always dreamed of doing something like that. Hunting my way around the country. You know, if you have time, you should really go down to Waynesburg and visit a guy by the name of Joe Riggs. He owns a sporting goods store in town. All the grouse hunters hang out there. Joe is Mr. Grouse around here."

"Wait just a minute," I said, exasperated, "I thought Les was Mr. Grouse. And what about this Professor Michaels, and George Bird Evans?

And Harold Pickens? What about Gordon Gullion? And Sam Pursglove? How many Mr. Grouses can there be?"

The grouse hunter lowered his voice. "Listen," he whispered, "take my word for it, Les here knows a lot about grouse, so does Michaels, and I recommend that you talk to both of them. And those other guys are certainly experts, too. But Joe Riggs has been around here forever. If you're really looking for Mr. Grouse, for my money, Joe Riggs is your man. In this area, Joe Riggs is *Mr. Grouse.*"

I decided that the only fair thing to do was to visit all of the aforementioned people, maybe even hunt with them if possible, and then decide for myself. Suddenly the Mr. Grouse title had become something of a contest in my mind, like the Miss America pageant, sans bathing suit competition, of course. I spent an hour or so talking to Les Zimmerman, who was indeed extremely knowledgeable about grouse, and who very kindly invited me to hunt with him on Monday down at his farm near Waynesburg.

The next day at dawn I drove back to Ohio to meet Harold Pickens for our appointed hunt. The morning was damp, chilly, and somber; a dense fog descended on the hollows.

Pickens, trim, fit, without an ounce of fat on his wiry frame, was still dressed in his running suit when I arrived, the first inkling I had that I might be in trouble here. A marathoner, he had already been out for his daily ten-mile run, *before* hunting. He changed into hunting attire, and we loaded gear and dogs—Sweetz and Harold's male setter, Thicket—into his four-wheel-drive vehicle.

Without Harold, I'd have spent days lost in the hollows, driving narrow winding roads, through tiny one-store villages, up and down the mountains, and in and out of the clouds, which seemed to be permanently settled in the bottoms, heavy as stones. Then you would drive up the next hill and break free of the cloudbank as if in an ascending airplane, and the warmth of the sun would feel wonderful for a moment, before you descended into the dank gloom of the next patch.

This was country of old hardscrabble, submarginal farms, with a few scrawny beef cattle grazing on the steep sloping meadows and faded Chew Mail Pouch Tobacco signs painted on the barns. We passed a number of abandoned coal mines in various states of reclamation. Over the past few years most of the coal mining companies had moved their operations out west where the coal has a lower sulfur content. "Strip mining actually created some fantastic cover for grouse," Harold explained as we drove. "Ironically, it makes better cover when they don't try to reclaim it because then it grows back up wild in brush and native plants. When they reclaim it they plant it all in grass, which doesn't provide much in the way of food or cover."

Harold was a sincere, low-keyed fellow, an extremely tidy bachelor sort, who knew virtually everybody in the area; eventually he fit them all for eyeglasses, at least those who would come off the farms or out of the tiny villages to go into town. Harold hunted every Saturday of the season, either alone or with one regular hunting partner, and he spent Sundays, a day on which hunting is banned in this region, driving around the country looking for new coverts or exploring them on foot with his dogs, but without a gun.

I liked Pickens right away; he was a conscientious sportsman, clearly less concerned with the size of his daily bag than he was with the totality of the hunt. "If you hunt the same covert every time you go out," he explained as we drove, "and the first time you have twelve flushes and two kills, and the next time you have ten flushes and two kills, it doesn't take much to figure out the mathematical progression. It always surprises me when hunters do that, and then wonder why eventually there are no birds left."

A dedicated, single-minded sportsman, Pickens joins a group of local bird hunters every fall for a three-week grouse hunting vacation in Michigan, and in the summer if he can get away from the clinic, he tries to take a week-long fishing trip to Canada. He confided to me that he had recently broken up with his longtime girlfriend, whom he had always expected to marry.

"A question of sport abuse?" I probed, following up on a theory I had formed that this affliction has doomed nearly as many relationships as alcohol abuse.

Harold laughed. "Could be. It's hard to explain the almost . . . addiction of grouse hunting," he said. "It's not just a hobby or a pastime, but a way of life. I feel sorry for people who have nothing in their life that keeps them fired up like that all year long."

We stopped at the general store in the little hamlet of Armstrong Mills so that I could buy a hunting license. The mist was beginning to part, and by the time we arrived at the place Harold had chosen to hunt for the day, the sun had finally gained the upper hand over all but the most stubborn clouds in the darkest north-facing hollows. It promised to be a lovely day after all. From northern Michigan, where fall had been all but spent by the time I left, I had come far enough south again that many of the trees and bushes here had not yet dropped their leaves, still red and golden, and the damp rich grass was still a deep summer green. I seemed to have gained a lead over winter again.

We drove up a rutted two-track road and parked by an old strip mine, in the process of being reclaimed in its own sweet time by brush, but unfortunately also discovered by the locals as a dump site. This country shared with all depressed regions a certain unkept look—litter and garbage abandoned along the roads or at any convenient pull-off.

But once we were afoot and away from the road, I began to like the country; I liked the wild, overgrown feeling here, the dense hawthorn thickets and wild grape vines, the impenetrable multiflora and wild rose. We climbed up and down the steep hills, working the ridge tops and bottoms and the slopes between. As in so much good game bird country, particularly that east of the Mississippi, everything that grew here seemed to have thorns or briars on it, everything hung on to you with grasping insistence or outright claims on your flesh. At one point I froze in the center of a multiflora rose thicket; with one eyelid and one nostril caught on thorns, I didn't dare take another step.

As might be expected of a man who runs ten miles a day, Harold moved fast through the country, neither winded by the steepest slope nor slowed by the densest cover. And eventually, I found myself moving easier, too. I had nearly forgotten what the open country of the West was like. It seemed years ago that I had hunted blue grouse in the thin air of timberline in Colorado, or sage grouse on the windy expanse of a Wyoming alfalfa field. It seemed impossible that it had only been a few weeks earlier that I had walked the wide-open plains of the Blackfeet reservation in northern Montana with Joe Kipp. Now I was beginning to feel comfortable in the tight grouse coverts, beginning to learn how to make myself a smaller target to the relentless tentacles of undergrowth, to pick and choose my openings, and to slip through the tiniest hole in the densest thicket.

After two solid months of hunting I thought I was in fairly good condition, but this would be the most physical hunt I had been on yet, the heaviest cover and most grueling uphill and down; and Harold, mild-mannered bespectacled optometrist by week, my hardest taskmaster. People in his kind of physical shape tend to take for granted that everyone else has similar endurance, and, for my part, I refused to be deadweight. I prided myself, and Sweetz, too, on being able to keep up with any hunter and any dog, respectively, in any terrain on any given day. And so we would. Harold was not the first and would certainly not be the last *gonzo* bird hunter I would hunt with in this long season. I had already survived Ford, Harrison, Swanson, and Reens; I had Bill Cheney in Vermont yet to go, Charles Gaines in New Hampshire, the Count in northern Florida, and Jimbo Meador on the delta of Mobile Bay. I still had the Simmons brothers to keep pace with in Texas, and my friend Baer in New Mexico. Why, I was just getting into condition, just warming up, and so was Sweetz, her lanky puppy physique beginning to take a new, more mature form, a new sleek musculature, which she would need in order to keep pace with all her canine cronies to come—the slight setters of New England, the lean houndish pointers of the South, and the quick busy Brittanies of the Southwest.

We worked the hollows and hilltops, hard going all morning, hunting in a wide circle back to the car, with only one point and one wild flush, and no birds in the bag by lunch. No matter.

Harold had offered to pack along a lunch for me, but wisely, I had brought my own—slightly stale french bread, hard salami, provolone cheese, pepperoncini, and Greek olives—the last of my provisions from the excellent Fogarelli's market in Traverse City, Michigan. We sat on the tailgate while the dogs rested in the shade beneath. Harold pulled a Ziplock bag of congealed slabs of last night's pizza from his cooler and poured himself a cup of coffee from a thermos. "I brought enough for you," he offered, holding out a wedge. "Cold pizza is my favorite." I couldn't help but think about Swanson and our lavish lunches in the U.P.—complete with wine, followed by naps before the afternoon hunt. I doubted Harold had taken a nap in his life, and certainly not in the middle of a hunting day, and though I had packed along a beer with my lunch, knowing now what to expect for the afternoon, I didn't even consider drinking it. It would have tasted wonderful with the salami and cheese, and then I wouldn't have minded lying around in the grass for a bit, possibly even dozing off for a few minutes, falling "into that sweet, untroubled sleep known only to hunters" as Turgenev, who was not above a little snooze in the field himself, so beautifully put it.

But no nap for Harold. After a niggardly two slices of cold pizza and a refill of coffee, he fairly bounded off the tailgate to continue our hunt. Probably just as well, because I was beginning to stiffen up a bit in the legs, and might never have been able to rise from my nap in the grass. I'd been doing almost exclusively flat walking for the past few weeks and my muscles had lost their mountain tone.

On we hunted. Not far from the car, Harold's dog Thicket pointed a woodcock; it flew and Harold shot it. A bit farther on, Sweetzer kicked a grouse out of a hawthorn thicket against the side of a hill; I had a decent shot at it but I missed. I was winded and off-balance, one of my three favorite excuses for missing chukars on steep mountain slopes out west. Amazing how well one's standard excuses translate into new country.

We climbed a long hill to gain the grassy clearing of an old cemetery at the top which offered a small vista over the surrounding country—a deep gorge on one side, with the resonating sound of a waterfall far down below. Large oak and hickory trees grew around the perimeters of the graveyard— the Martin family plot, we learned. Many of the headstones were canted at precarious angles, others toppled over and beginning to disintegrate.

Though some of the markers were dated from the early 1800s and the most recent from the 1940s, someone, presumably a descendant, was still maintaining the plot, as the brush and trees had been kept back and the grass, though grown up, had clearly been mowed at some point during the summer. I picked up a small chunk of marble that had broken off the top of one of the older stones. The engraving on the marker had weathered almost smooth but I could make out that it belonged to a young girl, Sarah, who had died in 1832 at the age of seven. The barely discernible inscription beneath the dates read: *It is Sweet to Fall Asleep in the Arms of Jesus.*

We sat down to rest for a few minutes by the little girl's stone. Her young death seemed no less poignant for having occurred over 150 years ago. I slipped the piece of marble in my game bag. I didn't think Sarah would mind.

That night Harold took me out on the town—Saturday night in Wheeling, West Virginia, the tri-state urban hub in these parts. Harold had been out of circulation for a long time, and was trying to get back into the singles scene after his recent breakup with his girlfriend.

Besides being somewhat of a "fitness nut," Harold was a conservative guy, and as I'd already guessed from his lunch, not much interested in food; for dinner at Ye Olde Alpha Inn, he ordered a light beer and a club sandwich. After computing that I must have burned several thousand calories in the course of our grueling nine-hour hunt that day, from which we had returned with only the one woodcock, I felt that I required, and deserved, somewhat more sustenance than that. I ordered a double Bombay gin and a platter of fried oysters. In the heartland one may as well throw caution to the wind re fat and cholesterol.

While we were having dinner, a tall, attractive blonde woman named Millie stopped by our table to say hello. Millie was flirtatious with Harold, having evidently heard via the grapevine that he was back in circulation. Millie wanted to know if we were planning to go to the disco after dinner. "Since you're from out of town," she said to me in a sugary Appalachian accent, "you'll surely want to get a taste of that Wheelin' feelin'!"

"That Wheelin' feelin'?"

"It was an advertising campaign that the city ran last year," Harold explained. "The slogan was, 'Get That Wheeling Feeling.' "

I took a big swallow of Bombay. I didn't know discos existed any longer and I was whipped from our trek, but what the hell, I wasn't about to cramp Harold's reentry into the Wheeling social scene. "I think I'm already getting it," I said.

It was dark, smoky, and noisy in the disco, lights flashing across the dance floor. I hadn't been in a place like this since the Bee Gees reigned and even then I wasn't exactly John Travolta on the dance floor. Millie spotted us as soon as we walked in and dragged Harold out for a spin. I made a beeline for the bar, purchasing a pack of Camels on the way, even though I'd given them up; I get a bit nervous in crowds and anyway, what with all the passive smoke in this place, I decided to take the offensive. At the bar, I struck up a conversation with a woman named Susan, a small, dark-haired criminal attorney, recently divorced, and with a young daughter.

"I don't usually come into places like this," Susan said apologetically.

"That's what we all say."

"No, really, I hate this sort of thing, but it's better than sitting home alone on Saturday night. And how else are you going to meet people?"

"You don't have to apologize to me."

"You're not from around here, are you?" she asked.

"How'd you know?"

"And you're married, right?"

"Right. How'd you know that?"

"I can just tell. You're the first guy that's spoken to me all night, so I knew you must be from out of town and married. That's the kind of luck I have. What are you doing here, anyway?"

"Getting that Wheeling feeling."

"Are you a criminal?"

I laughed. "No, I'm not a criminal. Why would you ask that? Is that a criminal act?"

"I spend a lot of time with criminals in the course of my work," she answered, cryptically. "Actually, that's the best part of the job. It's wonderful to see that our criminal justice system really works."

"Does it?"

"No!" She laughed. "If you'll excuse me I'm going to circulate now." She got up from her stool. "It's getting kind of late in the evening and I want to see if I can find someone to talk to who's not from out of town, married, or a criminal."

"I'm not a criminal," I insisted, but Susan had already faded into the crowd. I hunkered down to the bar and sipped my gin and smoked Camels, feeling vaguely criminal. I was suddenly terribly depressed by the state of loneliness in which so much of the world seems to exist. I hoped this wasn't that Wheeling feeling.

17

OLD HEMLOCK

The purist has never been understood by those who have let living get away from them.

George Bird Evans

Of all my stops along this upland trail, none was more keenly anticipated than my visit with George Bird Evans. In the relatively small world of ruffed grouse and woodcock hunters, Evans is widely held to be the living master of American sporting literature—a fine stylist and a great romantic, who, had he chosen a less arcane subject, might be a well-known writer. In his eighties now, Evans is also a controversial figure, with a reputation for combativeness and irascibility; at one time or another (and sometimes together), he has taken on the hunting establishment, state game managers, wildlife biologists, dog breeders, the Ruffed Grouse Society, and any sundry individuals who have managed to incur his displeasure, which, given Evans's unwavering code of conduct both in and out of the sporting field, is evidently not that difficult to do.

Besides having a better than passing familiarity with his work, I'd been hearing George Bird Evans stories ever since I'd hit grouse country. Depending on who you talked to, he seemed to be either respected and revered or despised and feared, with very little middle ground between the two extremes.

So the reader may perhaps also understand the narrator's slight sense of trepidation on that last Sunday afternoon of October when at exactly the appointed hour, I drove down the long, tree-shaded lane that led to "Old Hemlock"—the eighteenth-century hewn-log and stone cottage, near Bruceton Mills, West Virginia, home to George and Kay Evans since 1939.

I was visiting on a Sunday as it was the only day of the week (by mandate of state law) that Evans would not be hunting, and I was visiting in the afternoon as his wife, Kay, had explained to me over the phone that due to his writing schedule, "George does not receive visitors in the morning." It had never occurred to me to ask to hunt with George Bird Evans, which would have been as unthinkable as a club golfer asking Jack Nicklaus if he'd like to play a round, or a weekend softball player suggesting that Willie Mays shag a few fly balls for him.

Tiny and vine-shrouded, Old Hemlock appears as a kind of enchanted cottage in the forest, as if the setting for a Grimm's fairy tale. Kay Evans, an attractive, gracious woman, with gray hair pulled into a bun, greeted me at the end of the stone walk and led me inside. She offered me a cup of tea; George would join us shortly, she explained.

There is a distinct time-warp feel to Old Hemlock, the illusion of being transported back to an earlier, quieter era, a retreat from the garish excesses of the modern world. Wide-board pine floors and a large stone hearth bespeak an eighteenth-century simplicity, and on a table near the window, George Evans's ancient Remington typewriter seems a long way from the computer age. The Evanses were down to just one dog at the time of my visit, Quest, who lay on the hearth where the ghosts of his ancestors sleep—nine generations of George and Kay Evans's internationally re-nowned line of Old Hemlock English setters.

From some of the stories I had heard, I rather expected a severe, stern, if not downright intimidating man, but when George Bird Evans entered the room, I saw a thin, almost gaunt gentleman, with bright, twinkling eyes and a spry, vigorous, open manner. Beyond a certain angularity of figure and feature, there was nothing severe about him. And far from being imperious or remote, Evans was cordial, attentive, and inquisitive. He seemed very interested in my trip, wanting to know where had I hunted so far, what bird species, and with whom. Both he and Kay seemed almost hungry for news of the world outside, and it occurred to me that their decision to retreat has not been without sacrifice.

No one understands more intimately or has written more eloquently about the upland shooting life than George Bird Evans, nor has anyone lived that life more completely. George and Kay moved here fifty-three years ago from New York City, where George worked as a commercial artist. Though prewar New York might seem nearly bucolic by the standards of the modern urban jungle, even then the Evanses wanted out of the city. On one of several house-hunting trips to the area they discovered Old Hemlock, a safe haven where they have lived a strangely cloistered life together ever since, a life of nearly monkish devotion to sport, art, and each other.

The Evanses support themselves from the proceeds of George's hunting books which they publish privately and which George also illustrates, while Kay serves as editor and business manager. Anyone familiar with Evans's work will know that this arrangement is far more than a workable partnership, but a deep, abiding love affair as well. Though Kay does not shoot, at least not with a gun, she has hunted alongside her husband nearly every day for over fifty years. For many of those years, she carried a movie camera with which she recorded each point, each flush, each killed, and each missed bird.

George Evans has watched the grouse population in his Appalachian mountain region dwindle over the last two decades, and finally virtually disappear in the coverts he has hunted for half a century. He attributes the decline directly to gunning pressure, and lays the blame squarely at the feet of state wildlife managers who have extended the hunting season into February, causing higher mortality among those birds that have already survived the winter and thus provide the breeding stock for the following year. Evans has written passionately against the extended season and has angered state game officers with his uncompromising criticism of their management methods and motives.

Recent studies, among them Gordon Gullion's in Minnesota and an ongoing Pennsylvania Game Commission study, would seem to support Evans's contention, but state officials remain reluctant to shorten the seasons for two reasons: They will lose revenue from hunting licenses, and grouse hunters appear to be overwhelmingly against a shorter season. At the same time, the Ruffed Grouse Society, whose business it is to promote the sport—a growth industry which must be constantly fed by new members and more hunters—has been equally unwilling to finger hunting pressure as a factor in population dynamics, nor will most of the wildlife biologists with whom I spoke ("George Evans is an asshole!" snapped one ordinarily soft-spoken RGS biologist I queried). This may be a case of both hunters and the hunting establishment shooting themselves in the foot; one might expect conscientious gunners to be in favor of shorter seasons, especially if studies suggest the possibility of increased grouse populations. In Minnesota Gordon Gullion put it to me this way: "It's very simple. It's a matter of saying, do you want to have more birds to shoot or do you want to have a longer season? You'd probably have twice as many birds with a shorter season."

"Many of the grouse biologists I've spoken to," I said to Evans, "have suggested that although they think you're a fine writer, you're not much of a biologist. At least that's how the polite ones put it."

"And I can imagine how the impolite ones put it!" Evans said, laughing. "They dislike me intensely because I've spoken out against them. But they're quite right, I'm not much of a biologist. I have the viewpoint of the hunter, not the scientist. I have very little regard for biologists."

"They also suggest that your forest here has matured, grown too old to provide good grouse habitat, and that that's the real reason bird populations are so depressed."

"If you spend time around here," Kay interjected, "you'll see logging trucks going down the road all the time, full of logs."

"Well, you're exactly right, Kay," George said turning to her. The Evanses are as solicitous of each other as newlyweds, and I would notice during my visit that they have a charming habit of engaging in conversation as if there were no one else in the room, a habit surely formed from a lifetime together in relative solitude.

"I can show you coverts," George continued, "that used to hold birds and that still are prime grouse habitat, and that now are empty. But then perhaps they think that after over fifty years of gunning here, I don't know what good habitat looks like? And I wonder, how many of them actually know this country? It seems to me that biologists should be objective and open-minded. If I'm wrong, then let them prove me wrong. Close the season earlier for five years and see if the grouse come back. But you see, Jim, they're afraid to be proven wrong."

"It must be discouraging for you to have experienced the kind of grouse shooting that you once had here, and that you've written about, and to see what's become of it now."

"I'm very bitter. It's terribly, terribly bleak. You should have the best hunting when you're old. And though I tend to be eternally optimistic, I'm not sure that the birds here aren't below the point of no return. You have to have a great fecundity of grouse just to feed the predators and I don't know that they'll ever be able to come back."

Evans is equally outspoken against a new generation of bird hunters who seem to take the competitiveness of the modern business place with them into the field. He finds that the old definitions "avid" or "dedicated" now tend to describe those who exploit the "resource" most relentlessly, who cover the most miles in a day, and "harvest" the most birds. To Evans, this is a soulless operation, a numbers game. Even when grouse populations in his region were at their peak with fifty or sixty flushes a day quite common, he rarely killed more than one bird in a day, and never more than two. His own interest always lay in the individual specifics of "a clean kill over a grand point," a lovely phrase, itself anachronistic, redolent of an earlier era of gentlemen sportsmen.

"Does it ever concern you that your own writing has served to promote the sport of grouse hunting in this region?" I asked.

"If everyone hunted the way I advocate in my books," Evans said simply, "there wouldn't be a problem."

If George Bird Evans is discouraged about the prognosis for grouse hunting in the Appalachians, he remains a remarkably sanguine and fulfilled man. He has the memories of thousands of days in the field, recorded in loving detail in his sporting journal, and on film by Kay; the memories of each grouse killed over each of their nine generations of beloved setters as vivid in his mind as if it happened yesterday. The Evanses have never had children. ("I prefer your company," Kay says, looking lovingly at George.) They have each other, and they had their dogs. And these days they still hunt the ghost coverts of the past, country as familiar to them as other people's backyards, silent now of birds but palpable with memories—the points of long-dead dogs, the startling flight of grouse, the resonating echo of a shot. George had not killed a grouse since 1986.

It was late in the day and time to go. Graciously, George Bird Evans insisted on accompanying me out to the camper. He said he wanted to meet Sweetzer and to see my 20-gauge Belgium double. I had heard it said by his detractors that unless you owned an Old Hemlock setter yourself, the breeding of which Evans has strictly monitored and controlled over the years, that he would "run down" your dog, but I already knew him to be too much a gentleman for that. He cooed to Sweetz, told her that she was beautiful, and instantly charmed her.

Evans has had surgery in both shoulders, and it is difficult for him to mount a shotgun now; he must hold it with his left hand down on the receiver and painfully ratchet the gun into position. This he did with my shotgun, which, although a very plain, inexpensive field grade, he handled and spoke of as if it were the finest Purdey. I felt a bit as I did when I was a schoolboy and had the opportunity to meet my baseball hero, Nelson Fox, star second baseman for the Chicago White Sox. I asked Fox if he would touch my mitt; he did, and it seemed like impossibly good luck to me. And now, a grown man, I felt a similar absurd sense of good fortune that the great George Bird Evans was handling my shotgun.

It was dark by the time I drove back down the tree-lined lane of Old Hemlock that afternoon. I recalled a passage from Evans's lovely book *An Affair with Grouse* in which he describes how he and Kay ate each of the birds they killed, ". . . savored, before a log fire and to the sound of Mahler, two people in total harmony. . . . We will touch our crystal glasses and sip our Cabernet from the ringing edge in a toast, not to what is going to be but to our now."

KAY EVANS'S GROUSE
IN BUTTERMILK GRAVY

(Note: The Evanses skin their game birds.)

Flour lightly the breast, legs and upper back with inner joint of wings attached, liver, and heart. Brown in corn oil. After turning, cover with a tight lid and cook on low heat for an hour or more. Salt and turn occasionally and add a small amount of water, replacing lid, until golden brown and tender. Remove to a heated serving dish. Make gravy with flour and water in the browned residue in the skillet, thicker than desired. In the last minute or two, thin with buttermilk—about ¼ cup to a grouse. Serve around the grouse.

18

THE LAST GROUSE
IN GREEN COUNTY

If you believe that gun pressure has no effect on grouse, consider your favorite covert where you have found the most grouse this year. Would you tell about it, describe its location at the next Ruffed Grouse Society meeting? If you do, I suggest you check it the following week and next season.

George Bird Evans

"I've hunted this same area, about two thousand acres contiguous to my little sixty-acre piece, for fifteen years now," said Les Zimmerman, my original candidate in the Mr. Grouse competition. An energetic, talkative man, with sharp birdlike features and a quick bustling way of moving, Zimmerman, like so many of the hunters I had met so far, was an outgoing, hospitable fellow. "Up until about three years ago, I would guarantee you forty flushes a day," he said. "Today, we're just not finding the birds."

"What do you think happened?"

"We beat it to death," he admitted. "Our hunting here is mainly small woodlots, interspersed with fields. For years we supported more grouse in Green County than anywhere else and everyone started coming here to hunt our woodlots. We shot our birds out. And they all blame it on me, because I talked too much. You see, I brought a lot of those people in through my business."

"So you agree that the sport can be overpromoted."

"I don't do it anymore. I guess you would call it . . . how will I put this? I'm in the business of selling wildlife art and I specialize in ruffed grouse. I advertise in all the sporting magazines. I'm active in the Ruffed Grouse Society. I've been known for thirty years for grouse. . . . What would you call that? . . . Do I sell my body? Am I a prostitute? I get calls all the time, 'Are you hunting Monday, Les?' they ask me. They want me to take them out, friends and clients. But I won't do it much anymore. I've cut it way

142

back. I used to do too much of it. Yesterday I had Mr. Hunt, the president of Alcoa, call. I said I'd take him out, probably in the second week of November. But, you see, I have to find these guys birds first. I mean our birds are way down. You tell these bigshots that, and they don't care, they don't want to hear about it. They just want you to find them birds. They don't know that I have to go out first and find the coverts for them. And I don't really have the time to do it. But I don't bring as many people in as I used to. I'm not saying that I ruined the whole county, but I did show too many people too many coverts, back in the days when we thought that the grouse would never end. When you have it like that for fifteen years—forty flushes a day—you think that we've got heaven here, that we'll have grouse like that forever, that you can't shoot them out."

I had come to hunt with Zimmerman at his farm, a lovely spot in the hill country outside Waynesburg, Pennsylvania, where he was in the process of restoring a beautiful old log cabin on the property. The cabin, which Les had moved here from another site, was originally built in 1787 by a retired seafarer by the name of Captain Pindall.

Before setting out for our hunt, Les showed me around the place, while keeping up a running commentary. He explained that he was managing his small property for grouse in conjunction with a University of West Virginia study program. I had noticed as I drove up the steep drive to the house, on the crest of a hill overlooking the surrounding countryside, that he had the place posted: Grouse Preserve—No Hunting.

"I don't think it's all a result of shooting pressure, either," Les continued, "but that certainly contributed. There are many other factors such as the natural cycle, maturing forests, and a number of very wet springs which can affect nesting success. But we still have a lot of good habitat, you'll see some of it today. Our habitat here is a hundred times better than anything George Bird Evans has down in West Virginia. But there just aren't any birds in it. What's happening now is that all the local bird hunters are going up north to hunt, because there are so few birds down here. That in turn will take the pressure off Green County. It really will. And maybe what will happen is that in combination with the cycle turning up again and some clear-cutting, and a few dry springs, the birds will start to come back and by then maybe I'll be too old to hunt, and there will be some other young buck in the area who is taking advantage of the forty flushes a day, and bringing everyone in. And everyone will blame him."

"You really think you can get those days back?" I asked.

"I don't know. I doubt it. It's hard to see it because our woods are getting more and more mature, and there isn't much cutting going on. We're too far away from the pulp mills. You'd need a combination of all those things for it to work. You see, people don't realize that when I was a boy, we didn't have many grouse. Green County was all in pasture for sheep. And then the sheep industry went out and all those pastures started coming up in brush, and that's when we got all our birds. Merritt here came from the northern part of the state, and he goes back to the days when they carried gunnysacks and they had kids carrying their shells for them and when they came out of the woods after a hunt, they brought out hundreds of grouse. Isn't that right, Merritt? This was in the twenties and early thirties. That will never come back. In those days the lumber companies were cutting a thousand square miles at a time, and in a few years it came back all in brush and prime grouse habitat."

Les's hunting partner, Merritt, the retired president of a steel company, was a pleasant, soft-spoken man who raised his own line of setters, clearly the breed of choice in ruffed grouse country. He and Les were each hunting with one of his setters today. I was hunting with my trusty companion, who, if the truth be told, had been just as effective as the setters in this relatively grouse-free country.

We set out. It was pretty country, steep and hilly, dense with cover. A severe ice storm several years earlier had knocked down trees in a radius of miles and the cover had grown back in briars, which, with the tangle of deadfall beneath, made much of it totally impenetrable. It looked like spectacular grouse habitat, with unlimited food and cover for the birds— wild cherry, flowering dogwood, wild grape, greenbriar, multiflora rose, chokecherry, and a vine called bittersweet that produces an orange berry which is an important late season food resource.

Les and I hunted across a long hillside while Merritt worked the ridge top. It was hard going, the cover so thick you couldn't see your companion fifteen feet away, and it was difficult to keep track of the dogs. We fought our way through a heavy patch of multiflora rose, the most tenacious of covers; Sweetz had learned how to crawl on her belly through the stuff, like an infantryman under barbed wire, her sleek Lab coat somewhat an advantage over the long hair of the setters.

We finally broke out of the multiflora at the bottom of a draw, a kind of ravine with a small creek running down it. The cover opened up a bit and the walking became easier. Les and I heard a grouse flush wild in the undergrowth, but neither of us saw the bird. We tried to follow the sound, spreading out and working either side of the creek. Merritt had kept to the ridgetop.

I wasn't expecting to find birds, and looked upon this operation more as a hike-with-gun in interesting new country. Though in his early sixties, Les was in excellent shape, and kept up a brisk pace, though after my initiation with Harold Pickens two days before it seemed a relatively leisurely stroll. The creek bottom was lovely, verdant with ferns and mosses. I followed it for a while downstream, while Les cut back over to the hillside.

I came to a small glade between the creek bottom and the forest edge where tall mature oak and hickory trees led back up the hill to the cabin. Sweetz went into the trees while I stood for a while in the lush grassy clearing, reluctant to leave the warmth of the sun for the somber forest ahead. A moment later I heard the wingbeats, resonant and purposeful in the trees, and then I saw the grouse break from the edge of the forest into the glade, headed for the cover along the creek. It was a large, beautiful golden brown cock. I could see the pattern of his spread tail feathers as he sailed across the clearing. I had an easy, open shot, and plenty of time but I didn't shoot, didn't even mount my gun. I watched the grouse fly by and wished him well. "Did you just hear a bird?" Les called out from the forest.

"No, I didn't hear a thing."

After lunch we stopped over at Joe Riggs Sporting Goods, where Les introduced me to Joe. Les and Merritt stayed for only a few minutes and then took their leave. Never-say-die optimists, they were anxious to get back out for the afternoon hunt. I had decided to pass, to hang around in town a while and visit with Riggs.

Joe was a smiling, bandy-legged, cueball-bald ex-marine, who also raised a well-known local line of English setters. There seemed to be more grouse hunters and grouse dogs in this country than there were grouse. There seemed to be more Mr. Grouse candidates than there were grouse.

While he waited on a customer, I wandered around Joe's shop. It had a wonderful feel to it, a patina of authenticity that is sadly missing from the ubiquitous new style of trendy sporting boutiques, where the help, all attired in nifty Orvis wear, display their recently acquired expertise by treating the customer with haughty disdain. At Joe Riggs's one had the sense that the walls, the display cases, the floorboards, and countertops had themselves absorbed a lifetime of sporting tales, that if you could just squeeze them like a sponge you might have those days back again, after all.

"You come from out west, eh?" Joe asked after his customer left. "You ever hunt chukars out there?"

"Sure do, hunt them all the time."

"I hunted native chukars during World War Two," Joe said, leaning on the counter.

"Native? You mean in India?" I know a lot of chukar hunters but had never met one who had hunted them in their native country.

"In the mountains around Tsingtao, China. I was stationed there with the Sixth Marine Division, Twenty-ninth Regiment. My captain was an avid bird hunter and he brought his shotguns and all his gear with him over there. We also shot ducks and geese in the beanfields. You've never seen anything like it. They blackened the skies. Because of the war the natives were all starving. They had all that waterfowl—millions and millions of ducks and geese—but they didn't know to eat them. That's how we fed the troops; it was the first fresh meat we had eaten in two years."

I'd spotted an old Austrian double shotgun on Joe's rack that looked interesting to me and I went out to the camper and brought in my 16-gauge Fox. We negotiated briefly over a trade. Double shotgun aficionados are a notoriously fickle lot, as are bird hunters in general. Somehow, I had identified the Fox in my mind as the direct cause of my recent shooting slump, even though I had hardly been using it. I was convinced that a trade would make things right, although it was also instantly clear to me that Joe's trading skills were far superior to my own. In the end, I came to my senses and decided to keep the Fox.

Joe pulled an old scrapbook of sporting photos and newspaper clippings out from under the counter. In it were photos of his line of setters, with penned notations such as: "478 productives"—a productive being each grouse pointed by that particular dog, the total representing the dog's lifetime grand total number of pointed birds.

"See this dog here?" Joe said proudly, as we huddled over the scrapbook and he tapped a picture with his forefinger. "That was my son's dog. Five hundred and sixty-one productives. Now that was a great dog!"

"I've asked everyone around here this same question, Joe. What do *you* think happened to all your grouse?"

"I don't know for sure," Riggs said, "but I'll tell you what I think. I think a lot of it is due to an explosion in predator populations over the last few years—and by predators I don't mean just hunters, either. No one traps fox or coon for the hides anymore, and since they started protecting raptors, the hawks and owls have really proliferated. Don't get me wrong—I'm not saying you oughta shoot hawks or owls, but they do cause heavy predation on grouse, and the fox and coons are especially hard on nesting and young birds. I think that once the grouse population started to decline, whether by hunting or habitat loss or whatever combination of factors, the increase in predators made it real difficult for them to come back."

A complicated matter indeed, and, finally, I had grown tired of it. Joe's explanation made as much sense as any I had heard, and more than some. We thumbed through his scrapbook a while longer, reliving the old days, bittersweet memories for Joe, as he pointed out to me more great dogs of the past, the lifetime stats of each carefully noted beneath the picture.

After my visit that afternoon with Joe Riggs, I drove back to Les's place, where he had offered to let me camp for the night. He had gone back to his home in Washington. Les had once hoped to complete the house restoration and retire here, but his wife didn't care much for the place.

I had some difficulty finding a level spot for the camper in this hill country and I finally parked next to a tiny log cabin, on the crest of a hill above the main house. Les referred to it as the "hunter's cabin"—a plain one-room building with a plank table and an old cast-iron cot. He told me that up until two years ago, an alcoholic carpenter named Barney, hiding out from alimony payments, had lived here. Barney had been hired to restore Captain Pindall's house and had fallen in love with the old place. Les gave him free room and board for his restoration services, and judging from the exquisite work I had seen in the house, his carpentry skills had been considerable. Barney lived here for five years, working by day and drinking by night, until one day Les found him dead of a heart attack in his bunk.

Just before sunset, I wandered around in the hollow silence of Captain Pindall's half-restored house on the knoll. It was a wonderful old place constructed of massive hewn logs and plank floors, everything fitted together with the kind of old-world craftsmanship that is not possible to duplicate with modern mechanical tools. Without Barney, Les didn't seem sure that the job would ever be completed.

It was very still in the empty house in the lengthening afternoon shadows, too still. It gave me a chilly, uneasy feeling. Les had told me that the place rested directly on the site of a famous Indian massacre. There were too many ghosts at large in this country for me, like the silent sailing ghosts of vanished grouse. The next day was the first of November and Sweetz and I were headed out.

NOVEMBER

Vermont

New Hampshire

Maine

Manhattan

19

THE HUNTER
REVISITED

Man is a fugitive from nature.

Ortega y Gasset

We traveled north and east toward New England, the leaves stripping from the trees, color and life progressively draining from the land. A low time on this road, a time of apartness and loneliness of heart: a rural bar in northern Pennsylvania, where a handful of zombie patrons watched afternoon Loony Tunes on the television. Eyes riveted to the set, they guffawed at the antics of cartoon animals, repeating lines of dialogue and howling appreciatively at dynamite explosions. One of them went outside and taunted Sweetzer, who sat in her place in the passenger seat. He pressed his face to the windshield and made strange gurgling noises, a fool's noises, presumably learned from watching cartoons. Sweetzer, frightened, began to bark hysterically at him. I heard her howls and went out to investigate. "Get away from there," I demanded of the man.

"What's the matter with that dog?" the fool said, laughing. "Don't he like me?"

"Move away from there," I said again. "Or I'll open the truck door and she'll rip your fucking throat out." An idle threat because, of course, she wouldn't, but collectively the idiots had already put me in a foul humor. They reminded me of the group of Pennsylvanian hunters I met at the bar in Wisconsin. I want the world to be more polite.

The fool moved off, muttering. I drove on, away from this place, these louts.

The loneliness shadowed me through the gray reaches of New York's

Finger Lakes region. Maybe it was just the weather, the rapid loss of fall and sudden cold immersion in winter again, or simply the vertigo of too much changing country, all of it unfamiliar, none of it mine. I did not hunt.

My first day in Vermont, hunting alone, I shot a woodcock on the edge of a meadow at dusk. Sweetz retrieved it, but the bird was still alive and I made the common hunter's error of looking in its huge eyes as I dispatched it. Reflected there in the glint of twilight on iris was my own unshakable sense of autumnal despair. Did the woodcock feel lonely on the edge of the meadow at dusk when the dog bumped him into flight? The bird made a scared, plaintive, haunting piping sound as he flew straight up, then dipped down over the willows before plunging back to earth.

Afterward, driving unfamiliar rural lanes, looking for a place to camp for the night, a full moon rising over the mountains of New England, I thought that I had never felt so out of time and place in my life, an outsider looking in. I once lived in New England for a few years but the smallness and closeness of it bored and depressed me and while I was there some people I loved very much died. One tends to associate a place forever after with such events, in the same way that everyone of a certain age remembers exactly what they were doing when they heard the news that President Kennedy had been shot.

Now I thought that I would never be able to get the interrupted arc of that single woodcock's flight out of my mind, and, in fact, I haven't. I considered abandoning the trip; maybe I'd hunted enough already.

But that same night, I roasted the woodcock on a piece of thick toast and ate it, like the French, trail and all, as a kind of nostrum. By morning, just as suddenly as it had come, the blackness lifted.

20

OUR TOWN

On a visit to Zhizdra Uyezd in search of sport, I met in the fields a petty landlord of the Kaluga Gubernia called Polutikin, and made his acquaintance. He was an enthusiastic hunter; it follows therefore that he was an excellent fellow.

Ivan Turgenev

I spent a few days at Robert F. Jones's farm in southwestern Vermont. We had only just met, but we had mutual friends and had corresponded and spoken on the phone a few times, and as often happens between hunters, I felt as though we became friends immediately. Bob Jones is a consummate sportsman who has fished and hunted all over the world, and a fine writer who beautifully depicts loss, a good subject for one with an affinity for wildlife and the natural world.

Nowhere is the climate for bird hunting, or hunting in general, more precarious or polarized than in certain parts of New England, where the grouse coverts are being slowly whittled away by suburban development, posting, and privatization. Increasingly, urban refugees turned country squires are nailing up No Hunting signs on their properties so that, as my sometimes cynical friend Jones puts it, "Bambi, Thumper, and Flower can live out their lives in happy harmony." Bird habitat is also being lost as a result of strong antilogging sentiment among many new residents, as the forest, allowed neither to burn nor be cut, grows overmature. Added to these pressures are the steady inroads made by the emotional "don't eat anything with a face" antihunting, vegetarian campaign—the "posie fuckers" Jones calls them with a growl, which makes him sound much more like a macho, chest-thumping fellow than the gentle and articulate writer that he truly is.

Jones's old farmhouse which he shares with his wife, Louise, is filled with stacks of books on every available surface, sundry sporting gear, fishing rods, shotguns, hundreds of hats, and more books, with sheets covering the furniture, and dogs sprawled on the sheets. Clearly a sportsman's home.

Jones is a diehard Labrador retriever man, which further endears him to me. He had two of them when I visited: old Luke, a wizened, gray-muzzled, arthritic, flea-bitten black Lab, with fading hearing and cataract-clouded eyes, who spent the better part of the day snoring loudly on the sofa in the living room, presumably dreaming of his salad days in the grouse and woodcock coverts, when he rousted out birds to his master's gun; and young Jake, immediately fast friends with my own Sweetzer. They were about the same age and color and with about the same energy level and they spent the next several days chasing each other around the property or playing tug of war with sticks. Sweetz had more than met her match in Jake, who was a strong, chesty, brash lad.

Though he has owned pointing dogs in the past, Jones has always preferred hunting upland birds with Labs. "It's more existential," he explained, revealing his own naked literary roots. Any flushing dog owner knows exactly what he means.

With a Lab, of course, there are no birds pointed, no predetermined flushes, no time for the niceties of positioning and preparation; there is just the hunter following his dog's nose, trying to read his posture and attitudes—each flush, even if anticipated, an existential surprise. The Lab owner's bag may generally not be as full as that of the man who hunts with a good pointing dog—or better yet, two or three good pointing dogs—but the fullest bag is hardly the point, is it? In any case, to read Jones's shooting log, in which he has meticulously noted each bird moved and each killed over a period of many years hunting his cherished Vermont coverts, is to know that he and Louise have hardly gone hungry for want of game on the table.

Bob Jones was tied up with work my first morning at his place and so I had arranged a hunt with a fellow named Bill Cheney, from nearby Pawlet, Vermont. I'd been put onto Cheney's trail by our mutual friend Nick Reens from Michigan. The world of bird hunters is still relatively small and self-contained; they tend to know, or at least know *of* one another—a mysterious spiderweblike network that stretches all around the country. Like Reens and, indeed, like many of the best, Cheney had a bit of a local reputation as a loner, perhaps with leanings toward the eccentric—a very serious grouse hunter. And like all serious grouse hunters, especially in this New England region, he was extremely tight-lipped about his hard-earned coverts. "You won't show Bob Jones any of my coverts, will you?" Cheney asked suspiciously when I first called him and he learned where I was staying. Though for years they had lived less than thirty miles apart, he and Jones were barely acquainted, though each knew of the other's reputation as a grouse hunter, and they were always running across each other's trail in the coverts.

"No, of course I won't."

"Because one condition of going out with me is that you don't tell anyone where I take you. Understood?"

"You can blindfold me."

I met Cheney at his farm at 7:30 A.M. It was still cool when I arrived, a thin mist hanging over the valleys and hollows. He wanted to get an early start as an unusually late heat spell had settled over New England and though we were already into November, by midday it would be too hot for dog and hunter alike.

Cheney, a professional photographer and Vietnam veteran, is a tall, bearded, long-limbed, urbane man who lived and worked for some years in Paris and New York, and who bears rather a resemblance to the actor/singer Kris Kristofferson. I had left Sweetz back at Jones's to play with her new friend Jake; Cheney had a pair of English setters and I had gotten the distinct impression on the phone that he was somewhat less interested in the existential nature of hunting behind Labs. Today we took only one of his dogs with us, his young bitch, Willow, a lovely little dog, slight and feminine.

As we were driving out to the first covert of the day, I asked Cheney if he was a member of the Ruffed Grouse Society, which maintains a strong presence in New England. "No, I'm not," he answered. "To me grouse hunting is essentially a solitary pursuit, antipathetic to joining organizations. As far as I can tell, all they've done is create a lot of grouse hunters that we don't need out there."

As in so much of the rest of the country, the history of grouse hunting in New England is mirrored by its economic and land use history; the countryside here is dotted with small failed farms, now grown up into heavy cover, and old abandoned apple orchards no longer in production. It has been noted by others that the Great Depression was one of the best things that ever happened to game bird habitat in certain regions of the country, as formerly cleared and cultivated land came back wild. But many of the orchards here have gone by—that is, grown to maturity—and are no longer prime grouse habitat, and clearly more habitat is currently being lost in New England than is being gained. "People like the same kind of places to live as grouse," Cheney explained sadly, "high with a view. I lose a few coverts every year to development. It's like losing a member of your family. . . . I can get quite unpleasant about it. I really feel that I own these coverts. I've invested so much time and energy in finding them and hunting them over the years that trifles like deeds and bills of sale mean nothing to me."

Thus far, Cheney has been able to replace his lost coverts every year by finding new ones; he does a tremendous amount of prospecting during the off-season, but he's not particularly encouraged for the future. Besides the ubiquitous threat from development, he sees the burgeoning antihunting sentiment of so many new residents as yet another nail in the coffin of the esteemed tradition of New England grouse hunting. "You have to be careful what you say at cocktail parties around here these days," he said. "It's gotten to the point where it can be a real conversation-stopper to tell people that you hunt."

Cheney hunts with a 28-gauge Spanish double, and as I had already anticipated from his tall, long-legged build, and from the fact that he and Reens were sporting pals, he's no noodler afield, not one to dally or smell the daisies. He's the kind of hunting companion with whom those of us under six feet tall must step double-time to keep pace.

The grouse population was down, too, in New England this fall, though nowhere nearly as drastically as in the Ohio River Valley. Most local hunters attributed the decline to the natural cycle, a somewhat mysterious phenomenon not even fully understood by biologists, whereby grouse populations fluctuate in approximately seven-year cycles of peaks and valleys. In this part of the country, the grouse feed heavily in the fall on apples, in shorter supply than usual this year, which may also have had something to do with lower bird populations. Still, we found sufficient apples in the orchards we hunted that morning. Some, pecked by grouse, lay half-eaten on the ground, while a few still clung to the trees. Cheney and I both picked some and ate them as we hunted. Obviously unsprayed and untended, they were stunted and blotchy of color, many of them worm-eaten, but they tasted wonderful. Thinking now of their cool, tart, crunchy texture brings back that day as nothing else can.

We hunted one such high orchard on the top of a hill, with a spectacular view of the surrounding countryside. The ancient apple trees here were twisted and gnarled, the understory of briars, thickets, and vines grown up tight beneath them. Cheney's dog, Willow, though just two years old, was a superb bird dog, one of the best I had hunted behind so far. She reminded me a bit of Swanson's Joy, another top dog, for her ability to track a running grouse—to point, relocate, point, relocate, working the bird carefully, almost daintily, to avoid flushing it.

Cheney and I were following her in such a situation, he working the inside of the cover, while I hunted the edge where the orchard gave way to meadow. Willow tracked the bird exquisitely, pushing it to the edge of the orchard where she locked up into a final rigid point. The bird had nowhere to go from here but out into the open where I stood waiting for it, and when it flushed it came up out of the cover, turned along the tree line, and flew straight away from me, an open easy going-away shot by all grouse hunting standards. I fired my first barrel, so surprised that the grouse didn't fold that I hesitated a moment before firing the second. The bird sailed off down the hill following the tree line along the edge of the orchard. Willow and I watched it fly away. After her perfect work, I felt that I had really let her down. There are some missed shots that haunt the hunter's dreams for years to come and this would be one. I still see that grouse following the tree line on the edge of that high apple orchard, flying away over the New England hills, on the echo of my shots.

The midday heat drove us in before noon that day. We flushed two more birds and Cheney killed one. It was a fine morning hunt. I had eaten those delicious apples and seen some gorgeous dog work and some equally gorgeous country.

"Now don't tell Cheney about this covert I'm taking you to," Bob Jones warned, as we went out later that same afternoon, on the back end of the heat and the other side of the county. We had our yellow Labs, Sweetz and Jake, with us. "Or anyone else, for that matter."

"My lips are sealed." It occurred to me that if either Jones or Cheney knew of my poor sense of direction, they wouldn't have worried about me giving away their secret coverts. No need to blindfold this guest; one tiny, narrow, winding New England road through the hills and hollows had come to look much like the next to me, and I couldn't have led them to the other's grouse coverts if they had tortured me for the information.

If Cheney was a big walker, a ground-eater, Jones was a wily tactician, a strategist, and after the morning hunt I rather enjoyed the more deliberate pace in the afternoon. Flushing dog owners tend to hunt slower than those with pointing dogs, in order to allow the dog to work out every inch of the available cover. Jake was a better grouse dog by far than Sweetz; he'd certainly had more experience and he worked in close, whereas she still tended to range too far out. Beside our mutual affection for Labs, Jones also shares my dislike of electronics in hunting—beeper or shock collars; he hunts with a bell on Jake.

Though there may not be much in the way of shooting or tumbling birds to report about my first hunt with Bob Jones, there was a good deal of existential anticipation, the idea that at any moment a bird could flush before us, kicked up by one or the other of our dogs. We hunted around the base of a mountain, and then followed along an old stone wall, built toward the end of the eighteenth century to separate what must have been cleared fields then, now grown back to mature forest. The wall ran up over the knoll of the mountain and we hunted along either side of it, working our way to the summit which dropped off precipitously on the other side, offering a view of the quaint little village of Hubley's Gore below, a scene almost too precious. "Ah, the big country of Vermont!" I teased Jones.

"Yeah, it looks like one of those terrible paintings they give out as raffle prizes at Ducks Unlimited banquets," Jones admitted. He lit a cigarette. "It would be titled *New England Village in Autumn*." We stood there for a while, looking down on the village, as the sun slid behind the mountain.

That evening I had been invited for dinner to Bill and Kendra Cheney's home, a lovely, sprawling Vermont farmhouse, decorated with antiques and fine sporting art. Also at dinner were a writer (this part of the country full of them), the writer's wife, and the owner of a famous mail-order sporting goods store home-based in a nearby town.

Kendra Cheney is a marvelous cook and prepared a first-rate woodcock gumbo as an appetizer and superb roast grouse as an entree. Bill Cheney also shared his friend Reens's taste for fine red wine, and several bottles were consumed in the course of the evening; the narrator must be careful when he drinks red wine—it loosens his tongue like nothing else and gives him dreadful hangovers.

In the interest of research for this book, I asked the owner of the famous sporting goods outlet—a very pleasant gentleman—if he ever felt that the promotion and sale of outdoor sport, which was his business, had a potential downside, that of overexploiting a finite resource. I used as an example some of the famous spring creeks in Montana, now overrun with chichi fly fishermen. He neatly, and I thought somewhat disingenuously, deflected the question by blaming the decline of western fisheries on bait fishermen from Utah. This struck me as elitist nonsense, and I became testy; it may have been the red wine talking. A touchy moment ensued, but the subject was quickly dropped. I remembered with amusement that an outspoken sporting companion of mine from home, a populist and egalitarian, once referred to the sporting goods magnate as "a princeling of the evil empire."

A lively political discussion was entered into. The writer and the retailer, who identified themselves as conservative Republicans, were anxious about a local senatorial race.

"He's a goddamn socialist!" the retailer objected of the Democratic candidate.

"But so-and-so [the Republican candidate]," countered the writer, "is even worse!"

"No," insisted the former, "I don't think so, I think he's one of us." I'm never sure what exactly they mean by that, but I've noticed that conservatives frequently refer to one another as "one of us."

For a brief time, we argued about whether or not the vice-president of the United States (also "one of us") had matured while in office, possibly even gained valuable IQ points. The sporting goods magnate maintained that he had. Others of us remained more skeptical.

Perhaps everyone drank a little too much. Someone (*not* the narrator) did a very funny imitation of a well-known Democratic senator with a widely reported drinking problem crawling through a doorway at a party which she had recently attended with him.

The narrator then told one of those truly tasteless stories about this same well-known Democratic senator, the punch line of which is still hanging in your mind when you wake up the next morning in a state of utter incredulity that you could have said such a thing in polite company. Had my wife been present she'd have given me severe shinsplints under the table. I'm convinced it was the red wine talking; unfortunately, drinking never allows me to forget anything.

Then the sporting goods magnate mentioned that the famous Democrat Ted Turner had recently signed the even more famous Democrat Jane Fonda up for his store's shooting school down in Georgia, where both Turner and he own large plantations. There seemed to me to be something really quite peculiar about the notion of Jane Fonda at shooting school.

"Don't let her in," the writer, a very courtly southerner, said in earnest. The writer, like Cheney, was a Vietnam vet and had recently written a book about POWs from that war. Some of the men he had interviewed, he explained now, had been beaten and tortured for refusing to meet with Jane Fonda during her trip to Hanoi.

"If she were on fire," the writer hissed softly, "I wouldn't walk across the street to piss on her!"

Under the table, my canine girlfriend, Willow, lay with her head on my foot. Cheney had remained silent throughout most of our political discussion. Now he took this auspicious moment to say, "Listen, all you political intellectuals, I want you to hear Jim repeat what he said about Willow this morning." He looked at me expectantly.

On cue I repeated that the dainty Willow's hunting performance was one of the very best I had witnessed on my trip thus far, and I'd hunted behind plenty of fine dogs.

Hunters are inordinately proud of their dogs, and Cheney beamed and rewarded me with more wine. He had successfully rescued the evening from meaningless political chatter, and possible discord, turning the talk graciously to the far more important, and interesting, subject of bird hunting and bird dogs, the great common denominator at this table, crossing political and economic borders, uniting Republicans and Democrats alike, conservatives and liberals, rich and poor, them and us. I never had learned where Cheney's politics lay; he was far too wise to let on. And what difference does it make? But for the fact that I would wake the next morning with a killer hangover, it was a convivial evening: gracious hosts, a lovely home, superb food, fine wine, excellent company, stimulating conversation. What more could the hunter ask for than that?

Late one afternoon, after an interesting hunt with Bob Jones, I was nursing a solitary beer at the bar in the Dorset Inn. Bob and Louise had gone off to a local Ducks Unlimited banquet. After the Ruffed Grouse Society affair in Minnesota, I'd had my fill of such events and I declined their invitation to join them. I was sipping my beer and enjoying the quaint atmosphere of the inn when a fellow dressed in English shooting attire entered. He looked as if he had just come in off a driven shoot on the Scottish moors. He wore tweed plus fours, a tweed shooting jacket, and one of those little tweed shooting caps. He had a foppish, self-important stride, and a certain elfin look about him—small eyes set close together and big floppy ears that stuck out prominently on either side of his cap. Naturally curious, I struck up a conversation with the man. He introduced himself as Robin, and explained that he and his wife had moved here last year from Boston. Robin was retired from the commercial real estate business, and either he'd made a real killing in it or else there was some family money bankrolling his early retirement; he was quite a young man.

Robin ordered a sherry. "I've decided," he said, "to devote myself completely to a life of sport," which sounded to me more or less like the way I was spending my year, without the retirement part.

Robin had hunted all over the world, but he particularly loved grouse hunting, "the last gentleman's sport," he called it. "It's the grouse hunter's elite fascination with the sport," he explained, sipping his sherry, "that separates us from the rest of the shooting world."

He talked on for a while about the grouse hunter's "unspoken code of conduct in the field," and about his "regal respect for the bird." I wasn't sure about this last part and asked for clarification. Did he mean that the bird or the hunter was regal?

He talked about the "majesty of the ruffed grouse," and inevitably, as

I knew he must, he got around to the "intellectual challenge" of grouse hunting—"pitting my wiles against that of a wild creature, outfoxing that creature, and proving my mastery over him," which sounded almost kinky to me.

Trying to get a feel for how much grouse hunting Robin actually did, as opposed to sitting on a bar stool talking about it, I made the faux pas of asking him how many grouse he was likely to shoot in an average season.

He looked me over distastefully and sniffed the air as if I had farted. "The English have a saying," he instructed me. " 'A gentleman only counts his change.' "

Though Robin was the worst kind of sporting bore, I thought it might be interesting to spend a day in the field with him, or at least a half-day, but when I proposed this, he got cagey. He wanted to know whom I had hunted with around here already. I gave him four names of local grouse hunters with whom I had thus far been afield: Jones, Cheney, Geoffrey Norman (a consummate sportsman who has written one of the best instructional books on upland shooting), and a quite knowledgeable gunner by the name of Chris Hagen who'd taken me out the afternoon before. Robin assumed his fart-sniffing demeanor. "There are only two or three *real* grouse hunters in this entire area," he told me, the clear implication being that he was one of them and they weren't. "Tell me," he asked, trying to sound casual, as if he already knew the answer to the question, "where did they take you hunting?"

"Oh, come now, Robin," I answered, feigning shock, "you know perfectly well that I'm not at liberty to divulge that information. And frankly," I sniffed, "it strikes me as rather unsporting of you to ask."

The next morning I was headed for New Hampshire. I was sorry to be leaving my new friends in Vermont, and I knew that Sweetz would miss her pal Jake. On the other hand I had decided that I was glad I lived where I did, and not surrounded by so many writers, sportsmen, and sporting gentry, or in such proximity to New York, or having to watch each year the painful loss of favorite precious coverts, or secretly hoard those that I still had, although these things come to all hunters eventually, no matter where they live.

I couldn't leave Vermont without making one last small pilgrimage to the famous Orvis store in Manchester Center. I had been there once before, nearly a quarter-century ago with my father. I was fifteen years old at the time and we had driven all the way from Chicago for a fishing trip, and my father bought me my first fly rod at Orvis. It was made of bamboo, an inexpensive model, but how I loved that rod. I still have it, still fish with it occasionally. Sometimes I just take it out of its case to admire it, to touch it. It reminds me of my father, who died less than a year after he bought it for me. In terms of performance, that old bamboo stick can't compare to modern graphite fly rods, but like a fine double shotgun, it has a soul altogether lacking in the new high-tech gear. Who can wax romantic or even get mawkish over a graphite fishing rod? And, of course, like an old shotgun, that bamboo rod has a history—my history.

After I had admired a lot of fine sporting gear in the Orvis shop, gear that I didn't need and, in any case, couldn't afford, I wandered out to the casting pool in back. I remembered it from my last visit all those years ago. We had brought my new fly rod down here that day to try it out. Then, as now, they had trout in the pond. Next to the pond they kept a container of fish chow so that visitors could feed the fish, but it was empty now. Some Styrofoam packing bits had blown over from the catalogue outlet next door and the shells littered the bank of the casting pond. Idly, I toed one off the shore into the water, where it caught the wind like a sail and headed out across the pond. A trout rose to it, and sucked it under. I felt just terrible; it would probably kill the fish. Somewhere here lurked yet another sporting metaphor for our times: a trout feeding on Styrofoam packing shells in the Orvis casting pool. . . .

BILL AND KENDRA CHENEY'S PARIS GROUSE BREASTS

(Unlike some hunters who hang their grouse undrawn, Cheney believes that birds should be gutted immediately upon being shot [field drawn] so that portions of the meat are not spoiled by fecal matter traveling along shot paths that pass through the intestines.)

Bone and skin 1 grouse per person (breasts only). Sauté gently in butter and small amount of light olive oil, about 3 minutes per side (breasts need not brown). Set aside in platter in warm oven. To the sauté pan add ½ cup rich game stock (grouse, duck, or woodcock) and ¼ cup red wine. Stir to mix all juices and reduce to ¼ cup rich essence. Add 1 cup heavy cream and reduce again until thick enough to coat spoon. Add *small* squeeze lemon juice, salt and pepper to taste, and 1 tablespoon finely chopped parsley. Cover warm breasts in cream sauce and serve at once with white rice and small green peas on the side.

LOUISE JONES'S POMMES DE TERRE BECASSE AVEC AUBERGINE (WOODCOCK POTATO PIE WITH EGGPLANT)

³/₄ lb. eggplant
salt and pepper
3 tbsp. vegetable oil
breasts from 8 woodcock, boned
¹/₄ cup chopped parsley
2 tsp. chopped fresh thyme (or ¹/₂ tsp. dried)
1 tsp. minced garlic
5 large Russet potatoes
¹/₄ cup melted butter

Peel eggplant and cut into ³/₄″ strips. Place strips in nonreactive bowl, toss with 1 tsp. salt, and leave at room temperature for at least ¹/₂ hour.

Peel potatoes and cut into ¹/₈″ thick slices. Place slices in pan of cold water.

Drain eggplant on paper towels and fry in 3 tablespoons vegetable oil in nonstick pan. Drain on paper towels. In same pan, sear woodcock breasts very briefly—until they just change color. Remove from pan and set aside. Add herbs and garlic to pan and sauté briefly. Add herb mixture to woodcock breasts.

About 1 hour before serving preheat oven to 450 degrees. Lightly oil or butter a 9″ pie pan or shallow casserole. Drain potato slices and pat dry thoroughly with paper towels. Cover bottom of pie pan with half the potato slices, arranging them in smooth layers with some of the longest slices overhanging the edge of the pan by 2″. Season potatoes lightly with salt and pepper and drizzle with about ¹/₃ of the melted butter. Arrange eggplant slices over potatoes, then follow with herbed woodcock breasts.

Fold overhanging potatoes over woodcock and cover top with remaining potato slices, arranging in concentric circles. Season with salt and pepper and sprinkle with remaining butter.

Cover pan with aluminum foil and a heavy lid that will press the potatoes down. Cook in preheated oven for 20 minutes. Remove lid and foil, replacing any potato slices that may have stuck to it, and cook for another

30 minutes, until brown and crisp on top. If necessary, brown under broiler at end.

Before serving, replace lid on pan and, turning it upside down, drain out any excess butter.

Serve in wedges with a green salad. This dish is very rich and the woodcock is not tough despite the long cooking time.

(This is a variation on
a Paula Wolfert chicken recipe.)

21

GOOD SHOTS

Now Swing *is one of the secrets of good shooting.*

Lord de Grey,
second marquess of Ripon

In New Hampshire, I would be outgunned by a one-armed man. In Michigan, I'd been quite convincingly outgunned by a one-eyed man. No disgrace here; bird shooting isn't supposed to be a competitive sport and, in any case, one would hardly consider either of these men to be handicapped. They were simply both excellent shooters, who had managed to compensate for their respective physical shortages. I, on the other hand, was still in the black depths of my seemingly permanent shooting slump and had begun to make a more concerted study of what it was that made one person a good shot and another a hopeless bumbler. This would be the same way that a baseball player who was hitting nothing but infield pop flies might watch old newsreels of the Babe pounding homers in Yankee Stadium, to see if he couldn't pick up some pointers.

Indeed, even before leaving home I had already invested a certain amount of time, effort, and money trying to improve my shooting. I bought all the books on the subject I could get my hands on; I even bought a wonderful video demonstrating the famed English "Churchill" method. When it comes to the inviolable traditions of bird shooting, nobody does it quite like the English, who virtually invented the game, and parts of the video are really quite charming, with the shooters in their plus fours and stockings and brown oxford wing-tips. For some reason, it put me in mind of an oft-repeated story about the time Sir Randolph Churchill accidentally shot a woman's pet dachshund during an estate shoot. By way of apology, Sir

Randolph had the dog mounted in a glass case which he presented to the bereaved owner as a distinctly unsuccessful Christmas gift. Even the English version of "slob" hunting has a certain twisted elegance.

None of my research helped my shooting. In fact, the more I thought about shooting technique, the more I read, the more I watched that video, the *worse* my shooting got. It's one thing to be a competent skeet shot at the ranch dump with my friend Billy Cantrell, and something altogether different to go into unfamiliar country nearly every day with one great shooter after the next. So I decided to go right to the source, arguably the greatest wing shot in the history of the sport, not to mention the biggest game-hog ever.

England's legendary Lord de Grey, second marquess of Ripon, a.k.a. Lord Ripon (1867–1923), lived to be a mere fifty-six years old but had a total lifetime bag of 556,813 head of game. As Lord Ripon's main interest was in wing shooting, the vast majority of this mind-numbing figure were driven pheasant and grouse, with a fair number of hares, rabbits, and the odd deer that crossed his path thrown in.

To fully appreciate his feat, let's say Lord Ripon started shooting, however unlikely, when he was one day old, and shot every day thereafter until his gun fell silent over half a century later. That would account for an average bag of 27.24 head each day of his life, which computes to roughly 10,000 birds and mammals killed every year for fifty-six years.

A legend even in his own time, Ripon once filled this daily quota in a single minute, killing twenty-eight pheasants in sixty seconds. In another instance, he was reported to have had seven dead birds in the air at once, which sounds a bit like a western gunslinger trick.

I probably don't need to tell the reader that the second marquess of Ripon did not have a job, or that shooting was his life, as he was fond of remarking, and frankly anyone who discharged a gun that many times has no excuse *not* to be a great wing shot. So it was with some mild annoyance that I read in the first paragraph of Ripon's short treatise, appropriately entitled *On How to Shoot*, the following disclaimer: "That 'practice makes perfect' is in the case of shooting only true to a certain extent. For a man must be born with a certain inherent aptitude to become a really first-rate shot." Sure, Ripon, easy for you to say—besides being well born, this is a man who reportedly idled away his summers lying on his back in the grass of his estate shooting dragonflies with a .410.

Yet there was some pertinent information to be garnered here, too, as when Ripon opens with what may be the perfect description of my own fundamental shooting problem: "To be a first-rate shot necessitates the combination of two distinctly opposite conditions: a highly strung nervous temperament which keeps you ever on the alert, a cool head which enables you in moments of excitement to fire without recklessness or undue haste. This combination is naturally rare."

As I read on, I realized that as most of the shooting Lord Ripon and his Edwardian compatriots did was on driven birds (and the occasional driven dachshund), much of the information herein was, for my purposes, totally inapplicable, as when he explains how to quickly discharge your second and third guns, which will be handed to you by a loader. "Never look at your loader," advises Ripon, not exactly invaluable advice to the modern American shotgunner. But there was one more line that did seem potentially useful—Lord Ripon's personal shooting maxim: "Aim high, keep the gun moving, and never check." In other words, swing and keep swinging.

22

HENRY, CHARLES, AND CHIEF

Here is the dog, which has always been an enthusiastic hunter on his own initiative. Thanks to that, man integrates the dog's hunting into his own, and so raises hunting to its most complex and perfect form. This achievement was to hunting what the discovery of polyphony was to music. In fact, with the addition of dogs, hunting acquires a certain kind of symphonic majesty.

Ortega y Gasset

One evening I was talking to the proprietor of a country inn in a small town in central New Hampshire. I was trying to get a line on some local bird hunters. The innkeeper had recently moved up from Boston, and admitted that he wasn't much of a hunter; in fact, he couldn't bear to kill anything. He told me that his cat had once brought a wounded bird home to him and he didn't know how to kill it. (Cat lovers take note: By conservative estimate, domestic cats are believed to kill 4.4 million songbirds per day in the United States alone. Add to this the incalculable toll from feral cats on all species of birds, and the mind-boggling totals would indicate that the average suburban cat owner is a far greater threat to wildlife populations than is the average American bird hunter.) The innkeeper couldn't bring himself to wring the bird's little neck. He thought about holding it under water to drown it (the innkeeper made *glub-glub-glub* noises at this point), but he didn't think he was capable of that, either. The solution he finally hit upon was to put the crippled bird in a paper bag that he set out in his driveway and then back the car over it, crushing it under the tire. Just to make sure that the bird was really dead, he drove back and forth over the paper bag several times. This method for dispatching cripples is not recommended for game birds.

*   *   *

Early the next morning I stopped by the tiny police station in the town and introduced myself to the chief of police, a large, heavyset man named Stanley Martin. Chief Martin had the sleeve of his left arm pinned at the elbow. I asked the chief if he might be able to put me on to some local bird hunters.

"Well, it just so happens that I'm a grouse hunter myself," said the chief with an air of some self-importance. "In fact, you might say that I'm a grouse hunting fool. Ordinarily, I don't take people out with me but as long as you're not from around here I could probably show you a thing or two." He invited me to hunt with him on Saturday, two days hence. I was curious to know how Chief Martin handled a shotgun with only one arm, and I gladly accepted the invitation.

In the meantime, the chief suggested that I talk to a local farmer, a fellow by the name of Henry, who had some grouse and woodcock coverts on his property a few miles out of town, and who, the chief said, might be willing to show them to me.

I followed Chief Martin's directions out to Henry's place, pulling up in front of a huge old ramshackle farmhouse on the top of a hill, overlooking a rolling checkerboard of meadows, woodlots, and fields. Down below a few cattle grazed against the hillside.

A cold front had moved in overnight, the air crisp and wintry that morning. I could see the frost on Henry's breath as he came out to greet me. He was a bearded, stocky, sandy-haired, slightly bowlegged man who looked to be in his midforties, wearing a buttonflap undershirt and suspenders. "What can I do for you?" he said in that wry, oddly inflected New England accent. I explained that Chief Martin had sent me and Henry invited me in for a cup of coffee.

We sat at the kitchen table in front of a wood cookstove with a hot hardwood fire burning in it. The kitchen had the slightly skewed, disorganized look of bachelor digs, with lots of dirty dishes and empty food containers, and a crusted casserole of last night's dinner still on the table. Henry rinsed a dirty cup for me and filled it from an old brown-stained percolator on the woodstove. The heat from the stove felt good.

Henry apologized for the mess and explained that he was a recent widower and lived here alone with his son. A third-generation farmer on this land, a subsistence farm in the best of times, he said he worried about losing his land one day to "yuppies from the city." Henry raised a little beef cattle and a few dairy cows, some corn, potatoes, and grew a small vegetable garden for his own use. He made a little cheese which he sold locally, but because of FDA regulations he had to be careful. Like so many country people, Henry had a nearly inexhaustible disdain for government agencies and regulations. To make ends meet he was also a carpenter and small-scale contractor, as had been his father and grandfather before him.

Henry had hunted this land all his life, and, of course, he remembered the flocks of "paatridges" (ruffed grouse) when he was a boy. "You could walk out into any of these woodlots around here," he said, "and find paatridges then. In the morning they'd be on the edge of the fields or alongside the road. My faathah and I used to go out before breakfast and it was nothing to shoot a limit."

Henry was a refreshing change from the more genteel eastern sportsmen I had been hunting with so far in this part of the country. In fact, he reminded me of an eastern version of my resolutely western friend Cantrell, and though their country was altogether different, I had a feeling they'd have gotten along just fine. Henry was clearly a man who knew a little something about the land, a man who lived *in* the country and had paid close attention to it for a lifetime, noting each subtle change and transformation, and taking it personally.

Henry said he would be glad to take me out for a short hunt, and he dressed and grabbed his shotgun while I went out to the camper to get Sweetz and my own gear. No fancy hunting attire for Henry, he came out in Redwing work boots, jeans, and a fleece-lined jean jacket, carrying an old Ithaca pump gun with a banged-up stock.

"I was up on the mountain a couple of years ago and I saw a mountain lion," Henry recounted as we started out across a meadow headed for a woodcock covert on the far side, Sweetzer quartering ahead. "I watched it through my binoculars for quite a while. My, it was a beautiful creature, the way it slinked so graceful down the mountainside. I sat very still and just watched it. And when I came back down off the mountain, I went over to the game warden's office to report it. You see, there hadn't been a mountain lion sighting around here in a long time and I thought they would be interested. But when I told the game warden what I'd seen, he said, 'Oh, there aren't any mountain lions in New Hampshire.' And I said to him, 'Well that's what I'm trying to tell you, I *saw* a mountain lion.'

" 'Oh, no,' he said, 'that's impossible. You must be mistaken, there are no mountain lions in the state of New Hampshire. Haven't been for many years.'

"Now that made me mad. I know what I saw. And I know what a *goddamn* mountain lion looks like. So I said to the game warden, 'I'll tell you what, the next time I see the son of a bitch, I'll shoot him and I'll bring him in here and lay him right across your desk. Then maybe you'll believe me.'

" 'Why you can't do that,' says he. 'It's illegal to shoot mountain lions. I'd have to arrest you.'

"And I said, 'How can you arrest me for shooting something that doesn't exist!' "

It was a pretty little woodcock covert, an alder thicket on the edge of the meadow, the ground wet and spongy. Henry hunted at a slower pace than anyone I'd hunted with yet, certainly not because he was in poor physical condition but simply because that was his style. Perhaps because he hunted without a dog, he was extremely thorough, thoughtful, and deliberate, carefully investigating every square inch of cover. Between his and Sweetz's efforts had there been a woodcock in that alder thicket we'd have found it, but it was getting a bit late in the season for migratory woodcock; most of them had already come through this far north, though there were likely to be a few stragglers.

"We're losing the woodcock," Henry said sadly. "We don't get nearly the fall flights through here that we used to." In fact, woodcock populations have been declining steadily in the Northeast for the past decade. As usual, theories abound, the primary ones being loss of habitat in their southern wintering grounds, as well as overgunning of the birds in the South upon their return. Gunning pressure in the North has also increased substantially over the years.

"In the old days around here," Henry said, "all the faahmahs ran a few head of cattle, which kept the fields open, and the cowshit provided a steady supply of worms for the woodcock. When I was a boy there were hundreds of 'cock all over everyone's fields. No one hunted them much back then because there were so many paatridge."

Henry decided we should try to hunt up some partridge. He was not particularly encouraged about the future of grouse hunting in this area, either, believing that the forests around here had grown too mature, a situation he saw would not improve, as there was very little logging these days.

It occurred to me in the course of the morning that maybe another reason Henry hunted so slowly was because this was such circumscribed country, the coverts all small woodlots, corners, pockets, and edges, most of which only took ten or fifteen minutes to hunt out before we would move on to the next. A brisk walker would have covered all the available ground in under an hour, and that would be the end of the hunt. Henry's slow, careful pace served to extend the morning afield, making each tree, each thicket, each corner and pocket of cover seem specific and important. His was the pace of an attentive man, who knows the land not in generalities but in all its minute particulars.

As in Vermont, I frequently had the feeling that we were hunting in people's backyards, which, in fact, we often were, as suburban development was encroaching on all sides surrounding Henry's farm. At one

point, we stepped out of the forest into the back of a housing development—newly paved streets, fire hydrants, manicured lawns, and
recently planted shrubbery. It was a bit disconcerting. It would certainly
not do to shoot a bird here, or even to be spotted carrying guns here,
frightening the local populace. We ducked back into the woods, and the
illusion of the wilds.

But we didn't find any grouse, either, and Henry had to get back to
work; he was no gentleman sportsman who could devote the entire day to
this. I could tell he was disappointed that he hadn't been able to produce
any birds for me, but I didn't care. I had enjoyed his company, his open,
genuine manner, easy conversation, and deliberate pace. When we got
back to the farmhouse, I asked him about all the birdhouses I noticed that
he had put up on his barn and outbuildings.

"I put them up on the baahn to attract the swallows," Henry explained.
"When I was a boy growing up on this farm we had thousands of swallows
here in the summertime. But now every year fewer and fewer. I don't know
what's happened to them. You know, except for the sound of bulldozers, it
keeps getting quieter and quieter around here." He looked off across his
land, his brow knitted in thoughtful concern. "The birds are trying to tell
us something. And I think it's time we started listening."

I had arranged a hunt that same afternoon in the adjoining county with the
writer Charles Gaines (author of *Pumping Iron* among other books), who,
under the auspices of the Ruffed Grouse Society, had recently formed the
Woodcock Protection Fund to study the matter of declining woodcock
numbers. Gaines is the founder of Pathways International, a travel business
for well-heeled sportsmen, a business he cooked up at least in part as an
excuse to hunt and fish all over the world. He was also co-creator of the
National Survival Game, in which players run around in the woods shooting
paint bullets at one another, a sport that became quite popular in the last
decade with urbanites trying to recapture something of their lost manhood
and dulled wilderness survival skills. Though we hadn't met before,
Gaines had been described to me by a mutual friend as "the shootin'est,
fishin'est gentleman of them all"—a man who, depending on the season,
does one or the other nearly every day of his life.

I met Gaines at his Pathways office. He was dressed in brush pants and
L. L. Bean hunting boots—a tall, elegant, fit man, with a soft, courtly
southern accent, who seemed a decade younger than his fifty years. He
nicely fit the role of urbane international sportsman and gave the appearance
of being somewhat of a throwback to another, more genteel age.

Like a handful of others with whom I had hunted thus far across the country, there was nothing whatsoever casual about Charles Gaines's interest in sport. It was neither a hobby, nor a way to relax on weekends, nor an escape from or a tonic to the more mundane concerns of life. Gaines was simply one of those men at the top of the food chain, for whom being a predator was a perfectly natural, nearly full-time vocation. In the field virtually every day, he sometimes hunted with a regular partner, but often alone with his Llewellin setter, Arthur, a stockier, stronger, and, Gaines maintains, more athletic breed of English setter than the ganglier, more classic-looking Rymans and Old Hemlocks I'd hunted behind in Michigan, the Ohio River Valley, and thus far in New England.

One can learn a great deal about a hunter by observing his relationship with his dog—whether it is a partnership of mutual love and respect or a kind of mechanistic relationship in which the dog's sole function and purpose is to produce game. As we drove out to the first covert that afternoon Gaines talked about the "spiritual alliance" between man and dog that to him, and to so many bird hunters, is fundamental to an appreciation and enjoyment of the sport. "It's almost a primordial state that we achieve hunting together day after day," he explained. Though this sort of animistic description may seem at best incomprehensible to the nonhunter and at worst pretentious—the kind of romantic twaddle of which nineteenth-century sporting writers are sometimes guilty—anyone who has spent concerted time afield with a beloved canine partner will understand.

In a by now familiar tale of the region, Gaines claimed to lose five or six cherished coverts each year to development and posting, but he compensated for these losses by finding new ones, and he showed me some beautiful country that afternoon—remarkably large coverts by New England standards, mixed meadow and forest, alder thickets, hidden ponds and swamps, apple orchards, and poplar stands. It was country that still had a wild, unkept feel to it, the kind of country you could walk in for several hours without coming upon someone's house or a development.

Gaines moved easily and confidently through the woods, obviously at home here, and Arthur was an excellent hunting dog. Charles never had to raise his voice to him, and treated him in all ways as an equal. Even when he got mildly annoyed with Arthur at one point for a momentary loss of concentration and gently chastised him ("Arthur, you asshole"), he did so in the mild, soft-spoken, good-natured way that best friends sometimes speak to one another—no offense meant or taken. And when Arthur pointed his first woodcock of the afternoon and Charles walked in and killed it cleanly on the flush, and Arthur retrieved the bird to him, Charles, in his polite fashion, complimented his dog on a job well done. "Wonderful work, Arthur," he said. "Thank you very much." They were a fine team, a pleasure to hunt with.

Gaines is a superb wing shot, who shoots a 28-gauge double shotgun and rarely misses. Always the gentleman, he tried to put me into position for the best shot, gently coaxing me to walk in on each point where he thought the bird would fly to my advantage. And usually they did, and I, still mired in my slump, fired and missed, fired and missed. My shooting seemed to be getting progressively worse and I was getting pretty discouraged. One may joke all one likes about being a poor shot, but it can be debilitating, too, and as in any sport, a certain degree of proficiency makes for a lot more enjoyment.

Arthur went on point and a woodcock got up right in front of me, rose straight in the air with its now familiar and somehow heartbreaking piping sound, leveled, and flew straight away following the path of a dirt track through the forest. Charles happened to be standing directly behind me when I fired. And missed. Again. Such an easy shot. I was disgusted and ashamed of myself. With perfect tact, without a hint of the annoying know-it-allism that can strain relations between hunters, Gaines suggested that because of his position behind me, he had been able to notice that I wasn't leaning into the shot, that I seemed to have my weight slightly back on my heels. I knew he was quite right. I understood that this habit of rocking back on the heels reflected a loss of confidence, a certain timidity of commitment and faith, a lack of necessary aggressiveness.

On the next point, I walked in thinking about this, and when the woodcock got up, I tried to lean into my shot. Gaines and I fired our guns at exactly the same instant. The bird fell. Having watched Charles's faultless shooting that day, I'm quite certain he did not miss that woodcock, and given the current abysmal state of my own efforts I had no way of knowing whether I'd hit it or not. I thought I may have, but that might only have been wishful thinking on my part. But Gaines made a lovely gesture, the gesture of the consummate gentleman sportsman. As Arthur made the retrieve, he came over and offered me his hand. "Congratulations," he said, smiling broadly, "you've just ended your shooting slump!"

Later, after the hunt, over drinks at Gaines and his wife's beautifully restored eighteenth-century farmhouse with its sporting prints and old pine floors, full bookcases, soft lighting, and huge stone fireplace—amid the warmth, elegance, comfort, and effortless patina of privilege that is palpable in such surroundings, drinking the smoothest whiskey on earth and chatting contentedly, Gaines made a memorable remark, spoken with no trace of pomposity or elitism, although admittedly many of us bird hunters are hopelessly pompous elitists. "The older I get," said Gaines, "the more I'm of the opinion that life is too short to waste hunting with anyone other than gentlemen."

The next morning I asked the chief of police, Stanley Martin, what I should call him—Stan, Stanley, Chief Martin?

"Chief'll be just fine," he said in his serious, official bass voice.

We were headed out to the chief's coverts in his four-wheel-drive police car. He had the police radio turned on in case anyone needed him and a portable radio that he carried on his belt. His dog, an ugly cringing setter with slanty pink eyes and an upturned pink nose, rode in a kennel in the back. I never did learn that dog's real name; Chief just called him "Bub" and treated him abruptly and without affection, like the lowliest of employees. For the second hunt in a row, I had left Sweetz in the camper. The chief felt that she'd just get in the way; I gathered he had a pretty specific hunting routine, and to hear him tell it, he was "more effective at killing than the average hunter." Those were the chief's words exactly: *more effective at killing than the average hunter.*

The chief knew Charles Gaines by reputation and that I had hunted with him the day before, and he hastened to tell me that it was just as well that he himself was a "working stiff" and not an "idle rich man who could hunt every day of his life" because if he were able to do that, there wouldn't be a grouse or woodcock left in the whole country. "I don't miss too often, Jim," the chief explained solemnly. Evidently, the chief was a self-appointed, one-man conservation organization, who conscientiously limited his kill in order not to put "undue pressure on the resource."

The chief was what my wife sometimes refers to as a "wee-bit-o-windbag," and it was becoming more and more clear to me that it was going to be a difficult day. He seemed to approach hunting with somewhat the same grim, cheerless attitude which he took to law enforcement, as if the game were criminals to be apprehended in the act.

The chief carried a customized Remington automatic with a sawed-off barrel, for quick mounting with his one arm. It had a deadly riot gun look to it. Anyone who wants to find out how truly hard it is to shoot a shotgun with one arm need only try it once, as I did later, and I had to give the chief credit for the remarkable manner in which he had overcome his disability. Indeed, he was a better shot than most men with two arms.

First we hunted a small covert off one of the interstate exchanges, a reclaimed borrow bit replanted in mixed pine, fir, and olive. It was boggy at the bottom; some poplar and alder had volunteered up and the beavers had been active—there were many freshly gnawed stumps and downed trees.

Actually, it wasn't bad-looking cover if you could ignore the interstate traffic rushing by above, which to my mind puts a bit of a damper on a day in the field. The chief said he'd discovered the spot a year or so earlier while investigating a dead body that had turned up out here; it was eventually determined that the victim had been killed elsewhere, the body driven here on the interstate and dumped.

"Right over there is where we found the victim," Chief pointed out to me. "Caucasian male, approximately twenty-eight years old, no identification. One bullet wound to the back of the head. Execution style. Which leads me to believe that it was a professional hit." The chief nodded his head, satisfied with his conclusions. "Well, now, let's get on with it," he said, as if we were sweeping the area for yet another corpse.

It didn't surprise me to learn right off that the chief was what another hunting partner of mine describes as a "neo-Nazi, fascist dog handler." He was tough on poor Bub, constantly shouting at and reprimanding him, controlling his every move as if he were a slightly dimwitted rookie deputy. "Close, close, close now you, Bub! Whoa! Get in here! What in the hell are you doing? Get in here! Come around! Whoooa! Wait, goddammit! Wait! What are you doing, you asshole! Do you hear me! Get the hell in here!" Bub was a nervous wreck, anxious and panting, and foaming at the mouth. After five minutes of this, I tried to strike up a conversation with the chief. I was already tired of listening to him yell at his dog and I thought that I might be able to divert him and give poor old Bub—and me—a break. But the chief cut me off abruptly. "Jim, you *cannot* speak to me while we're hunting," he explained, "because then I *cannot* control the dog."

"Right, Chief, sorry," I muttered, and I didn't try to speak to him again.

The chief obviously liked his dog to work in close. There's a fair amount of disagreement about this among grouse hunters. Largely because they are hunted so intensively in this part of the country, ruffed grouse are notoriously spooky, do not hold well for a point, and tend to flush wild at the slightest provocation. Consequently, many hunters are of the opinion that if a dog ranges too far out he will simply bump and flush birds out of range all day, whereas a close-working dog is at least likely to bump the birds within range of the gun. Taken to its extreme, this theory might seem to recommend a flushing dog like a Lab or springer spaniel. And it seemed to me that the chief might have been just as well off with one of those breeds; he kept Bub in closer than any pointing dog I had hunted behind yet, completely overriding the dog's natural hunting instincts. Every time poor old Bub set out to hunt, his efforts were met with, "Whoa! Whoaaa! Get in here, Bub! Goddamn you! You hear me? Close! Close! Come around! Get *the hell* in here! Close! What in the hell do you think you're doing?"

Every so often Chief would set down his gun and chase poor Bub, catch him, and whip him severely for ranging too wide. Bub would howl piteously, white foam bubbling from his anxious pink mouth. Bub must have had some terrible neuroses as a result of this treatment.

Then the chief would come back to collect his gun, shaking his head. "I hate to do that," he would say in his official voice. "That's what you call a negative contact, but he needs to learn. There are some hunters who might think I overhandle my dog, but I want that son of a bitch in close!"

I kept my mouth shut. Interfering with another man's dog handling is as taboo as telling a man how to raise his children or stepping in during a marital dispute.

We hunted out the interstate exchange covert but we didn't find any birds—or any dead bodies. We got back in the car and drove to another of the chief's coverts, along an abandoned railroad bed by the river. The chief had me walk along the tracks up above, while he and Bub worked the cover below. I liked it up there on the railroad tracks; it gave me a certain hobo feel and I was daydreaming about hitting the rails when suddenly Bub went on point, and the chief walked in and flushed a woodcock. It was a very strange flush from my perspective because I was standing above the bird, and had to wait for it to gain enough altitude so that I wasn't shooting down at it. I watched it rise as if in slow motion and looked it right in the eyes when it was level with me and not ten feet away; it kept rising and veered off over the tracks above my head, creating that lonely sound of wind through wing feathers that was beginning to put me off woodcock shooting. I swung my gun in an arc overhead, and pulled the trigger.

Did I hit the woodcock?

I did not. I guess Charles Gaines had deceived me and my slump wasn't over, after all. But honestly, I believe I missed that woodcock intentionally. I didn't want to shoot any more woodcock this season. The bird landed in an alder thicket on the other side of the tracks.

"Did you mark him down, Jim?" the chief asked sternly.

"More or less, Chief," I equivocated.

The Chief and Bub came up onto the tracks and the three of us went down the other side to the alder thicket. I stayed on the edge while the chief and Bub went in to hunt the bird up. In fact, I had marked the woodcock down precisely and though I tried to steer them away from it, Bub found it anyway and pointed it, and the chief walked in to make the flush. The bird got up again and headed for the outside edge, toward me, flying practically straight at me. I really wanted it to escape from the long arm of the law, and I was thinking that I might have to miss it again, when the chief whipped his gun up with his one arm, using the stump of his other as a rest, and fired. He was smooth and fast, and he got his man. I felt a little sad about that. It would not be the first or the last time I had rooted for the game.

"Sorry, Jim," the chief said. "I just couldn't afford to wait any longer for you to shoot."

"I know, Chief. He was getting away."

CHARLES GAINES'S WOODCOCK BREASTS WITH COGNAC

Cut 4 woodcock breasts into ½" strips and sauté in butter for 1 minute. Set aside in warm oven. In a food processor make a *foie gras* paste of the trail and liver, sauté briefly, and set aside. Add game stock to pan drippings and reduce. Thicken sauce with ½ cup cream and add 2 tablespoons good cognac. Bring just to a boil. Spread toast with *foie gras*, lay woodcock strips on top, and cover with sauce.

23

ONE MAN'S
FOOD

A few fallen woodcock may be located without a dog, but to shoot those delightful little birds other than over a pointing dog would be like drinking Chateau Haut-Brion from a paper cup.

George Bird Evans

I made a brief hunt one morning outside New London, New Hampshire, with my friend, writer and editor David Seybold, in whose driveway I had parked for a few days. And that same afternoon, I hunted with another fine local hunter by the name of Peter Stanley, the fire chief of New London and a talented professional sign painter and small farmer. Stanley was missing a hand, which didn't seem to slow him down in the least and, like the other, armless, chief, he was also an excellent wing shot. Stanley, too, believed in the efficacy of the close-working setter for grouse, though he tended to be less tyrannical about it.

For his part, though Seybold didn't produce any birds for us in the field, he came up with a few in the kitchen, cooking some magnificent game dinners during my visit. And I enjoyed our hunt for no other reason than that it provided an excuse to wander around in the woods for a few hours with a friend. Not that this activity necessarily requires an excuse, but sometimes the act of hunting, successful or not, provides added dimension, direction, and focus to a walk in the woods, as well as special purpose and cement to a friendship. Sweetzer had fun, too, even though we didn't find any birds.

I was not able to get together with several people in New England with whom I had hoped to hunt. One was the fine writer Annie Proulx in Vermont, who always hunts alone or with one regular partner, and without dogs, one person on either side of a wooded ravine, creek bottom, or logging road, "one walking point," she explained to me in a letter, "to bump the birds out into the narrow corridor of air over the stream. A slow, very watchful kind of hunting that is not suited to many and takes a long time to get into. It would probably not be fun for you if you are used to a fast-paced hunt over a dog." Wrong, Annie, it would have been plenty of fun for me; I had become accustomed to all kinds of hunting, fast paced or slow, though I do prefer hunting with dogs.

Nor was I able to hunt with the poet Sydney Lea, also of Vermont, with whom I spoke on the telephone and who told me of his own, by all eastern grouse hunting traditions, downright heretical style of hunting. Lea hunts behind big running English pointers—favored by some western bird hunters and most southern quail hunters—who get way out of sight and sound and go on point deep in the woods far from the hunter. This is exactly the opposite tactic espoused by Chief Martin, and Lea maintains that what causes grouse to flush wild is all the noise made by approaching hunters, the crashing and thrashing in the underbrush, and the talking. By this theory, then, it wasn't poor Bub's fault that grouse were bumped, but the chief's for making such a racket with his incessant commands. According to Lea, his pointers, left to their own devices, quiet and stealthy in the forest, held the birds just fine, until he, presumably locating them with beeper collars, walked in as quietly as possible for the flush. He claimed a remarkably high success rate with this approach, and I had no reason not to believe him. I'd have liked to have seen it.

All of this is to say that in the pursuit of one seemingly specific form of bird-hunting—ruffed grouse and woodcock gunning, so storied in sporting lore and literature—there exists a remarkable and mutually contradictory array of styles, theories, approaches, and prejudices, none of them necessarily wrong—or right for that matter. Let us say that on one extreme we have my pal Merlin, road-hunting with a six-pack of beer, and on the other end of the spectrum, the great George Bird Evans who would sooner suffer the indignity of drinking Chateau Haut-Brion from a paper cup than to hunt in any other manner than behind one of his beloved Old Hemlock setters. In between, we have Bob Jones, existentialist Lab man; Nick Reems with five setters on the ground at once; Bill Cheney with his delicate, light-footed tracker, Willow; farmer Henry, who, like Annie Proulx, hunts slowly and carefully, sans dog; Chief, with his cringing Bub; gentleman Charles Gaines, with his equally well-mannered and gentlemanly canine companion, Arthur. And then, of course, we have our trusty narrator, with his trusty partner, Sweetzer, both of them confirmed generalists rather than specialists.

And so Sweetz and I were off again, back on the road and pointed north still and east, winter closing fast behind us, headed for the blustery coast of Maine where we had arranged yet another hunt with an accomplished woman who hunted with yet another distinct style and behind yet another breed of dog: grouse driven by springer spaniels. When I told some of my new grouse hunting friends about this novel method, they said flatly that it could not be done, that it was quite impossible. "Why, you can't drive ruffed grouse," they said skeptically. "I'd like to see that!" Well, Sweetz and I would just see, wouldn't we?

I spent the night camped alongside the Kennebec River near Bath, Maine. It rained hard all night, turning to wet sleet by morning, a cold, spitting, windy Sunday, a better day for traveling than it was for hunting. After a leisurely, meandering drive up the jagged Maine coastline, with frequent stops for chowder and lobster bisque and a huge plateful of assorted seafood, I arrived that afternoon at Jo-Ann Moody's house in the country outside Belfast.

A talkative Down-Easter with a Gordian knot of springer spaniels of all ages and colors intwined on a huge dog bed in the kitchen, Jo-Ann was a woman with grouse hunting convictions of her own, foremost among them the idea that springers—forget setters, forget pointers, forget Labs—and specifically *her* springers, were the best, the only grouse dogs in the world. Indeed, I'd yet to meet a single hunting dog breeder, a notoriously opinionated and contentious lot, who didn't fervently believe that his/her breed was *the* breed, and his/her dog the *only* dog worth owning.

We sat in Jo-Ann's kitchen that first evening and talked about dogs, hunting, dogs, hunters, dogs, dogs, dogs. The television droned on in the background with disturbing tales of impending war. We ignored it, in favor of more dog talk. It occurred to me, and not for the first time, what a strange, insulated, charmed life I had been living these past few months, totally immersed in the arcane and rather less than earth-shattering pursuit of game birds, while the rest of the country, glued to their sets, prepared for the armchair thrills of modern warfare.

That night I parked in an old apple orchard below Jo-Ann's house, the coastal weather still wild and windy, the camper pelted throughout the night by flying apples hurled like baseballs from the trees.

It was snowing by dawn and still blowing and Sweetz and I huddled deep under our comforter, trying to keep each other warm, and reluctant to face the chill brutalities of the outdoors. How keenly the hunter who takes to the field day after day with the same regularity as most men go to the office experiences the weather—the variances of temperature and moisture, the subtleties and the not-so-subtleties of changing climes. Just a week ago, I had hunted in Vermont in the tongue-dragging dog days of a brutal heat spell, and now in Maine, checking the outdoor thermometer mounted by the window above the camper bed, I marked the mercury hovering just below twenty degrees.

I got up finally, turned the burner on under the coffee, and dressed warmly in long underwear, flannel shirt, and insulated hunting boots, thankful that I had packed for all possible weather conditions, every one of which I would eventually encounter.

Sweetz and I met Jo-Ann and her passel of springers by the house at the appointed hour. "It's going to be hard hunting today, Jim," Jo-Ann said in the kind of heavy coastal Maine accent that puts one in mind of weathered, hearty seafarers and lobstermen. "With this wind we won't be able to hear the grouse fly." Without benefit of a point to signal birds, hunters with flushing dogs must rely as much on the sound of beating wings as they do on sight to identify the bird's location and direction of flight.

Jo-Ann Moody would be only the second professional bird hunting guide with whom I had hunted thus far. A friendly, self-reliant, no-nonsense Down-Easter, she had been divorced a few years earlier from her longshore-man husband. "I remember one time I saw a pair of pants that I wanted in a catalogue," she explained of the demise of her marriage, as we drove out across the wild, blustery landscape of Maine on the way to the day's first covert. "I asked my husband if I could send away for them and he said, 'Do you really need them?' And I thought, You can take those pants and stick 'em where the sun don't shine. I decided that I would never ask him for anything again. And I never did, either." These days Jo-Ann supported herself by guiding grouse hunters and raising her own fine line of springers.

We pulled off the highway and followed a rutted muddy two-track through the trees until it dead-ended in a clearing of thick yellow fall grass, whorled on the ground, heavy with the wetness. I had Sweetz with me at heel and Jo-Ann had two of her springers, one-year-old Pepper, who was just learning the ropes, and her mother, Cricket. We came to the edge of a thicket, to the left of it a line of old apple trees and behind them a dense forest of tall, mature pine. Jo-Ann directed me to follow the edge and stop at the second apple tree I came to, and to position myself right next to it. She would go into the thicket with her springers quartering ahead and bump the birds out. "When the grouse flushes," Jo-Ann explained, "it will fly out just to the right of that apple tree, headed for the forest behind you."

"How do you know it will come that way?" I asked. From what I had seen of ruffed grouse hunting so far, and of the unpredictability of the bird, I may have had a trace of skepticism in my voice.

"You just take my word for it, Jim," Jo-Ann said. "Stop at the second apple tree. And be ready. I'll yell when we flush the grouse."

Sweetz and I walked out to the second apple tree as directed, stopped, and waited. This seemed a strange kind of hunting, relatively sedentary compared to what I had been doing thus far, and reminiscent of the driven grouse shoots of England that I had read about and watched in my English shooting video. I stood there for a minute. I couldn't hear Jo-Ann or the bells on her dogs' collars over the howling of the wind. Unlike most dog handlers, Jo-Ann does not use a whistle, believing them to be too noisy, and in three days I would never hear her raise her voice once to her dogs. Rather she "speaks" to them when they need correcting in soft conversational tones, and they "listen" to her. "The quieter your approach," she had explained, "the closer you can get to the birds before they flush."

I waited under my designated apple tree, and then for some unknown reason, perhaps just out of restlessness because I was used to walking when I hunted, or because I was getting cold standing there, I decided to reposition myself on the other side of the tree, and as I was moving, I heard Jo-Ann's sharp call, "Bird, Jim! Coming toward you!" I turned; I still couldn't hear the wingbeats of the bird for the wind, but damned if the grouse wasn't flying right out of the thicket, silent and ghostly, gaining altitude as it passed the apple tree, exactly where Jo-Ann had told me to stand. Of course, I was out of position now and I swung around awkwardly, mounting my gun and fumbling the safety off with stiff fingers. I managed to squeeze off a shot but the grouse continued its uninterrupted flight for the forest beyond. I caught the faintest sound of departing wingbeats on the arriving wind.

Jo-Ann came out of the thicket, preceded by her eager springers who were running in the direction the grouse had flown, presumably expecting to make a retrieve of a dead bird. "What happened, Jim?" she asked in her direct manner.

"Well, Jo-Ann, for starters, I wasn't standing where you told me to stand. So I didn't see the bird as soon as I should have. Then by the time I did see it, I was facing the wrong direction. And then I had trouble getting my safety off," I answered, trotting out all my excuses at once.

"Why weren't you standing where I told you to stand, Jim?"

"I don't know, Jo-Ann."

The icy wind blew all morning, making the hunting difficult. Still, I could see that Jo-Ann's unusual technique was highly effective, and after that first bird I didn't try to second-guess her again. She knew her coverts and game so intimately that she could put the birds out almost exactly where she positioned the shooter, usually on the edge of a clearing. The shooter had a brief "window of opportunity" as the birds flushed out of the cover and entered the clearing before disappearing in the trees on the other side. But today, due to the wind, they often sailed by without enough warning to offer a shot. He who hesitated in that split-second window was lost. "If you have to think about whether or not you're going to shoot," Jo-Ann instructed me, "you've already missed your chance."

We broke for lunch at a small country café. It felt good to get out of the wind, sip some hot soup, and have a conversation that didn't necessitate yelling at each other to be heard. Sometimes the best parts of a hunt are the lulls between it or after it. Jo-Ann talked about growing up in a family of three brothers and two sisters. Her father and brothers were all hunters, and early on she found that her interests lay beyond the common pursuits of young girls, in the silence of the woods. "I am what I am," she said with a shrug as we hunched over our soup. "I tried to fit in for years, and I was very unhappy." As a teenager, Jo-Ann came home from school every afternoon during the grouse season, changed into her hunting clothes, gathered her gun and her half-Brittany/half-beagle mutt and headed out to the grouse coverts where they would hunt until dinner time. She hunted with that dog for fourteen years. "That was a good grouse dog," she remembered softly. "That dog taught me to be quiet. That's one of the things I like best about grouse hunting. I like quiet."

The wind did not die down overnight, and the following morning was even colder, ten degrees at dawn. Still, we would hunt. Jo-Ann had another free day; it was late in the season for her guiding business, and on days when she didn't have hunters booked she generally went out anyway, to work her dogs and to explore new coverts. She didn't usually carry a gun.

As we drove out that morning, Jo-Ann voiced the by now familiar concern, the common litany of bird hunters everywhere, that of losing habitat each year to development, posting, and the clearing of formerly wild or overgrown lands that provide prime food and cover for birds but might seem unruly to the new breed of country residents who prefer their landscapes tidy, neat, and trim. It would hardly seem necessary to point out that we need wildness of flora to promote wild fauna.

That morning we hunted the state land on nearby Frye Mountain—old meadows and fields that had once been farmland carved out of the forest in the early part of the century and abandoned during the Depression. Now the state kept the fields open, rather than letting them succeed back to forest, for the grass and openings they offered the wildlife. It was gorgeous-looking bird habitat, with edge plantings of various berry bushes as food for the grouse, apple trees, and plenty of cover.

The country was perfect for Jo-Ann's style of hunting—a strip of meadow alternating with a strip of forest. She would position me on the edge of the trees and walk the middle of the cover with her spaniels. I had by far the easier job, but in truth, I prefer to do my own walking, finding, and flushing. And so does Sweetzer, who was envious of the role the springers played and bored with our own stationary posture. This kind of hunting seemed best suited to an older, more sedentary sportsman who preferred the shooting to the hunting.

Perhaps due to the wind and cold weather, the grouse seemed to have moved out of their usual lies, or they were flushing wild and out of range, or we simply couldn't hear them when they did fly.

After lunch we decided to explore some new coverts and I prevailed upon Jo-Ann to carry her gun, making us more equal partners. The wind had finally layed down a bit as we drove into some very pretty upland farm country of rolling meadows and pulled into a long drive, up the crest of a hill to an ancient clapboard farmhouse in bad need of a coat of paint and beginning to crumble on its foundation corners. A wizened old man, who looked to be of the same vintage as the house, peered out from a crack in the kitchen curtain. I waited in the truck while Jo-Ann went to the door to introduce herself and ask permission to hunt the old man's property.

I liked the way the springers worked—busy, eager dogs, gentle and much lighter afoot than my more oafish Sweetzer. I have a memory of that afternoon, of watching Jo-Ann Moody crossing a high upland meadow with her brace of springers, mother and daughter, quartering ahead. A network of old stone walls dissected the expanse of fields below, dotted with strips and pockets of cover. We had split up to work one of these cover strips from opposite ends of the field, and as I watched Jo-Ann and her dogs walking away, I thought about the ineffable aura of aloneness that seems to surround so many hunters I have met, a separateness that is quite different from loneliness, and is perhaps best summed up by Jo-Ann's simple remark, "I like quiet."

I particularly enjoy the kind of hunting we did that afternoon: walking through meadows and along edges with the dogs working inside the cover. At one point, Jo-Ann and I were on opposite sides of such a strip, with the dogs quartering through the undergrowth, when one of her springers put up a grouse. I heard the bird get up between us and just caught a glimpse of it as it flew through the trees behind me. I mounted my gun and swung but Jo-Ann fired first and the bird tumbled on my side of the cover. I marked it down and called to tell her that she had hit it. Sweetz ran in to make the retrieve while I tried to stop her with the whistle; this wasn't our bird, but belonged to Jo-Ann and her dogs. But our training had not progressed to the point where I could call her off a retrieve with any regularity; she was of the belief that all downed birds belonged to her. I set my gun down and went into the cover after her, and though she was trailing the bird I managed to stop her and get ahold of her collar, intending to wait for Jo-Ann and the springers to come through from their side. I knelt there and held on to Sweetz; she was trembling with excitement and suddenly managed to wriggle backward, leaving me holding an empty collar; she was not to be denied this retrieve. I lunged and grabbed ahold of her leg, just as Jo-Ann and her dogs arrived on the scene. I was determined to save the retrieve for its rightful owners, and Sweetzer was equally determined to pick up that grouse. Now I was stretched out on the ground holding tenaciously on to her back leg with one hand as she dragged me through the leaves. Labs are incredibly strong, and Sweetz really wanted that bird, which now lay only a few yards away. Jo-Ann and her dogs were the picture of composed New England dignity. They stood and looked down at us as we grappled on the ground like adversaries in a greased pig contest. "What are you *doing*, Jim?" Jo-Ann finally asked.

The next day, my last in Maine, would also prove to be my last hunt in New England. Jo-Ann had hunters in for the day and so Sweetz and I went out on our own, to a covert she had taken us to on our first day and that she had given me permission to hunt again.

The weather remained cold but less windy, and we hunted through the woods along a wide, slow-moving river. Thin, glass-clear ice had formed along its edges. Sweetzer flushed the same woodcock twice, but I didn't shoot at it. As far as I was concerned, woodcock season was over, and I wished safe passage south for these last stragglers.

Then Sweetz got birdy and I knew she was on a scent trail, her tail stiff and wagging furiously. I hurried to keep up with her. She pushed the running bird to the edge of the woods, where it flew and headed out across the river. I shot it and it dropped into the water. Sweetz bounded in, shattering the shelf of thin ice on the river's edge and arcing downstream to intercept the dead-drifting grouse in the gentle current. She swam back to shore with the bird in her mouth like a duck retrieve and delivered it to me on the bank. This would be my final ruffed grouse of the season and I took it from my dog and smoothed its wet feathers. I remembered something Jo-Ann had said the day before about those strange mixed emotions that the hunter feels at this moment. "Sometimes when the dog presents that bird," she said, "you just want to throw it up in the air and let it fly away again."

I went over and sat down on a log by the edge of the woods overlooking the silent, black, slow-moving river. The last of the leaves were down and it was winter now for sure. I could see songbird nests exposed in the bony skeletons of the trees, the birds long gone south. As much as I had enjoyed Jo-Ann's company, I was happy to be hunting alone again, at my own pace, in my own style, which now involved sitting on a log. Sweetzer lay down on the leaves at my feet and fell asleep instantly. She seemed to understand that the hunt was over. I opened the bird's crop and sorted through the contents—yellow birch catkins, raspberry leaves, and acorn meat. I set the grouse down on the log next to me by my gun, and then I sat there for a long while, not thinking about anything in particular, just sitting by the silent river at the edge of the dark woods, in the wintertime on the coast of Maine, with my yellow dog asleep at my feet.

DAVID SEYBOLD'S
DOVE/WOODCOCK QUENELLES
(MOUSSE FORCEMEAT)

(This recipe is perfectly suited for birds ruined by shot or freezer burn.)

> *¹/₄ lb. each of woodcock and dove meat, picked*
> *from carcasses and chopped into large pieces*
> *1 oz. pancetta, trimmed of fat and diced small*
> *1 shallot, chopped into large pieces*
> *2 tbsp. chanterelles, or other wild mushrooms,*
> *diced small*
> *1 egg white if egg is large, 2 if small*
> *³/₄ cup heavy cream*
> *2 tbsp. cognac*
> *¹/₄ tsp. cayenne*
> *2 tsp. fresh parsley, chopped, rinsed and squeeze-*
> *drained through a cloth*
> *2 tsp. chives, chopped*
> *¹/₈ tsp. salt*
> *¹/₄ tsp. fresh cracked pepper*

Remove meat from the dove and woodcock, reserving carcasses for stock and sauces, and mix with shallot and egg white. Place in refrigerator until chilled, then purée to a smooth paste in food processor. Spoon the mixture into a stainless steel mixing bowl and place on a bed of ice cubes.

Add the cream a few drops at a time, whisking all the while until the cream is used and the mixture emulsifies. Next add cognac, cayenne, parsley, chives, salt and pepper, diced pancetta and mushrooms. Taste-test by forming a quenelle between two soup spoons and easing into simmering broth.

Make quenelles and poach in chicken or game stock for approximately 10 minutes. Serve with a traditional tracklement, such as a bread, caper, mustard, or Cumberland sauce.

24

A HUNTER
IN NEW YORK

With no standard nothing has merit, and man is capable of using even sublimity to degrade himself.

Ortega y Gasset

The reader may be wondering what in the world Manhattan has to offer in the way of bird hunting, and the narrator freely admits not much, other than some sporting pigeons in Central Park. Think of all the homeless people who could dine on Central Park squab, if only they had bird dogs and shotguns. I once wrote to several large outdoor sporting equipment retailers, suggesting that, as business appeared to be booming, they outfit some of the homeless families in America with good tents, down sleeping bags, and proper camp cookware. I never heard back from any of them.

In any event, in spite of the case the narrator has tried to make to the contrary, there is more to life than bird hunting, and I had arranged to meet my wife in New York for Thanksgiving. We hadn't seen each other in almost three months. Sweetz and I were both tired and a little frazzled around the edges, thin and sinewy from months in the field. In Maine we hadn't been able to get dry or warm, the constant damp soaking into our bones; we were beginning to mildew. It had been months since we'd slept in a real bed, and since I'd had a real shower. It was time for a break from the road. The idea of eating in a good restaurant and walking down a sidewalk instead of through a thicket, and of not lugging a shotgun, seemed rather appealing. Even the hunter needs to come to town now and again.

Because it was off-season on the eastern seaboard, I couldn't find any open campgrounds as I drove down from Maine to New York, and I was finally reduced to parking for the night in the lot of a mall and multiplex cinema off the interstate outside Providence, Rhode Island. I tried to park down in a corner of the lot, but it was impossible to get away from the ubiquitous quartz vapor lights. With the sudden bustling urban environment of the East Coast, the crowded highways and the endless expanse of concrete, I experienced a certain momentary culture shock, a kind of car lag. Already my rural wanderings of the past few months seemed a fading memory. It seemed impossible that just the evening before I had been parked in the most silent of apple orchards with stars overhead.

I took a shower in the camper, and for the very first time on my trip cranked up the television antenna on the roof and hooked up a five-inch portable set I had packed along with me. It had seemed terribly inappropriate until now, but I was back in civilization.

After my shower, I fixed a cocktail, watched the news, cleaned my shotgun, and prepared dinner. When one has not seen it in a while the television news has a certain surreal quality, especially when it involves going to war. Watching the troops eating dust in the moonscape of the Middle East helped to put my own minor discomforts of the past months into proper perspective. I was the luckiest man on earth.

For dinner, I was having a Maine lobster, which Jo-Ann's neighbor, a burly young lobsterman, had given me the evening before as a going-away present. I liked those folks up there; they had been generous and hospitable to this hunter. Last night, the lobsterman and his wife had come over to present me with the lobster, caught that very same day, and to show off their own yellow Lab bitch, the biggest Lab I've ever seen in my life—as big as a mastiff. The enormous beast was straining at its leash, held by the lobster-man's wife, which gave sly Jo-Ann the opportunity she'd been waiting for to tease me about Sweetz and my wrestling match the day before. "Why Jim," she said to me in her lilting, wry, Down-Easter way of speaking, "how is it that this tiny little woman is able to control that great big dog and that little Sweetzer of yours dragged you all over the forest floor?"

As I was enjoying my cocktail and finishing my gun cleaning, there came a sharp knock on the camper door. Startled out of a sound sleep on the cab-over bed, Sweetz howled and leapt up, raising the hackles on her back. I tried to quiet her as I opened the door. It was a policeman, the sight of whom standing outside in his uniform and holding a flashlight, which he shined in my face and which he certainly didn't need what with the floodlights in the lot and the lights I had on in the camper, sent her into further paroxysms of terrified howling.

"Evening, Officer," I said, stepping outside and closing the door. It was impossible to talk over her barking. "Sorry about the dog. She's kind of timid."

"May I see your driver's license and registration, please, sir?" the policeman asked. He looked me over disapprovingly. The fact that I was dressed in bathrobe and slippers did not escape his attention.

"Well, sure, but I'll have to step back in the camper to get it. Is there something wrong, Officer?"

"What are you doing here?" he asked.

"I'm parking for the night. I couldn't find a campground that was open."

"You'll have to move along, sir. Overnight camping is not permitted here."

I desperately did not want to move along. I'd had my shower and I was settled in for the night. I was in my bathrobe and slippers. I had a cocktail and my lobster water was just coming to a boil. I had the table set, the TV antenna up. It wasn't my fault there were no open campgrounds, nor any open country in which to park around here. "I didn't see any signs prohibiting overnight parking," I said. "How about giving me a break, Officer? I'll be gone first thing in the morning. Besides," I added, "I've already had a cocktail and I really don't think I should be driving."

"You've been drinking?" the officer asked.

"While I was cooking my dinner," I explained, "I had a drink. I hadn't planned on doing any more driving tonight."

"I need to see that driver's license and registration, sir," the officer said, sternly. "This isn't a public campground. And alcoholic beverages are not allowed on the premises."

Great, now I was going to be arrested. And just then I remembered that my shotgun was broken down on the table where I had been cleaning it. There would probably be some kind of charge involved with that, too—drinking, illegal firearms—I'd probably miss Thanksgiving in New York and my much-anticipated reunion with my wife. I'd probably spend the holiday in the slammer. I decided to come clean, to throw myself on the mercy of the law.

"Officer, I'm going to go back in and get my driver's license now, but I have to tell you that I've been traveling around the country for the last few months researching a book about upland bird hunting. I just came down from hunting in Maine, and I was cleaning my shotgun when you knocked on the door. It's sitting right there on the table, so do me a favor: If you happen to see it when I go back inside, don't mistake it for a weapon and reach for your gun. I'm really a law-abiding citizen and quite harmless."

"Upland bird hunting?" the policeman asked, suddenly less coolly official.

"Yeah."

"No kidding? Boy, I love to bird hunt."

"Really?"

"Oh, yeah, I do it every chance I get. What kind of shotgun do you have in there?"

"I have several with me. All side-by-side doubles. A sixteen-gauge A. H. Fox, a twenty-gauge Parker and a little twenty-gauge Belgium gun."

"No shit? I shoot a model twenty-one Winchester. I love double shotguns. That's all I'll hunt with. I save the autoloaders for the line of duty. Would you mind if I took a look at your guns?"

"Not at all."

"So you're traveling around the country, bird hunting, huh? Man, I've always dreamed of doing something like that. Tough job you've got there!"

"I know, but somebody's gotta do it, Officer."

"Say, I don't suppose you know the writer George Bird Evans, by any chance?"

"Why yes, as a matter of fact I do. I just visited with him a few weeks ago."

"Get outta town! You know George Bird Evans? George Bird Evans is my hero! I have signed copies of every one of his books."

"No sense in talking out here, Officer. Why don't you come inside, and I'll show you my guns. The dog'll probably bark at you at first, but just ignore her."

We stepped in the camper. "Man, great rig!" the officer said, looking around.

"Sit down. Make yourself comfortable. I guess you're on duty, or I'd offer you a drink."

The officer looked at his watch. "My shift's over in fifteen minutes. Maybe I could come back out after I get off and have a beer with you. I'd really like to hear more about George Bird Evans."

I didn't dare bring the camper into the city, unless, as a New York friend suggested, I wanted it turned into a flatbed overnight, so I arranged to park it in a garage on Long Island. I was trying to change lanes at the toll booth at the Throgs Neck Bridge, but no one would let me in. I didn't have the right change and I was in the wrong lane. A swarthy fat man smoking a cigar and driving a Cadillac with New Jersey plates crept along next to me, his bumper practically kissing the car in front of him for fear that someone might try to cut in front of him. It was warm and I had the window down, and I gestured imploringly to him to see if he might let me in. I knew quite well that he saw me, but people in this part of the country are masters when it comes to ignoring one another.

"Say!" I finally hollered at him, "would you let me in here, sir? Please?"

He continued to ignore me, refusing to look at me and leaving not an inch of space between his car and the one in front. I began to lose my temper. I hadn't been grinding my teeth in months, but now my jaws were clenched tight. I wished I was driving my old Jeep; I'd have rammed the son of a bitch. "Hey, you!" I screamed at the man. "Yeah, that's right, you! I just wanted to say, *thanks a lot, motherfucker!*"

Ah, welcome to New York.

Of course, I couldn't risk leaving my guns in the camper at the garage on Long Island, so I loaded a duffel bag with clothes and gear, took my guns in their cases and Sweetz on a leash, and called a cab from a pay phone.

"I can't take that dog," the cab driver said when he pulled up to the corner.

"Well I can't very well leave her now, can I? I'll give you an extra ten bucks."

"He'll get hair all over my backseat," the cabbie said. "People don't like to get dog hairs on them in cabs. That dog looks like he could do some serious damage to a blue suit."

"Fifteen bucks. For that you can get the seat vacuumed."

"I could probably take him for twenty." As we were loading my gear in the trunk of the taxi, the cabbie noticed the gun cases. "You a terrorist?" he asked casually.

"How'd you know?"

"Just a wild guess."

It struck me that for the most part people seemed friendlier in New York than they did a decade ago. There is nothing like the common bond of horror to bring people together. Still, it always takes me a few days in the city before I get used to that air of unflappable indifference at which New Yorkers become by necessity so proficient. I remembered years ago as a young man coming to the city for the first time to visit my sister who lived there. Walking down the sidewalk, I actually nodded, smiled, and said hello to people passing by. My sister was incredulous, embarrassed by her hayseed brother. "You don't look at or talk to people on the street in New York," she had explained, "unless you're insane, or a bum. Or unless they're celebrities—then it's okay to gawk a little." Which advice strikes me as still sound.

On our very first day in the city, I was walking Sweetz down Columbus Avenue on the West Side. Sweetz seemed to have adapted more quickly than I to the life of the city, and was interested in all the people and all the activity. She could hardly stop rubbernecking and didn't mind the bustle at all. People tend to be nicer to you when you're in the company of a pretty dog, and often they even look you in the eye sympathetically and smile. Yes, even in New York.

Though I had read all about the homeless and had seen endless reports about them on television, I was unprepared for the reality, the legion of dispossessed, alcoholic, and mentally ill people on the street and in Central Park. One need only come here from the country to understand that these people are a kind of biological indicator for the decline of a culture.

So we were strolling down the street, Sweetz and I, when a homeless fellow, swaddled in rags and sitting on the steps of a church, called out to us. "Sir!" he called. I knew he was talking to me but I kept walking, feigning deafness, just like the natives, staring straight ahead. "Sir!" he repeated. Still I went on. "Sir! Sir! Sir!" he said more insistently. I thought about my friend Cantrell out west, about how he always stopped to help stranded motorists, or anyone else in need, and I wondered how he would react to such a place as this, where practically everyone is in need. Burning with shame, I stopped and turned toward the man. "That dog you have there?" the man said, posing it as a question.

I waited. Did he want my dog?

"That's a real nice dog you have there," the man said.

"Why, yes she is. Thank you."

The next day my wife and I went over to the East Side to see the smart shops on Madison Avenue. We went in a store that sold $5,000 cowboy boots. A Japanese businessman was trying on a pair. I made my wife come over and look at the boots. I had never heard of such a thing, and made a mental note to tell Cantrell about them. On the sidewalk just outside the store, a black man sat with a coffee can in front of him and serenaded the wealthy shoppers with a better than passable rendition of "*I wanna be loved by you . . . uh-uh . . . and only by you, you, you . . . uh-uh . . .*" The shoppers, laden with packages from the expensive stores, quickened their step past the man.

While in New York, Sweetz and I took long walks every day through Central Park, the only country available in these parts. She was interested in the park pigeons because she'd been trained on pigeons at home and at first she strained at the leash when we passed flocks of them pecking around on the ground. Being accustomed to New York dogs, the New York pigeons are pretty complacent and just sort of hop or flutter out of the way, hardly bothering to fly. And it wasn't long before Sweetz learned to affect a certain New York indifference of her own, ignoring the pigeons altogether.

One afternoon, as we were passing by a particularly large flock, just out of curiosity, I stopped, leaned down, unhooked Sweetzer's lead, and whispered a command to her. Fast as lightning, she wheeled and pounced on an unsuspecting pigeon; it fluttered up ineffectually but she batted it right out of the air like a cat, pinned it on the ground, and gathered it in her mouth. Then she retrieved it smartly to hand. I took the startled pigeon from her. Sweetz had carried live pigeons in her mouth hundreds of times without mishap; other than being surprised and, I think, embarrassed at the indignity of being caught by an out-of-town dog, the pigeon was quite unharmed. I released it and it flew away, a bit wiser for the experience. Half a dozen people had stopped to witness the incident, and after I let the pigeon go, several of them applauded. Other normally jaded New Yorkers gathered when they heard the applause and I could hear people telling each other, "That dog just caught a pigeon!" Suddenly Sweetz was a bonafide Central Park celebrity. A little boy with his mother called out to us: "Hey, can you do that again?"

"Don't let it go to your head," I advised Sweetzer as we walked off to the admiring looks of the crowd.

At a cocktail party on Thanksgiving day at my brother-in-law, Laton McCartney, and his wife, Nancy's, apartment, I got talking to a stockbroker, a soft-spoken southerner from South Carolina named John Snyder. I was headed south next, for quail country, and I was interested to learn that John had grown up quail hunting, and that his father had raised a line of English setters. "Every day after school, I'd come home and change into my hunting clothes," he said, smiling. "And we'd go out hunting. We hunted for food. We often ate quail for breakfast." As we talked, John became more and more animated. He sat on the edge of his chair and leaned toward me. "For a long time I wanted to be a gunsmith," he remembered. "I saw an ad for a gunsmith school in Trinidad, Colorado, in one of the magazines and I sent away for information. I loved guns. I was fascinated by them."

"I've got my shotguns with me here," I said. "Maybe you'd like to take a look at them?"

"Why, I'd like that very much. I was going to ask."

We went out to the foyer and I uncased my shotguns. John took my A. H. Fox and held it in his hands reverently. "My father shot a twelve-gauge Fox grade B," he said in a soft voice. "God, this takes me back." He mounted the gun. "This *really* feels like a Fox. It reminds me so of my father's gun."

"You don't hunt anymore?" I asked.

"No, I don't. Those days are over. I stopped hunting when I went away to college and I haven't hunted since. I don't like what's become of the sport, the artificiality of it—the preserves and the released birds . . . to me it's like a slaughter now. In those days, it was just something we did, something that came naturally as a part of the fabric of our lives. And of course, the birds were all wild, not planted. Now the land use in our county down there has changed so drastically. No one raises cotton anymore, there aren't any stubble fields, and hardly any small farms like the ones we used to hunt. In those days you could hunt everywhere. Oh, sometimes the farmers chased us off, but you could always find someplace to go. And you could always find birds. Now the land is all owned by huge plantations."

In the living room, the New York party continued, but out there in the foyer with my shotguns, we were in our own world, the world of John's childhood in the quail fields.

"I'll tell you a story about quail hunting in the old days," John said. "This will give you an idea of the southern mentality at that time. My father wasn't a rich man, but all the rich guys in the area—the cotton gin owners and the plantation owners—always wanted to go hunting with him because he was such a fine shot. He was sort of locally renowned as a great quail hunter. He almost always shot a double on the covey rise. So one day these rich fellows came over to show my father this new car one of them had just gotten. Of course, this was before they had four-wheel-drive vehicles, or dog trailers. This car was designed with a new kind of vent pipe so that they could carry their dogs back in the trunk. It had only recently been invented, and I remembered this one fellow telling us that they decided they needed to test it out before they risked putting their valuable bird dogs back there; they were very worried about the dogs suffocating in the trunk. And the way they tested it, they explained, was to get a local black man and have him climb into the trunk, and then they drove him around town for a while. And the black man didn't suffocate, so they decided that it was safe for their bird dogs."

Over Thanksgiving dinner that day, I had a conversation with a woman seated next to me who owned a small farm in Connecticut that she used as a weekend retreat. She had what she described as a "wild turkey problem"; her place was overrun with them. "I'm afraid of them," she said. "They travel in packs. And every year there are more of them. They're so big. They come right up to the house. They're very bold and aggressive. They fly low to the ground, right toward you. I always go in the house when I see them." She might have been describing an inner city gang.

"Why don't you shoot a couple of them?" I suggested. "Have them for dinner. They're wonderful to eat."

"Really?" said the woman, surprised, pausing with a forkful of Butterball halfway to her mouth. "I didn't even know you could eat them!"

It didn't take long in New York, a week or so, before Sweetz and I were ready to resume our journey. Other than the park pigeons, the bird hunting was slow there and we were itching to get back into the field. We'd both put on a few pounds with this sedentary city living and we were well rested, although truthfully I hadn't slept particularly well because of the wailing car alarms that go off all night long on the streets below my in-law's apartment. Sometimes I would get up in the middle of the night and sit in the dark by the window and watch the car burglars at work or the passing gangs of youth or graffiti artists spray-painting on the wall of the building under renovation across the street. There was razor-wire strung up along the second floor so that no one could climb up the scaffolding and gain entrance to the building. It looked just like a war zone.

A short trip to New York can make bird hunting seem like the most sublime, and benign, activity on earth, can't it? I said good-bye to my wife again, and put her on a plane; we'd see each other in a month for Christmas in Florida. Sweetz and I went back to Long Island, collected the camper, and headed south, looking for bird country.

DECEMBER

Florida

Georgia

25

THE COUNT

On one of my excursions I received an invitation to dine at the house of a
rich landowner and hunter, Alexander Mikhailich G——. . . . I put
on a frock coat, an article without which I advise no one to travel, even
on a hunting expedition, and betook myself to Alexander Mikhailich's.

Ivan Turgenev

Before I introduce the Count, let me state this as baldly as possible, for
there's no point in trying to sugarcoat it: For a sportsman in America these
days the next best thing to being wealthy is having a few well-placed
wealthy friends scattered around the country, for the obvious reason that
rich people have access to better sport. This has always been true—the
general rule of thumb under every social, political, and economic system in
history from feudalism to communism to Reaganomics—and never truer in
this country than today.

I offer this preamble by way of introduction to my friend, the Count,
who, as such things go, is the real thing—a wealthy man with grace. No
pretender to the title, the Count grew up on his ancestral estate in France
with a shotgun in hand nearly as soon as he could walk; as a consequence he
handles one as naturally as if it were any other appendage. He was taught to
hunt by the butler at the family chateau, and while still a child participated
in driven estate shoots in France and England, conducted with all the pomp
and circumstance of the days of Lord Ripon—lunch served in the field on
sterling silver platters, wine consumed from goblets. In his mid-fifties now,
tall, lean, and of noble carriage and royally chiseled countenance, full of
generosity and *joie de vivre*, a man who gives and inspires undying loyalty
among friends and retainers alike, a man who loves great food, great wine,
great literature, great women—this is my fine friend the Count.

The Count would have none of Sweetzer and me staying in the camper.

Indeed, I'm not sure he wanted it parked in front of his plantation-style farmhouse in northern Florida. He had me pull it around back, out of sight behind the guest wing of the house, where he insisted we install ourselves. I had made a rule early on in this trip not to stay in anyone's house, but to remain as self-sufficient and unobtrusive as possible. I was beholden enough to all my hunting friends and acquaintances, and friends of friends and friends of acquaintances, and total strangers, for their having taken me afield into their favorite coverts, without the added imposition of also requiring food and lodging (though as the reader knows many of them have also fed me quite lavishly). But the Count insisted, and I was unable to resist his slightly imperious nobleman's manner, the manner of a man who is accustomed to having people do as he wishes. And, of course, I *was* his guest; if the Count wanted us in the guest wing, so be it.

Over cocktails that first evening, the Count expressed his disapproval of my dog's name which evidently didn't translate well to his French ear. "*Sweetzer?*" he asked. "What kind of name is that, *Sweetzer?*"

"She's named after a summit in Idaho," I explained. "Sweetzer Summit."

"But that's the worst name I've ever heard," protested the Count. "I'm going to call her Susie."

"Susie?" I had to draw the line here. Even if I was the Count's guest, I could hardly have him changing my dog's name. "But that isn't her name. Her name is Sweetzer."

"Susie," proclaimed the Count.

"Sweetzer."

"Well, I can't call her that—*Sweetzer.* Here her name must be Susie."

"How about plain old Sweetz? That's not so bad."

"*Sweetz?*" the Count wrinkled his nose. "No, absolutely not. Susie."

"How 'bout Swiss, then, or Swissy?" I offered, in the spirit of compromise. "Sometimes my wife and I call her that at home."

"*Swiss?* God, that's even worse. I *detest* the Swiss."

The Count always keeps his pockets full of dog biscuits for his own two dogs, and during the rest of our visit he tried bribing Sweetzer into changing her name. "Come, Susie," he would call, and when she came to him he generously doled out the treats. He could have called her anything, and Sweetz would still have gladly accepted the Count's offerings. I'm happy to report that the name change did not take; except for at the Count's house, Sweetzer is still Sweetzer.

That first evening, the Count, great gourmand as well as gourmet chef, prepared a simple, hearty dinner for us—plump free-range chicken spit-roasted over the fireplace in his professionally equipped kitchen. With old-fashioned European male sovereignty, the Count had sent the Countess off to visit her family in south Florida for the few days (which would stretch into a week) of my visit, so that we might pursue our sport without the encumbrance of other social or domestic commitments. The Count is distinctly not the sort of person one hears referred to these days as a "nineties kind of guy."

As with Sweetzer's name, the Count also pooh-poohed my genetic intolerance to cholesterol (no royalty coursing through these plaque-choked veins, only death-by-heart-attack in early middle age), dismissing such bourgeoise American dietary nonsense with a regal wave of his arm, the way we commoners shoo flies, as he added an extra stick of butter to his baste, recommending that I drink more red wine as a precautionary health measure.

Bombay gin on the rocks while the chicken turned golden on the spit, a bottle of fine wine with dinner, Calvados in the study afterward, dogs, sated with table scraps, lounging at our feet as we discussed in no particular order sport, art, literature, mutual friends, food, women—this is what I remember of my evenings at the Count's. And a soft feather bed for the night, Susie curled contentedly on the down comforter.

I slept in the first morning, rising briefly after dawn to peek out the curtain at a thick southern mist shrouding the massive live oak trees, which were a deep, deep green, draped in gray Spanish moss. I returned to the decadent comfort of my bed until nearly nine o'clock.

When I went in the kitchen, the maid had finished cleaning our dishes from the night before, and had brewed a fresh pot of coffee. The Count had insisted that I give her my dirty laundry to wash and iron this morning, though I was a bit uncomfortable about that, accustomed as I was to doing my own wash. "Count's up and around," said the maid, whose name was Blanche (the Count pronounced her name in the French manner to rhyme with *launch*, while Blanche said it in American to rhyme with *ranch*), a string bean of a woman, in a starched white uniform; she had short steel gray hair, a leathery complexion, and a nearly incomprehensible deep-South accent, "but he's gone back to his room."

I sat down at the table with a cup of coffee and the newspaper. Blanche was a friendly, chatty sort, and I being the sort of person to whom strangers are never shy about unburdening themselves, it wasn't long before she had engaged me in conversation, even though I had really wanted to read the newspaper.

"Countess says I'm not allowed to talk to Count," Blanche began. "Except to ask him if he needs anything. She doesn't want me to disturb him. So you just tell me to shut up if I'm talking too much." This was a sly way for Blanche to entrap me in a conversation, because I couldn't very well tell her to shut up; it's not in my nature, and she's not even my maid. But now it was too late to take the paper and my coffee back to the guest wing.

"That's all right," I said, "you're not bothering me." I started to read the newspaper.

"You a friend of Count's?" asked Blanche. (She pronounced it *Caaaawwnt*.)

"Yes, I am. I'm visiting for a few days of bird hunting."

"Bird hunting? You know my daddy got shot in the face by our neighbor with both barrels of a twelve-gauge shotgun when I was sixteen years old." Blanche turned to look at me directly, pursing her lips and nodding her head wearily.

"Boy, I'm really sorry to hear that. A hunting accident?"

"Nossir, neighbor shot him because our dogs had got into the neighbor's yard."

"Did it kill your father?"

"Both barrels of a twelve-gauge in the face at point-blank range? I guess it did kill him. Blew his *goddamn* haid clear off."

"Just because the dogs got into the neighbor's yard?"

"Yessir, that's right."

"Boy, I am really sorry."

Blanche sighed deeply. It was clear that she had been much put upon by life, her troubles indelibly etched in an arroyo-like network of lines on her face. I had the sinking suspicion that I was going to hear the cause of each and every wrinkle. "One of my boys got shot, too, a few years ago," Blanche said, nodding. "In a bar fight."

"Oh, no." I wasn't sure I could take Blanche's life story first thing in the morning and I was beginning to understand why the Countess had forbidden her to talk to the Count. "Dead?" I ventured anxiously.

"Just as daid as can be," Blanche said, sighing, her voice trailing off. "Just as daid as daid can be. . . ."

"I'm so sorry. That's really a tough break."

Blanche nodded thoughtfully, a faraway look in her eyes. "Lost one of my little girls, too. . . ."

"Not shot?"

"Oh, no, she was run down by a car. Hit and run. Just a little bitty thing, she was, too."

"*Jesus*, I am *really* sorry to hear that."

"God's will," said Blanche. "God has a plan for us that we can't understand. For each and every one of us. If I didn't have my faith, I wouldn't have been able to live through all the terrible things that have happened to me in my life."

Just then, the Count came in, and Blanche immediately clammed up. "You got some laundry that needs washing you just leave it in a pile on the floor of your room," she told me before withdrawing to the laundry room.

After breakfast, the Count took me on a tour of his farm, pointing out the ongoing quail habitat improvements he was implementing—cover crops, prescribed burnings, plantings of sorghum, lespedeza, and various other food crops. Of all game bird species, bobwhite quail can be managed for most successfully, and what has been lost in so much of the South through the demise of the small farm, and to the attendant sterility of agribusiness—enemy to man and wildlife alike—can be recreated by the private landowner on large or small scale. Consequently, in this region of the country, the best, and in many cases the only, available wild quail hunting exists on the huge "old-line" plantations, or on smaller managed properties such as the Count's. Because quail are also easy to raise, a number of commercial shooting preserves have sprung up throughout the South. Though some boast wild birds, most of them stock domestically raised quail, a pallid imitation of the real thing and about as interesting to shoot as fat, sluggish, hatchery-fed trout are to catch.

The Count's farm was a beautiful place, the perfect marriage of wild and manicured: a long winding, dogwood-lined entrance, passing by a kidney-shaped bass lake on the banks of which sat the Count's art studio (the Count was quite an accomplished painter). A little jetty ran off the porch of the studio where the Count could practice his fly casting (it has been said of the Count, by those who would know, that he is the most consummate amateur sportsman in America, a charmingly anachronistic title these days). Scattered around the property were a number of massive, ancient live oak trees and groomed forests of loblolly and long-leafed pine—classic southern quail habitat—interspersed by gently rolling hills and open fields that had once been under cultivation but have now gone back to native grasses and weeds. Small feed plots for the quail and other wildlife were strategically planted around the property, one end of which was bordered by a dark, damp, wildly overgrown swamp, dense with slash pine and honeysuckle, wild blackberry, and dewberry. Of wildlife, besides quail, the Count's farm held white-tailed deer, wild turkey, the South's ubiquitous feral pigs (whose ancestors were escapees from the original small farms back in the days when everyone raised a few hogs for slaughter), migratory mourning doves by the thousands, and all manner of raptors and birds. It seemed like heaven to me.

The Count had arranged a quail hunt for me the following day on a nearby old-line plantation owned by relatives on his American side, a well-known blue-blood family descended from a famous northern industrialist, and so my first day was spent in leisurely fashion, not hunting, just touring the property—a long walk with the dogs, lunch, reading, a nap. Back in my room all my laundry had been washed and neatly folded in a stack on the bed. Blanche had even ironed my boxer shorts.

The next morning we rose early and after coffee left for the plantation, and an extraordinary day afield.

Horses were saddled and ready when we arrived, a team of mules hitched to the hunting wagon, which was freshly painted a crisp red and white, with forest green upholstery on the seats. The driver, George, was a heavyset black man, while Lonnie, the dog handler, also black, was trim and wiry. Freddy, Lonnie's assistant, a tall, lanky white man with blond hair and mustache, had something of the look of a western cowboy. The dogs, all English pointers, rode in cages beneath the seats of the wagon, while the Count's little English springer spaniel, Laska (named after a hunting dog in Tolstoy's *Anna Karenina*), who would serve duty as a retriever, rode up on the seat beside George. Sweetz had had to stay back on the farm as outside dogs were not allowed on the plantation.

We slipped our shotguns into scabbards on the side of the saddles and mounted our horses. Older hunters or those not inclined to ride horseback may ride on the wagon, but today it was just the Count and I.

This was the classic style of southern plantation quail hunting, as storied in the shooting lore and literature of this region as the tradition of grouse shooting in New England. Though phonied up on some shooting preserves with stocked birds, this authentic form of the sport exists today on only a handful of such plantations. Increasingly, the old-money plantation owners, feeling the heat from all that nouveau wealth, and recognizing the economic potential of their resource, are running their quail hunting operations as commercial ventures. Today, a quail hunt such as this, with wagon, horses, and wild birds, can cost several thousand dollars per gun. Setting out that morning on a hunt that most bird hunters only dream about, I felt more than a little fortunate to be the Count's guest.

It was cool and cloudy and still misty as we embarked, the dogs quartering in front, followed by the horsemen, and the wagon bringing up the rear. The Count's cousin, Laura, who managed the hunting on the plantation, rode with us for part of the morning. She was a young, athletic woman with a wry, amused manner, dressed in jeans and cowboy boots. She wasn't shooting, just spectating. "I like it when the birds get away," she confided to me.

"Then you're going to love the way I shoot."

Two dogs were on the ground at a time, rotated every half-hour. Lonnie controlled them, speaking to each by name, in a soft but authoritative voice. The dogs all had utilitarian names like Buck and Lady, and they seemed to listen to Lonnie, perhaps in part because he had shock collars on them. These he used judiciously, every now and again a little yelp signifying that he had "corrected" one of the dogs, but he didn't need to do so often.

The plantation, over ten thousand acres, was gorgeous, and there was no better way to see it than the leisurely view afforded by horseback, the variations of country unfolding slowly and intimately. One tends to think of Florida in terms of its Gold Coast—crowded highways, sea-level flat, and choked by condominium development. Now the interior of the state has been taken over largely by Universal Studios, Sea World, and, of course, Disney World—tourist country with so much construction going on that the fragile peninsula seems likely to snap right off the mainland and sink in the Atlantic from the sheer weight of concrete and steel. But this was big, expansive, open country we were in today, with nothing to break the horizon but more country. From on high, the hills ran off to Lake Jackson, steel gray in the flat, overcast morning light. Dark, verdant live oaks, hung with Spanish moss, drifted in and out of the mist, while the paler green, soft-needled pine trees had been carefully thinned by prescribed burning so that soft morning light fell all the way to the grassy forest floor. Not a patch of concrete as far as the eye could see.

There is a great deal of country left in America, I was heartened to learn on my trip, and a lot of prime wildlife habitat—although statistics tell us that we are losing nearly half a million acres per year to the growth monster. Much of the best of it, like this, is in private ownership, though even some of that is being chipped away at, especially in such rapid-growth states as Florida. In this plantation country of the panhandle where some massive acreages still remain in relatively pristine condition, rising property taxes or the irresistible carrot of economic enrichment prompt even old-money families to divest themselves of bits and pieces of their land, the pie progressively smaller as chunks are carved from its edges.

But for now, entering this fine landscape to the gentle creaking of a mule-drawn wagon, the easy, rhythmic gait of my horse, gun scabbard slapping time against his flank, it was easy to pretend to a less congested and slower era.

I was jolted out of this reverie when Lonnie, riding in front of us, raised his arm in signal. "Dog says birds there," he announced softly. Indeed, one of the dogs was locked up solidly on point on the edge of a clump of low-growing bushes. "Whoa, Buck," Lonnie said, as the second dog backed the first. The Count and I dismounted, as did Lonnie, flushing whip in hand. I handed my reins to Freddy. Hoping to take my cue from the master, I kept one eye on the Count, who has walked in on thousands of points. He carried

a beautiful little 28-gauge English Purdey double shotgun, worth somewhat more than my home. Lonnie walked up the middle and motioned for
me to walk around one side of the dog, while the Count moved in on the
other. Passing the dog, still locked in a rigid point, Lonnie switched the
grass in front of him with his whip. I was already tightening up, icy sweat
trickling down my ribs, my heart beginning to pound; how I regretted that
second cup of coffee. I sneaked a nervous glance at the Count, who, of
course, was calm and stylish, a slight patrician smile playing at his lips.

Having spent the better part of the past two months hunting the solitary
grouse and woodcock, which generally flush one at a time, I was altogether
unprepared for that first covey rise of the morning, the fabled whirring of
wings that stops the heart and blurs the vision. The birds got up all at once,
like a couple of dozen whirling eggbeaters. I rocked back on my heels and
shouldered my gun, trying to pick an individual bird out of the buzzing
melee. I jabbed my gun at it with no trace of fluidity, discharged my right
barrel, missed, jabbed again, discharged my left barrel, missed. Oddly,
the Count, who almost never misses, also whiffed twice on this first covey
rise; perhaps, anticipating his guest's nervousness and trying to put me
more at ease, he was simply being polite.

"You must have enjoyed that covey rise," I said to Laura, as I slid my
gun back in the scabbard and prepared to remount my steed.

"It was great! I loved it!" she said, enthusiastically. At least I was
ingratiating myself with my hostess.

We broke for lunch at midday, and met the Count's aunt, Laura's
grandmother, at the main plantation house, a huge, imposing, vine-covered
antebellum stone mansion. Mrs. Fitzhugh we shall call her, in the interest
of privacy, a grande dame in the old tradition, certainly the last generation
of such women—gracious, lively, and welcoming, gray haired, fine boned,
impossibly thin with tiny wrists and long, elegant fingers; she wore slacks
and sporty tassel loafers, her ankles as delicate as an egret's legs.

Lunch was served in the formal dining room, where french doors
opened onto a stone patio, an enormous expanse of manicured grounds
slipping away to the lake below. Exotic pigeons smuggled in years ago from
Europe by Mrs. Fitzhugh herself performed tumbling aerial acrobatics for
us above the lawn. I thought way back (another lifetime, it must have been)
to the broken-down trailer of my friend Pigeon Man at home in northern
Colorado—how he would love to see these pigeons, to have a pair. Briefly, I
considered the impracticality of trying to obtain one for him.

Mrs. Fitzhugh rang a small silver bell between courses (the clearest,
most perfectly toned bell I've ever heard), and lunch was served by a
plump, ample-bosomed maid dressed in a crisp white uniform, who looked
(I must say this), exactly like Scarlett O'Hara's maid in *Gone with the Wind*.

There are aspects of the South that take some getting used to and if one mourns the loss of the more gracious, slower-paced "old" South, the days when "cotton was king," one is almost certainly not a black person.

"I went to the doctor the other day for a checkup," said Mrs. Fitzhugh, over lunch. "He poked around for a while, and finally he said, 'You know the only thing I can find in there is that you're full of gin!' " She laughed merrily like a schoolgirl.

Oyster soup was followed by the South's famous dove pie, a salad, and a simple baked apple for dessert, after which Mrs. Fitzhugh took the Count and me on a leisurely stroll down the network of paths through her world-renowned garden, naming the various flowers and plants for us. She picked up a piece of Spanish moss and scraped away the gray sheathing. "You see how it looks like hair?" she said of the thin strand in the middle. "The colored people used to hang this until it dried and then shake it out and use it to stuff their mattresses. And the Spanish used it to pack their household belongings for shipment."

Reluctantly, we took our leave of Mrs. Fitzhugh to head back out to the quail fields and the afternoon hunt, where I hoped to redeem myself. She gave the Count a kiss; it was clear that they were very fond of each other. I thanked her for the lovely lunch and offered her my hand, but she insisted on kissing me, too. I was in love; I wanted Mrs. Fitzhugh to be my aunt.

We put up twelve coveys that afternoon, a superb afternoon of shooting. The Count shot doubles on virtually every covey rise at which we had an opportunity to shoot. The Count is what is known as a "snap" shot, lightning fast and instinctive. It was a marvel to watch him.

And even I began to relax a bit by midafternoon, exhausted finally by my own ineptitude, until I didn't care whether I hit anything or not. The sky had cleared completely, and the afternoon was cool with the lengthening shadows. When the dogs went on point, and Lonnie raised his arm and we dismounted and slid guns from their scabbards and walked up, I no longer felt so tense and out of place, but suddenly a part of the scene, and when the covey got up before us, the whirring rise no longer seemed so frenetic to me, but slower, clearer in my mind's eye; I could actually see each individual bird and pick one out, calmly swing on it, pull the trigger, and watch it fold. I'm not saying I did this on every covey rise that afternoon, but on a few, anyway.

Riding back in at the end of the day, the sun setting before us across the lake, I wondered if Lonnie had ever shot one of these wild plantation quail, thousands of which he must have watched shot over the dogs he trained. I doubted that he had, as quail in the South are strictly reserved for the lords of the manor, for family and guests. I was going to ask him about this as we rode in, about whether or not he ever dreamed of walking in on a point with a shotgun in hand instead of a flushing whip, but I thought better of it. He was a professional and we would leave it at that.

We didn't get back to the Count's farm until after dark. We cleaned our guns in the gun room and took showers, and then we had a drink while we prepared dinner, or rather the Count prepared it and I served as his sous chef. The day's bag was left undrawn in the feathers, placed on the bottom shelf of the refrigerator to age for several days. That night we ate quail that had already served their time. We drew and plucked the birds and the Count browned them quickly in butter, stuffed them with veal sweet-breads, and roasted them in a very hot oven, serving them with a delicate game sauce.

26

THE SPORTING LIFE

While they [the shooters] were both talking, Laska [the dog], pricking up her ears, looked up at the sky and then at them, full of reproach.

Now's the time they've found for chattering, she thought, and here they come flying. . . . Yes, there it is, they'll miss it, thought Laska.

But just then they both suddenly heard a piercing whistle that seemed to flick them by the ear; they both seized their guns, there were two flashes of lightning, and two shots rang out at the same moment. The high-flying snipe folded its wings instantly and fell into a thicket, bending down the slender young shoots.

"Wonderful! Both of us got it!" cried Levin, and ran off to the thicket with Laska to look for the snipe. . . .

"Got it? There's a clever dog," he said, taking the warm bird out of Laska's mouth and putting it inside the gamebag which was almost full. "I've found it, Stiva!" he called out.

Leo Tolstoy, ANNA KARENINA

For the next several mornings, the Count and I would walk out the front door with guns and dogs, to hunt the quail on his property—a splendid thing, indeed, to walk right from the house first thing in the morning with gun in hand and the dogs racing excitedly ahead. The mornings were cool, wet, and foggy, the fog burning off fast as the sky reddened to the east with the rising sun; beautiful days walking through the misty forest at dawn with the Count, his Purdey in the crook of his arm, Laska and Sweetzer at heel, and Belle, the Count's little English pointer, hunting out in front. Through the forest, across fields and clearings, Sweetzer's coat wet with dew, sleek as a seal's, brown fall seeds stuck to her yellow head; skirting the swamp, the lush jungle sounds of the waking birds, the warmth of the morning sun cutting the dampness.

In the afternoons, the Count organized dove shoots for my amusement on one of his several dove fields, inviting six or eight guests in what is a venerable and rather more democratic tradition in the South than quail hunting. Often the larger dove shoots are also social events, followed by barbecues and dances, but in this case, they were small, impromptu affairs, with only a few shooters—the Count's farm manager, a tiny, sinewy little man named Billy Black; Billy's cousin, and near twin in stature, Bully Black; and another local plantation manager, a somewhat dour old fellow, known as Mr. Christian—in attendance.

An elaborate southern-style etiquette governs the dove shoot—the choice spots in the dove field (those that provide the greatest number of incoming birds) awarded to the best shooters, or to those to whom the host might owe a favor. At the same time, there is a certain spirit of reciprocity to the southern dove shoot and the host can expect to be invited to his guests' dove shoots.

By definition dove shooting is just that—shooting rather than hunting. The shooters are stationed at different positions around the field, dressed either in camouflage or muted-colored clothes. They kneel or sit on stools, trying to remain as motionless as possible so as not to flare the birds when they come in. The doves have rather predictable eating habits, and generally come in at regular times (morning and evening) to feed in the fields, which are planted by the landowner in various favored dove foods—brown-topped millet, corn, sunflowers. Doves are fast, tricky flyers, who seem literally able to dodge buckshot in the air, and one bird in hand per four shells fired is considered a respectable average. First-rate dove shots such as Mr. Christian might do considerably better than that average, while a poor shot such as your narrator might go no better than one for ten. Or worse.

Once, a few years ago, I was invited by another of my friends on a white-winged dove shoot in Mexico, where it's nothing to shoot four boxes—a hundred shells—in well under an hour. Though I tend to be less interested in that kind of volume shooting, doves do offer fine sport in terms of fast-flying, challenging game.

I especially enjoyed watching Mr. Christian and the Count shoot doves—two entirely different styles of shooters. Mr. Christian, given the position of honor in the field that day, was a distinguished gray-haired gentleman with a wide, stern, down-turned mouth who looked rather like a vaguely reprobate old-style politician. Dressed head to toe in camo, he sat on one of those special camo dove buckets with a camo swivel seat. He never stood up to shoot, but rather pivoted like a gun turret on a tank, giving him a full 360-degree shooting radius. And he was deadly, a whirling dervish, spinning and firing, doves tumbling; he rarely missed.

The Count, in contrast, knelt in the field or sat on his haunches, motionless until the birds were in range, then very quickly and with his inimitable form standing and leaning elegantly forward to take his shot. He had Laska retrieving for him, and Mr. Christian also had a springer, which make excellent dove field dogs. At the other end of the field, I was stationed with Sweetzer, who had never been on a dove shoot before and, as is often the case with young dogs, got a bit overly agitated when the birds started coming in and the shooting began. She grew quickly frustrated with the spotty performance of her own shooter and kept looking longingly across the field at all the birds raining from the skies around Mr. Christian and the Count and their busy springers. Finally, she could take no more of it, and broke at a dead run across the field, deserting her master for the promise of more steady retrieving work with them. It was the ultimate indignity, abandoned by my own dog—embarrassing, too. I called and whistled for her, but she pretended not to hear. *"You cheap slut!"* I hollered after her. Fortunately, Laska had no intention of sharing retrieving duties with this ill-mannered interloper and promptly chased Sweetz off the first bird she tried to pick up. Too timid to try it again, she came slinking back to me then, tail tucked between her legs. Now it was my turn to ignore her.

That night for our dinner the Count grilled doves, brushed with a simple baste and cooked to perfection, *au point,* as all red-meated fowl should be eaten. Exquisite!

Out the Count's back door, near the bass pond, was a smaller dove field where we shot one afternoon. I was positioned on one end of the field, next to a large live oak tree, its canopy of leaves shading me and partially hiding me from incoming doves, the Count at the other end. I had noticed before that the Count had a habit of warming up before a shoot by mounting his gun and swinging it, first left and then right, his barrels cleaving the air in incredibly fast, precise arcs, as fluid and deadly as a martial arts move. Then he sat back on his haunches, and right afterward, a lone dove came in over him. He stood with his straight, thin, elegant posture, leaning forward slightly on the balls of his feet, and raised his gun, late afternoon sunlight glinting off the barrels. He fired and the dove folded, and many seconds later his spent shot came trickling down through the leaves of the live oak tree I was standing under on the opposite end of the field; it fell overhead like a fine rain.

The next day we were invited to a dove shoot back on the big plantation; it was so big that the entrance to the dove field at which we were told to meet was off an entirely different highway, miles from where we had gone for the quail hunt a few days earlier—a truly "western" distance.

It was a very pretty dove field, surrounded by pine trees, and the shooters ringing the field were primarily young men—Mrs. Fitzhugh's grandchildren and their guests—down visiting for the Christmas holidays from college and boarding school. A few of them were slightly older, in their early twenties, recent college graduates with starter jobs at the family estate offices in New York, or at "Uncle Bill's" office on Wall Street. They were all extremely pleasant young men, good-looking, well brought up, and very sophisticated. In spite of their tender ages, they already knew the best restaurants in Paris, their conversation studded with references to $1,000 dinner tabs at the Closerie des Lilas, they'd shot driven grouse and pheasant in Scotland, white-wing doves in Columbia, and guinea fowl in Africa.

It was an unusually slow dove shoot, and I sat beneath a pine tree, quite content to watch the afternoon light soften, the colors deepen. Turkey buzzards circled lazily overhead, while ducks hurried purposefully by in formation. I watched them set their wings in unison and quickly lose altitude, dropping behind the trees to land in the lake on the other side. Clouds of busy blackbirds flew over the field, the thin high cirrus clouds taking on definition with the setting sun. I may have dozed off for a few minutes. I did not fire my gun.

The shoot was declared officially over, and we walked back to the vehicles. Apologies were issued for the lack of doves; no one likes to put on a bad dove shoot. One of Mrs. Fitzhugh's grandsons invited us back the following morning for a "driven coot shoot."

"It may be the only driven coot shoot in America," he said proudly. I'd never heard of a driven coot shoot, and asked him to describe it to me. Evidently, the shooters are paddled and poled around the lake by local black men from the plantation. "It's wonderful to talk to these people," said the young man earnestly. "It's very interesting culturally." The coots are herded by the boats into a corner of the lake until they start to fly and the shooting begins. "It's a slaughter," the Fitzhugh boy admitted, his brow knitted thoughtfully. "That bothers me a bit. It's not fun if you're not into slaughter."

"You don't eat the coots, do you?" I asked.

"Oh, God, no, they're terrible to eat! We give them to the colored people."

The Count and I declined the kind invitation; it was clearly a young man's sport (although I've since learned that there is such a title as World Coot and Crow Champion, a title actually held by a grown man). Heading back to the farm, we pulled off the plantation road onto the highway, and passed a pull-off down by the river. It was Friday afternoon and several vehicles were parked there, a group of young black men standing or leaning against the cars, drinking beer on this balmy southern evening. They all wore blue service station attendant uniforms with their shirttails out. They must have all worked at the same place and had just gotten off for the weekend; they were laughing and talking and having a fine time. They might have been a group of young stockbrokers in the city meeting for Friday Afternoon Club, and I knew their conversation was equally universal—money, weekend plans, women. For some reason, after our afternoon dove shoot on the plantation with the children of America's ruling class, it made me happy to see these working men drinking beer and enjoying themselves down by the river. And though I knew I would never fit in, I wished I could join them for a beer. Maybe I could get a good coot recipe.

Early the next morning I met a fellow named Ben Boynton in a cafe in Havana (pronounced by the locals *Hay-vana*), Florida. Boynton was a solid, round man, with short, strong arms, a round belly and round face, small, close-set round eyes, and a thick "cracker" accent. Friendly and easy-going, a local boy without artifice, Ben was what is sometimes referred to as a "good ol' boy," and I say that without prejudice.

Though I love the Count and had immensely enjoyed all our hunting together, sometimes it's nice to go out in the field with someone who grew up locally, who shoots a pump gun, and has a "couple a bonehaid dawgs, cain't smell shit, no sense a-tall," as Ben described his own hunting dogs in a moment of pique. Freckles and Lacey, they were called, a male Brittany and female English setter respectively. I had Sweetz with me.

After breakfast in the cafe, I followed Ben into the country outside town to an old abandoned farm that had originally been farmed for shade tobacco, from which cigar wrappers were made. There were several huge, falling-down tobacco barns on the property, but the land had long been "layed out" as Ben put it, meaning no longer in production.

We parked our vehicles next to one of the barns, unloaded the dogs, and let them run around for a few minutes to do their business and get acquainted before setting out. Ben and I took pees by the truck, while Freckles tried unsuccessfully to mount Sweetzer.

"That dawg always got pussy on his mahnd," Ben said, shaking his head. "If he don't behave himself, I might have to peel him down. You know what I'm sayin'?"

As a boy, Ben had worked on this farm in one of the tobacco barns for twenty-five cents a day, back in the days "when tobacco was still king around here"—hard work, ten hours a day, hanging up the tobacco leaves to dry from hooks on the rafters of the barn. Children were used for this operation because they could scramble up on the rafters.

Ben showed me his very first shotgun, which his daddy had given him when he was a boy and which he still kept in his truck for his own son; it was an old Stevens single-shot 12-gauge hammergun. We set out down an overgrown farm road.

I enjoy hunting abandoned farms; they provide some of the best natural game bird habitat, and offer the encouraging sense that the land survives, restores itself in its own good time. The reclaimed labors of past tenants and owners were palpable in the old crumbling barns and outbuildings, the grown-over cattle pens and loading chutes. Ben knew the country as intimately as only a native can, he knew the flora and fauna as well as any biologist, and he pointed things out to me as we hunted. He showed me a place where feral pigs had been rooting wild turnips from the ground, and he identified the lush diversity of tree and plant species in an ecosystem edging toward the tropical—oak, magnolia, and hickory trees interspersed with palmettos and clumps of the aptly named Spanish bayonet, with its dangerous razor-sharp spines. He showed me the differences between the needles on the three standard southern pine trees—loblolly, slash, and long leaf—and pointed out the yellow-flowered honeysuckle vine, the wild blackberry, and the hog plum ("a sour-assed thing'll turn your mouth inside out"). We saw several species of hawks and flushed a cumbersome blue heron off a tree-shrouded pond.

We were hunting through a patch of coffee weed, a favorite quail food, when Lacey went on point. "Easy, easy, easy, Lacey," Ben cautioned her as we moved in. The covey got up and Ben emptied his gun, all five shots in rapid fire from his pump. "Aw shit," he said, sheepishly, as the birds, all of them, dispersed untouched. "Son of a bitch, I oughta know by now not to covey-shoot like that. You never hit anything that way. You know what I'm sayin'?" Yes, I knew exactly what Ben was saying. We hunted on.

All told we put up six coveys that morning. Several of them flushed wild and didn't present shots, and on those that did neither of us particularly distinguished ourselves. We spotted the last covey of the day before the dogs found them, feeding by the tree line on the edge of a high field. By the time we walked up on them, they had melted into the forest. We followed them in, walking along the edge of the trees, into a dark, old woods that sloped away gently to a tiny fern-covered brook at the bottom. The brook had a sandy bottom and the water was perfectly clear. Freckles went briefly on point but the birds flushed wild, came buzzing up off the forest floor at all directions and angles. It reminded me a bit of grouse shooting, but with a dozen birds flushing in the trees at once. One flew right back over me and I swung my gun straight overhead, almost toppling over backward as I fired, and the bird dropped dead in the brook a few feet behind me. Ben, too, killed a bird on that covey rise in the forest.

I still remember how extraordinary that dead quail looked floating in the gin-clear water of the little brook that flowed through the woods, with the deep green ferns growing along the banks and the perfect sandy bottom. Though between the two of us we had less than one limit, it seemed like a good time to call it a day, and we walked back down the road toward the old tobacco barn.

WILD QUAIL WITH DOMESTIC DUCK LEGS

("Voici une recette pour oiseau," writes the Count.)

Buy a duck, Barbarie by preference but Monsieur Long Island will do. Cut off the legs at the top of the thigh. Carve off the breast and use it the next day to make duck salad or grill it with a cream and poached garlic sauce.

To 2 cups of chicken broth (fresh or the least salty brand available), add a glass of good white wine, 1 large onion cut in two with the skin caramelized in butter and olive oil on both sides in a separate skillet, the duck carcass, carrots, herbs, and whatever else pleases. Cook at least 1 hour, pass through a sieve (mashing the vegetables through) into a fresh pot, and reduce the stock down to half a glass.

Separate the legs from the thighs and brown the pieces in the skillet used for onion. Puncture the skin of the duck a few times to release its fat. Cook for about 10 minutes. Do not overheat. No smoke!

Move the duck pieces to a cast-iron casserole along with a peeled apple cut into thin sections. Add to the casserole a small bay leaf and a pinch of thyme (if not already used in the stock), along with half a glass of port.

Cook 4 plucked quail (trussed, if you have the patience and know how) in the same skillet for 5 minutes, or until they look like little brown frogs. Add them to the duck legs, pour in 2 shots of brandy, heat, flame, and when the fire is out pour in the reduced stock. Bring to a boil, cover the casserole, turn the heat to low, and cook for about 10 minutes. Degrease the sauce and serve *les oiseaux* with glazed carrots for color, a green salad, and french bread for the jus. A Merlot will do nicely if you can't afford French wine. Ho!

27

TWO COUNTRY GENTLEMEN

I have already had the honor, kind readers, of introducing you to several of my neighbors; let us now seize a favourable opportunity (it is always a favourable opportunity with us writers) to make known to you two more gentlemen, on whose lands I often used to go shooting— very worthy, law-abiding persons, who enjoy universal esteem in several uyezds [counties].

Ivan Turgenev

I had another friend in this Florida/Georgia plantation belt, Guy de la Valdène, a half-Frenchman himself (but unlike the Count, thoroughly Americanized) and a cousin of the Count's, although the two had a bit of a falling out a few years ago over an incident with a bird dog. This is another story altogether, and not mine to tell—let it only be said that it very nearly came to a duel, which is how people of the Count's position like to settle disputes. (The Count is always threatening to "cane" miscreants, or anyone with bad manners, for that matter, a wonderfully archaic practice which has fallen into some disuse in this country and which in the opinion of the narrator could stand reviving; the Count once actually did cane a tradesperson simply because the man called him "pal").

De la Valdène is the author of a fine book about woodcock (*Making Game*), a world-class wing shot, a superb game cook, and a gentleman sportsman of the first order. It's a shame that he and the Count are no longer speaking because they have much in common, right down to the royal blood in their veins. I had hoped that I might be able to get them together for a hunt during my visit to the region, and possibly even effect a reconciliation, as they are both good friends of mine, but now neither of them will have anything to do with the other. They are both stubborn men.

De la Valdène, too, grew up with a shotgun in hand, and is also a very stylish, snap shot. He was once described to me by the novelist Tom

McGuane (no slouch himself in the nimrod department) as "the best wing shot on rising birds that I've ever seen and I've seen a truckload of them." Having, myself, seen a fair-sized truckload of shooters on this trip, and having hunted with at least a half dozen truly superb shots, I concur with this assessment. While I'd never describe de la Valdène as precisely portly, his strong, heavyset build belies his speed; he wields his 28-gauge like a baton, and on a covey rise, would sometimes have two birds down on the ground while I was still mounting my gun. He was the fastest shot I'd ever seen.

On the day in question, de la Valdène and I drove to Thomasville, Georgia, the heart of plantation quail country, for a hunt with his old friend the singer/songwriter Jimmy Buffett, who leases a farm there.

Buffett lived in a huge old log house on the farm with a long, wide front porch overlooking an expanse of deep green lawn shaded by stately live oak trees. It promised to be a warm day, and we set out early, the seemingly constant morning mist in this part of the country just beginning to burn off.

Jimmy Buffett is a pleasant, cheerful, unpretentious man of great energy, talent, and many interests, to which more recently he has added game bird shooting. If one is going to take up such a pursuit in middle life, and money isn't a problem, it can help a lot to acquire a couple of professionally trained bird dogs, which Buffett had done—a handsome male English springer spaniel, named Spring, and a chubby female German shorthair, named, inexplicably, Biff. De la Valdène had a sister to Spring, Robin, and an English pointer, May. I had Sweetzer with me. This gave us collectively, one Lab, two springer spaniels, a German shorthair, and an English pointer; we had the bases covered.

I was really hoping that Sweetz wasn't going to embarrass me in front of all this professionally trained canine talent. She and I been having some difficulties of late, especially since we'd hit quail country. Having cut her teeth as a flushing dog and fresh off a couple of months of grouse hunting, she was having trouble adjusting to being at heel while the pointing dogs did the actual hunting and her own duties were restricted to retrieving. Impatient at heel, she wanted to hunt, and was constantly trying to slip away and get in on the action. Worse, after a few hunts with the Count and his pointer, with Ben Boynton and his dogs, and then with my friend de la Valdène and his, she had figured out what another dog on point indicated—that there were birds on the other end. Being still young and overenthusiastic, she hadn't quite gotten the idea that she was supposed to wait for the shooters to get into position before she flushed the birds. She had taken to watching the pointers very closely from her position at heel and when they locked up she would break, ignoring my commands to stop and racing off to jump in the middle of the covey. This is not a quality in a flushing dog likely to endear its master to serious quail hunters with finely tuned pointers, and can make hunting invitations dry up altogether.

We hunted first through a fire-thinned loblolly pine forest, with strips of brown-topped millet planted in clearings or along the edge.

Three can be a crowd in upland bird hunting, requiring particular vigilance of the man in the middle, whose shooting window is restricted to a fairly narrow corridor down the middle. In many cases it's easier, and safer, for the third man to lag behind the other two, taking birds that fly back over their heads. De la Valdène, above and away the best shot of our group, generally took this rear position while Buffett and I walked abreast.

Guy's little pointer, May, was working beautifully. The day before he had been so exasperated with her habit of hunting too far out, busting coveys out of range, and not coming back in when called that he had seriously considered giving her away. In fact, he had offered her to me. De la Valdène has somewhat of a temper, but he is also a great dog lover and won't have any of his bird dogs live in kennels. He believed that if a dog slept in his bed with him, she would also hunt for him, the kind of bonding between man and dog that can't take place with kennel dogs. Nor had he ever used an electronic shock collar on little May, either. He abhorred the idea—that is, until yesterday, when, driven to the point of desperation by her antics, he had put a shock collar on her for the first time, turned it down to the lowest setting, and when she got out too far and ignored his command to come around, hit the button. May yelped once, more in surprise than in pain, and immediately came back in to him, and had hunted perfectly ever since. "Well, so much for letting them sleep in bed with you," de la Valdène had remarked philosophically. "All she really needed was a little juice!"

For her part, Buffett's shorthair, Biff, was a well-trained, naturally close-working dog, and Robin and Spring stayed obediently at heel. Sweetz, too, seemed to be taking their cue, heeling nicely today, at least until the first time she saw Biff lock up on point. True to recent form, she broke and ran. I blew my whistle for her to stop; I hollered. She ignored me, leaping in front of Biff before we were able to get into shooting position, her head held high, proud, and alert in anticipation of the flush, chest bulled forward. Then birds were flying everywhere, and I was alternately issuing apologies and yelling at Sweetz, who had just earned a new nickname from an amused Buffett: Csonka (after the famed Miami Dolphin fullback, Larry Csonka, whose posture going up the middle, I admit, she resembled).

Then we dropped down out of the pine forest into a low-lying bottom along a spring, a tangled undergrowth of cover, and a different ecosystem altogether, vivid and lush after the spare simplicity of the forest above. The foliage was so thick that we could barely see one another and had to keep in voice contact. A covey of quail got up in the middle of it, in a confused, staggered rise. I heard Guy fire his gun from the other side of the thicket and thought I saw a high bird go down behind me out of the corner of my eye. He immediately came around to look for the bird as he thought he had only broken a wing, and this would be difficult terrain for the dogs to track a running bird. Sweetz partially redeemed herself by suddenly appearing from the undergrowth with his bird in her mouth.

We climbed up out of the bottom to gain higher ground again and almost immediately flushed another covey, the birds coming up in a tight cluster this time, fanning out from beneath a small bush which the dogs had each investigated in turn, but all passed by. The quail must still have been on their roost under the bush (in disk formation, like spokes of a wheel, tails touching and all members of the covey facing outward to guard against predators), and they hadn't put out enough scent for the dogs to find them. Buffett and I both whiffed on the covey rise while de la Valdène shot a quick, tidy double behind us. Again Sweetzer made a smart retrieve on one of the birds, relearning the unfortunate lesson that my companion's gun was usually more productive than my own.

Some days the birds fly for you, and other days they don't. I was finally becoming philosophical about this shooting business and had decided at the same time that there is a certain amount of luck, or at least good fortune, involved in bird hunting and, as in life, some people are blessed with more of it than others. My friend Collector has a wonderful way to rationalize missed shots: "It was not that bird's day to die," he will say, which neatly lets the shooter off the hook re his own incompetence, while putting the matter squarely in the hands of a higher power (and one with a native American sensibility to boot). And on this day, the birds did not fly for me, and for those few that did, it was not their day to die.

It was getting hot by midmorning and we were thinking about quitting, walking along casually chatting, and as usual, I wasn't paying the attention I should have been to the hunting. I had stopped to make some remark and when I resumed walking, my next step was like stepping on a land mine of birds; they came up directly under my feet, the sound of buzzing wings nearly overpowering; I felt the wind from their wings on my face. It gave me a kind of vertigo, this closeness, a thrill so intense and immediate that I simply laughed out loud and never did discharge my gun. Later, I would relive the rise at my leisure, in slow motion; if I could shoot in retrospect, I would never miss, I'd shoot doubles every time.

We hunted up the singles then, and several got up behind me. I didn't have a shot but I turned and had a wonderful vantage point of de la Valdène, backlit by morning sun, shooting a difficult double on either side of him, sunlight sparking off his barrels. Buffett fired just a split second later, but it was clear to me that Guy had killed both birds. I began to congratulate him on the beautiful shooting, but he quickly silenced me with a look, and let Jimmy claim the second bird as his. "Well done!" de la Valdène congratulated him. It was a fine gesture of sportsmanship that reminded me of Charles Gaines in New Hampshire, and made me think back to a few birds I had shot over the last several days in Guy's company, and wonder how many of them he may have shot for me, always adding "Well done!" "Nice shot!" "Good boy!" so polite and convincing that one began to feel like a competent sportsman after all.

We decided to call it a day then. We had seven birds in the morning's bag among the three of us, and if the truth be told, which it will here, de la Valdène had shot all seven of them, with seven shells. But Jimmy Buffett was very pleased; he walked back to the car with a new jaunty bounce, a confidence in his step. "You know," he said, "I'm real pleased with that last shot I made!" The next day, he shot beautifully.

28

A BRIEF
CHRISTMAS TALE

*Day after day I went up into the hills, Aesop at side; and I wished for
no more than to be able to go there day after day, although the ground
was still half covered with snow and soft ice.*

Knut Hamsun

At a Christmas Eve party in south Florida, I got to talking with a woman
who had recently returned from safari in Africa. She had done some bird
shooting while there. She told me that they use Masai warriors as bird
retrievers. "They don't have anything to do," the woman explained (the
Masai warrior business is slow in these postcolonial days). "They just hang
around camp all day, and so they're quite happy to retrieve birds for you. I
had a wonderful Masai named Mubu. He just loved my tennis shoes; I gave
them to him before I left. They wear strips of tire rubber on their feet for
shoes. I'm not a very good shot," the woman admitted, "and I kept
winging the birds and off Mubu would go . . . it was extraordinary to see
this huge Masai warrior running through the bushes after the birds."

The Florida Gold Coast is no place, finally, for a bird hunter, or a bird dog
either, and besides the pleasure of seeing my wife (Sweetzer's mistress) for
a few days, both the dog and I were itching to be off again. My wife waved
us away on the day after Christmas; we had a lot of country to see yet and
couldn't seem to stop moving, driving north, hanging a left at the top of
Florida, pointed west again to complete the loop we had begun four months
earlier, heading toward home. Our driving days had settled into a predictable routine: before departure, Sweetz would sit alertly in the passenger seat
staring out the window until I got in and turned the key; this seemed to

serve as a signal, a kind of soporific, and she would curl up on her seat or stretch across it with her head on my lap, promptly falling asleep, not to regain consciousness until the engine was turned off again—whether it be five minutes or five hours later. Labs are championship sleepers and they generally travel easy in cars, but I never said they offered much in the way of company on the road. Still, there was something comforting about her rhythmic snoring and the feel of her warm head, heavy as a brick on my lap as the miles rolled away behind us.

On the way through Tallahassee, we spent another night parked at the Count's farm. The Count and Countess were out of town for the holidays and we had the place all to ourselves. It was very peaceful and quiet there, a wonderful change from the crowded, noisy frenzy of the Gold Coast. More than anything, the hunter seeks solitude, and like his prey, fears noise and crowds.

We got up early the next morning to hunt for an hour before leaving for Alabama, where I had arranged to spend a few days in the Mobile Bay area. It felt good to be back in the field at dawn after a few days of holiday inactivity, and it was good to be hunting alone again. I think Sweetz liked it, too; under no subordination to pointing dogs, she was allowed to run out and hunt on her own, without constraints. We were both just happy to be afield on a warm muggy southern morning, a full moon still in the sky and the final night calls of the coyotes receding through the mist that was settled on the ground beneath the live oak trees. Mainly I was taking a leisurely walk with gun in hand, hardly caring if we found birds, and I was somewhat surprised when Sweetz put a covey up right away. I killed one that fell under a massive oak tree. Sweetz gathered the quail in her mouth and retrieved it to hand, and we walked back to the farmhouse, where I made a brief entry in the Count's gun log, changed out of my hunting clothes, and headed for Alabama.

JANUARY

Alabama

Louisiana

Texas

Oklahoma

Kansas

New Mexico

Arizona

29

DR. DEATH
AND THE DELTA

To exterminate or to destroy animals by an invincible and automatic procedure is not hunting. Hunting is something else, something more delicate.

Ortega y Gasset

"You want to take a boat ride out to the delta this morning? See if we can hunt up some snipe?" Jimbo Meador asked as we stood in his driveway on Mobile Bay at 5:30 A.M. on the first day of the new year. The air was cool, damp, and salty. "Or would you rather go quail hunting again?"

"I don't care. Which would you rather do?" I was trying to remember the last time in my life I had been up at this hour on New Year's Day, unless, of course, I hadn't been to bed yet.

"Doesn't make a bit of difference to me," said Jimbo. "You're my guest, you decide. Maybe you'd rather stay home and watch the football games today?"

"Watch the football games? Not a chance! I don't care about the football games. But maybe you'd like to see them?" I decided that I'd never been up at 5:30 on New Year's morning, at least not in my adult life.

"No, not me, I want to hunt."

"Good, then that's settled."

"Just think of all the people who are in bed right now with hangovers," Jimbo said. "And you and I are up and we're going hunting!" Jimbo quit drinking a few years ago and like many ex-drinkers rediscovered a quantum energy level that he applies now primarily to the pursuit of sport. Lean and fit, he has a large bushy mustache, and speaks with a deep-toned, leisurely Alabama accent. Though we had just met a few days earlier, Jimbo and I had several sporting friends in common.

"Now you tell me, which would you rather do," he asked again, "quail or snipe?"

"Well, I haven't done any snipe hunting yet on this trip. Maybe we should try that. And I wouldn't mind taking a boat ride and seeing the delta. On the other hand, I wouldn't mind at all going quail hunting again. Whatever you think, Jimbo. It's your last day of the holidays. You decide." No gentleman sportsman, Jimbo actually had a real job as the manager of a seafood company.

"You want to go snipe hunting? It'll be about a half-hour boat ride. Now it may be a little rough, I haven't looked at the bay yet. But I'm just as happy as can be to do whatever you want to do." Jimbo was the most polite, solicitous host I'd ever seen, but what we needed now was a decision. It was getting cold standing out here in the dark, and I was growing mildly nostalgic for my misspent youth when New Year's morning was passed hunkered down under the covers with the makings of a mighty hangover.

"Snipe," I said.

"Snipe?" Jimbo asked.

"Snipe," I repeated.

"Well, good!" Jimbo laughed. "Thank God one of us finally made up his mind. Otherwise we'd be standing out here the rest of the morning."

A cold ride at dawn, the sky flat and overcast above a choppy gray sea; it was Sweetzer's first boat trip, and she responded to the excitement of the experience in typical Lab fashion by curling up next to me and falling asleep. I think she mistook the boat for the camper. Jimbo got us up on a bouncy plane and we followed the coastline of Mobile Bay up into the delta. He pointed landmarks out to me as we went, his words often snatched away by the wind before they reached me. I nodded blankly and smiled.

A trucker honked and waved as we passed under the bridge of I-10, which spans the bay to Mobile. We ran up into the delta just as the sun cleared the coast. Jimbo dropped the throttle back and we cruised easier in the flatter, more protected waters. Graceful, curve-billed ibis and gangly great blue herons waded the shorelines in motions precise and elegant. Jimbo pointed to a huge flock of white pelicans flying in formation directly overhead, their long black-tipped wings fanning in unison. He had a broad smile on his face, a childlike, mischievous grin under his bushy mustache. He clearly loved the delta with the singular passion and intimacy of one who had fished, hunted, trapped, and wandered this country since boyhood.

"I used to duck hunt out here with my Lab, Eb," Jimbo said. "People always told me that I shouldn't be coming out to the delta alone but that never bothered me. I had duck blinds hidden all over out here. I knew it like I knew my own house. We used to hunt every day. I was absolutely obsessed with duck hunting. It was like an addiction. It got to be a bit of a problem. I actually quit school at one point so I'd have more time to hunt." An osprey winged heavily by, clutching a large fish in its talons. "I don't shoot ducks much anymore," Jimbo added. "Knowing how their numbers have declined, I just don't enjoy it anymore."

Jimbo cut the engine and we drifted up against the grassy shoreline, the quiet sudden and complete. Our wake lapped gently against the shore. The water in the delta was brackish, brown and muddy, ribboned with fingers and spits of land. It had a dank, swampy, fecund smell to it, a wonderful smell.

Sweetzer came alive, leaping eagerly from the boat. The damp richness of the land must have offered a smorgasbord of scent to her canine nose because she raced wildly in circles, snuffing loudly. Then she picked up a scent trail and followed it as if on a mission. Soon she was involved in a face-off with an enormous ratlike creature that snapped at her with vicious clacking teeth. She barked hysterically at the swamp creature, her hackles up.

"What the hell is that?" I asked Jimbo.

"A nutria. You'd better call her off. They can tear hell out of a dog."

Nutria, large members of the rodent family, once popular as women's coats, were introduced to the southern coastal region from South America some years ago in the hopes of creating a new fur industry here. In one of those economic schemes gone awry, the demand for nutria fur dried up, while the rodents proliferated. Now they cause considerable ecological damage to the delta from their habit of digging up the land into a muddy network of channels and burrows. Vain attempts are made periodically to control their ever-multiplying numbers and in the Mobile Bay region a "Nutria Rodeo" is held every year in which the rodents are roped, shot, and otherwise disposed of.

The nutria nipped Sweetz on the nose; she howled and redoubled her barking efforts. I'd never seen her so intent upon tangling with another mammal. Fortunately, the nutria was young and not fully grown, and nearly as timid as Sweetz, or it might have caused more serious harm to her. I finally had to go over with her lead and drag her off like a crazed police dog.

A light drizzle had begun to fall, and the wind picked up. It was shaping up to be a blustery day on the delta. Jimbo and I both donned waders and raingear, then we spread out to work our way across the peninsula. The land was muddy and spongy, dotted with potholes and crisscrossed by nutria trails. Thick yellow winter grass matted the ground, obscuring like booby traps the swamp rat dens. I stepped in one almost immediately, sinking to my hips, mud sucking like quicksand at my legs. Jimbo laughed. I finally had to lay my gun down on the grass and crawl out of the hole on my stomach.

The snipe started flying right away, flushing wild ahead of us, zigzagging on swift crooked wings, flying low and straight away before rocketing

up like tiny jet fighter planes. Their shrill cries drifted on the wind. I
followed Jimbo's lead and knelt in the mud when the birds got up in front of
us; sometimes, gaining altitude, they circled back, presenting a high shot.
But they seemed way out of my range and considerably beyond my skills
and at first I didn't even bother shooting. This was the most difficult game
I'd seen. I watched Jimbo make what looked to me like a few impossibly
long shots. He was another superb shooter.

Sweetz made her first snipe retrieve on a high bird he knocked down,
its flight heavenward suddenly truncated, dead against the gray clouds; we
watched as it fell endlessly from the sky, Sweetzer racing across the delta to
retrieve it. I felt a strange joy in the moment—no sadness, no apology, just
thanks. She delivered the snipe, a slighter, more streamlined version of a
woodcock, lovely little birds with their long beaks and sleek angled wings.

A popular target of nineteenth-century American sportsmen and market hunters, and a favorite table fare of that era, the snipe was gunned
relentlessly until populations became so suppressed that by the 1920s most
states had closed their snipe seasons, not to reopen them again for nearly
thirty years. In many areas, the bird is quite plentiful again, and usually not
hunted much by modern shooters, who have lost the taste for snipe. In this
hunter's opinion, they are fine sport in the field and superb on the table,
though, happily, I don't think they'll ever catch on again in a big way with
the shooting public.

We had a wonderful morning on the delta—the blustery wind and rain,
the snipe flushing wild before us. I floundered in the dank black mud,
soaking wet, alternately laughing and cursing the nutrias. Sweetz made a
couple of good retrieves on birds that fell in the center of potholes too deep
and wide for us to wade; she arced powerfully and purposefully through the
sucking mud to snatch the bird in her mouth, turning ponderously and
making her way back to solid ground, delivering the snipe to hand, and
shaking splatters of mud in my face. Soaking wet, yellow coat black
and sleek with mud, she was beginning to look like a swamp rat herself.

We worked our way out to the channel at the end of the peninsula,
turned, and hunted our way back to the boat against the gusting wind. We
stripped off waders and toweled down guns and I threw Sweetz into the
channel off the bow of the boat in order to wash the mud from her; she hit
the murky water like an anchor, disappearing beneath the surface, dragged
down by her dense Lab bones. Several long seconds passed and for a
moment I worried that she wasn't coming back up, but then finally she
bobbed back to the surface, and I helped her over the gunwale. She was
yellow again.

The wind had shifted and the bay was calmer on the return trip, but we
were wet and cold. I sat on the floor of the boat with Sweetz curled in a

tight shivering ball between my legs. I wedged cold, numb hands under her haunch for warmth. It was not 10:00 A.M. yet and already we'd completed a successful snipe hunt. I thought about all those New Year's revelers just waking up with dreadful champagne hangovers, and I was quite happy to be right here. I dozed for a few minutes, as we planed back across Mobile Bay.

Jimbo and his wife, Lynn, and two teenage children live on the bay in a beautiful old antebellum home, which has been in her family for several generations. Jimbo and I took hot showers at the house, warming our bones and washing away the last of the black delta mud, changed into dry clothes, ate a hot lunch, and by 1:00 P.M. were headed for the quail fields. No sedentary afternoon in front of the television watching New Year's football games for these hunters; Jimbo makes full use of his weekends.

On the way out we stopped off at the farm of a fellow named Orville to inquire about a dove shoot that Jimbo had heard the farmer was holding later that afternoon. As we were driving in, Jimbo explained that Orville's wife had dropped dead suddenly of a brain aneurysm several days earlier. "You mean to say his wife just died," I asked, astonished, "and he's still putting on a dove shoot?"

"Well," Jimbo explained in his slow, wry way, "Ah believe it was already scheduled."

We found Orville in a field working on a tractor. He was a short, heavyset man, with small red-rimmed eyes, who looked a little bit like the cartoon character Elmer Fudd. "Let me tell you something about *duuvs*," Orville said to me, grasping me firmly by the elbow and leaning in close; possibly he'd been drinking. Who can blame him?

"The later on in the season," Orville whispered with hot, tangy breath, "the earlier the *duuvs* feed. That's goin' in the book a'm writin' about birds." He relinquished my arm and smiled, nodding sagely.

"*Sumtames* Orville?" Jimbo explained as we drove back out, "is a little bit full a shit."

We decided to skip the dove shoot and spent the rest of the afternoon hunting the edges around small local farms, lovely old-time row cover, the kind of country that used to cover so much of the rural South before the onslaught of agribusiness—strips of live oak trees between soybean and potato fields, dense pocket cover of briars and brambles, old house foundations and ditch banks overgrown in vines—fine, romantic country.

Jimbo had a little English setter named Becky, who hunted beautifully, quartering the cover at just the right range, neither too far out nor too close in. But Sweetz gave me fits that afternoon—winding birds and taking off after them, busting them out of range or jumping in the middle of Becky's points before we were in shooting position. I was really in despair over this new habit of hers and didn't know how to break it.

Jimbo hunted at a steady pace. There are some hunters with whom one falls naturally in step and he was one—a generous hunting companion far less interested in the number of birds killed than in the number of coveys his dog pointed, and in showing his guest the country. Jimbo shot a Model 21 Winchester that had belonged to his father.

On one point, Jimbo sent me in behind Becky while he hung back and held Sweetzer, and afterward he remarked on what a pretty picture it had been: dog on point, shooter silhouetted against the horizon, birds flying. . . . I knew just what he meant. Sometimes it is just as satisfying to watch such a scene unfold as a spectator.

Walking in together on the next point, Jimbo whispered, "Mah damn heart is just pounding!" How many points must he have walked in on in his lifetime, I wondered, and still his heart pounds.

As we were hunting, Jimbo told me that he had recently become very serious about bird watching. He had started a life list and spent hours stalking and observing birds. "It's kind of like hunting," he explained, "except you write them down instead of killing them." Many of the most conscientious bird hunters I know are also dedicated birders; there is no contradiction implicit in this fact.

As we were working the edges of a meadow later that afternoon, we spotted a man across the field, riding along a line of cover in a four-wheel all-terrain vehicle.

"Uh-oh," Jimbo said.

"What's the matter?" I asked.

"Dr. Taylor."

"Who's Dr. Taylor?"

"Dr. Taylor is a local doctor and quail hunter. He drives around the county in a customized truck with dog kennels mounted on the back, pulling a trailer for his ATV. He rotates eight big running pointers, two on the ground at a time, and he follows them on his four-wheeler. When they go on point, he climbs off and shoots the covey rise. Then he hunts down the singles. Dr. Taylor can cover the whole county in a day. Usually he hunts with a partner, a local state trooper. Last year the two of them killed seven hundred and eighty-three quail."

"Seven hundred and eighty-three quail?" The idea that they had bothered to make such a precise tally seemed as inconceivable to me as the total.

We watched Dr. Taylor following the tree line on his ATV, the high insistent whine of the engine drifting ominously across the field. It was a vaguely sinister scene that made my heart sink. This kind of relentless motorized pursuit of game seems to me to badly miss the point of upland gunning.

"We'd better go somewhere else," Jimbo observed, sadly. "You don't want to be hunting behind Dr. Taylor."

A cold front was moving in, the weather taking on a chill wintry feel. The wind had picked up again off the bay, pushing dark gray storm clouds across a white sky. A huge orange sun fell into a gap in the tree line, the short winter wheat in the fields an intensely bright green.

Becky locked up on point, as Jimbo and I walked in on either side of a fence row. The birds came up in perfect unison, the tight covey fanning and banking, sliding away. The twin boom of shotguns reverberated. Becky delivered a crippled quail to Jimbo, who held it to his mouth and severed its spine at the neck with a nip of his teeth, an intimate gesture.

We walked down a red clay farm road between forest on one side and a field on the other. Dusk was coming on. Becky quartered in the forest, her bell sounding, while Sweetz noodled along the side of the road. Then Becky's bell fell silent, signaling a point, and Sweetz winded the birds a moment later, broke from heel, and dove into the forest. I couldn't stop her, and I ran in behind her, to hear the departing wingbeats of the birds she had busted through the trees. Becky hunted up the scattered covey deeper in the woods and Jimbo went in behind her and shot a double while I, losing my temper with Sweetz, angrily performed what the Monks of New Skete refer to in their recently published dog training book as a "takedown." This involved rolling Sweetz over on her back and disciplining her by assuming the role of alpha dog. I don't know if this technique works or not, and I'm not altogether sure about those monks, who, in any case, are obedience trainers of German shepherds, but I was getting desperate about Sweetzer's bad habit and willing to try anything now short of a shock collar. Were it not for my aversion to high technology afield, I might have fried her.

Sweetzer didn't seem to think much of the monks' disciplinary tactic, and didn't seem to take me seriously as alpha dog. She just looked at me wild-eyed and panting from her position on her back, her tongue hanging out the corner of her mouth, and when I let her up she raced off through the trees hoping she wasn't too late to pick up one of the birds that she seemed quite certain Jimbo had down in there. Having seen Jimbo shoot, when his gun went off, Sweetzer looked for dead birds. And as a matter of fact, in this instance, she did find one of his birds in the woods.

And that's how we spent New Year's Day. It was nearly dark by the time we walked back down the red dirt road toward the truck: Jimbo, Jim, Becky, and Sweetz.

That evening Lynn, a schoolteacher and Jimbo's high school sweetheart, served the traditional southern New Year's dinner, which always includes "collard greens for money and black-eyed peas for luck." I figured I could use a little more of both and I ate heartily after our long and varied day afield. A dime is dropped in the beanpot and whoever gets it on their plate can expect a particularly prosperous year, but although everyone had a second helping that evening, the dime never turned up.

The next morning Jimbo and Lynn went off to work, and before I left, I went out to the end of their long dock on the bay to dress a few birds—a wonderful mixed bag of snipe, quail, and doves from our several days of hunting here. The sea and sky were a flat gray as if welded together at the seam, not a breath of wind. I sat with my legs dangling off the dock. Sweetz lay beside me. It began to drizzle lightly. The tide was out and the sea smell of the exposed flats mingled with the deep scent of the birds' intestines: the often indistinguishable scents of life and death the hunter carries in memory.

Later that night in a dark pine forest in a campground outside Baton Rouge, Louisiana, I grilled a pair of snipe over coals and ate them with leftover black-eyed peas that Lynn had presented me as a little gift for the road.

I put the lucky dime in my totem bag.

GRILLED SNIPE

(Any recipe for dove or woodcock is suitable for snipe, and the simpler, the better.)

Grill over a hot fire for 6–8 minutes, rolling frequently, and basting with butter (or olive oil), Worchestershire sauce, ground pepper, and lemon juice.

30

EVANGELINE

"Allow me to introduce myself," he began in a soft and insinuating voice. "I am a hunter of these parts—Vladimir. . . . Having heard of your arrival, and having learnt that you proposed to visit the shores of our pond, I resolved, if it were not displeasing to you, to offer you my services."

Ivan Turgenev

I stopped to eat crayfish at a cafe in Lake Arthur, Louisiana, and as I was looking the menu over, an enormous Cajun fellow who must have weighed close to four hundred pounds came through the door, assisted by two tiny identical Latin women. The twins, like little bookends, walked on either side of the huge man, holding his arms and supporting his vast bulk into the cafe. He was short of breath and wheezed thickly.

After the twins had negotiated their companion to a table and seated him in a chair, he said to one of them, for no apparent reason, "You know, you're a *real* pain in de ass." The little twins looked at each other with dark twin regards and began to chatter together in Spanish, obviously discussing their companion. "You shud da hell up now, you two, awright?" said the Cajun. The women looked at each other again with those same inscrutable regards and fell silent.

I was sitting at a table next to them and the Cajun turned in his chair in the ponderous manner of seriously overweight people to face me. The motion seemed to cost him a great deal and he breathed heavily from the exertion. He looked at me for a long while before he could speak. Folds of fat on his forehead hooded his eyes, which were small and mean.

"Dat your rig out dere wit de Labrador dog?" the Cajun asked me.

"That's right."

"Dat Lab a duck dog?"

"Sure."

"My name is Rober' Evangeline. This heah is Rosa and Theresa. How you like to come out duck hunting to my place? Got a lake and plenty ducks."

"Thanks, but I'm headed for Texas. I'm going to do some duck hunting there."

"Texas? We got just as many ducks right heah. Why you goin' to Texas? You come out to my place. I show you ducks. I got a lake and plenty ducks but no dog to retrieve dem. You come out dere dis afternoon, bring dat dog, and we shoot some ducks, awright?"

I looked beyond the big Cajun to the little twin, Rosa (or maybe it was Theresa), behind him. Her brow was knitted in consternation and she was shaking her head vehemently at me.

"Uh, I really don't think so," I said, puzzled.

"Dat dog prob'ly ain't no duck dog. Dat dog prob'ly don't know how to retrieve at all," scoffed the Cajun.

"She knows how to retrieve just fine," I said, rising to the bait. Rosa and Theresa were whispering together again in Spanish. I got the feeling that Rosa was translating for her sister. Soon they were both looking at me with knitted brows, shaking their heads. I was getting a little uneasy. I ordered my crayfish and a bottle of long-neck Dixie beer. Rober' ordered two fried seafood platters for the three of them, but when the platters arrived the waitress set both down in front of him.

"You shud up, you two, awright," he said to the twins every time they started speaking in Spanish. I really wished I spoke some Spanish so I knew what they were saying. Rober' sighed deeply. "I can't shoot all dem ducks at my place no more," he said sadly, his back to me now as he ate his lunch, "because I got no dog to retrieve dem. Sometimes I make de girls paddle out in de boat and pick dem up, but it ain't de same as a having a duck dog. Oh, I love a good duck dog."

"Why don't you get one, then?" I suggested.

"Had me a good old dog, but he died," Rober' said, mournfully. "Maybe you let me just borrow dat dog of yours dis afternoon for a couple hours, awright?" Now Rosa was really shaking her head. I was wondering if maybe Rober' was a dognapper.

"Not a chance."

I got up to go to the men's room, and when I came out, the waitress was waiting by the door. "You don't want to go out to Evangeline's place to duck hunt," she whispered. "And you especially don't want to take your dog out there."

"Why not?" I asked.

"Gators," she said. "He's got a lake full of gators. He used to have a bunch of dogs out at his place but the gators got every one of them. Now he tries to get other people to come out hunting with their dogs but everyone around here knows about Evangeline's gators. Sometimes he gets a stranger like you to bring their dog out there to retrieve ducks for him. Gators get 'em every time. Pull 'em right under the water when they're swimming out to get the ducks. Evangeline thinks it's a big joke."

Sweetz and I didn't go duck hunting in Louisiana.

31

DUCK DOG

Although wild ducks offer no special attraction for a genuine sports-man . . .

Ivan Turgenev

I don't know at exactly what point on the road it stopped feeling like the South and began to feel like the West again. It was nothing as tidy as the Texas/Louisiana border, I know that; it was past Orange and Beaumont, which still have a distinctly antebellum feel to them; it was somewhere west of Houston, I'm going to say, say around Egypt, Texas, where the driver of a pickup truck flashed the index-finger salute as we passed—that's when I knew for sure that I was back in the West.

There are upland bird hunters and then there are waterfowl hunters. Which is not to say that upland hunters don't sometimes enjoy waterfowl hunting and vice versa. But the two are often very different breeds altogether, and a hunter truly adamant about one of these forms of gunning is likely to have only a lukewarm interest in the other. Thus, the reader has undoubtedly noticed by now that this is primarily an upland book, the narrator's own interest in waterfowl hunting tending toward the lukewarm. I like the motion involved in upland gunning, the walking and physical exertion, and I like the country. And though I love to eat ducks and geese, I don't much care for freezing my ass off in duck blinds, or for the general physical inactivity of the sport, which is certainly more of a shooting than a hunting sport.

At the same time, it strikes me that ducks have enough troubles these

days, given the continuing loss of wetlands and steadily declining populations, and under the circumstances it seems almost painful to shoot them
now. I think they need a break. (As with upland species there is considerable disagreement among experts and hunters alike whether or not gunning
pressure has an appreciable effect on duck populations. But that's a story for
a waterfowl aficionado to explore. For now, suffice it to say that if our
political representatives, including the man in the White House, were less
spineless on the issue of wetlands protection, and land and agricultural
developers less insatiable in their need to fill and drain wetlands, ducks
would not be in their current dire straits.)

All of that said, I think there ought to be one duck hunting chapter in
this book, and in any case, I couldn't take a trip of this nature, or pass
through the state of Texas for that matter, without making a hunt with my
old friend Barney Donnelley.

Whereas the Count is an upland hunter who occasionally hunts ducks,
Donnelley, a world class shooter in his own right, is a duck hunter who under
duress will hunt upland birds. He's the duck huntin'est gentleman I've ever
known, his lifelong passion for the sport having survived a bout with obesity
in his twenties, the attendant triple bypass surgery in his thirties, and four
marriages in as many decades. Now in his mid-fifties, Donnelley has two
new young daughters by his fourth and (I'm going to take a chance here)
final wife. Still, I know where to find him during duck season: neither the
constraints of illness, children, matrimony, or the end of matrimony can
keep him from his appointed place; in the past thirty-six years during the
duck season, he has spent no less than twenty-five days and, barring major
life-threatening surgery, up to forty-five days in a duck blind. He divides his
hunting time between southern Illinois, where he has belonged for years to
one of the oldest duck clubs in the country, and Texas, where he owns a ranch
near Garwood, in the heart of Texas waterfowl country.

I got lost driving into Donnelley's place, but having been lost on back roads
in every region of America, I had grown somewhat sanguine about it,
knowing that in spite of the temporary frustration involved, I would eventually be found again. So I stopped at dusk to reconsult my directions, and
then retraced my steps down county roads, farm roads, and section roads,
recounting the tenths of miles past silos, grain elevators, abandoned farmhouses, all of it somehow familiar in the common landscape lexicon of rural
America.

The country here was flat and wet, and incredibly rich with waterfowl.
Enormous flocks of geese and ducks passed overhead in the evening
twilight, while great blue herons and sandhill cranes lifted up out of grain

and rice fields as I drove by, the ponderous breadth of their wingspans offering the illusion of slow-motion flight.

It was dark by the time I finally drove into Donnelley's ranch—right where he said it would be, after all—down a long, winding entrance lined by live oak trees. Their limbs scraped the camper, while numerous pairs of yellow eyes gleamed in the headlights. Wherever there is an abundance of game, there is a corresponding abundance of predators and scavengers—a wild and perfect profligacy of life—deer, rabbits, squirrels, ducks, geese, coyotes, foxes, raccoons, hawks, owls, buzzards, snakes. Any country with game is good country for all.

I arrived, propitiously, just in time for a duck dinner. I have known Barney Donnelley for twenty-five years, and in that time have eaten hundreds of game dinners in a half dozen of his various residences with each of his four wives, but in all those years, I had never gone duck hunting with him. I don't know how to explain this, other than that earlier I had no interest in the sport, and later, even after I took up gunning with some passion, I was never much of a duck hunter.

Barney's son, Reuben, was also visiting for this last weekend of the waterfowl season. We hadn't all been together in some years and it was a treat to sit down at the table with them again. It occurred to me that we had known each other since Reuben was eight years old, I sixteen, and Barney thirty-two. In the strange symmetry and compression of time, and by multiples of eight, Reuben was now thirty-two, I forty, and Barney fifty-six—lifetimes marching by at this table.

Up before dawn and down to the duck pond in the cold, early morning twilight. Bill Hobaugh, Donnelley's ranch manager, had joined us with his young golden retriever, Sonny. Much to her dismay, Sweetzer had been confined to quarters, not allowed to come with us this first morning. She had never been in a duck blind nor retrieved a duck before, and Barney was worried that she might get in the way. In any case, there wasn't room in the blind for two dogs.

We set decoys out on the glassy stillness of the pond and then positioned ourselves on the bench in the blind. Reuben lit a cigarette and Barney packed a wad of Redman chewing tobacco under his lip. I liked the spearmint smell of it and bummed a chew from him.

It was comfortable sitting there in the duck blind, flanked by these old friends. There are things that go unsaid between fathers and sons, subjects better not discussed, opinions best unaired, and it occurred to me sitting there in the predawn silence that the sporting life brings its own solace to such relationships, and that these long quiet periods of inactivity and anticipation—the before and the after—can heal wounds and bridge gaps. I believe that.

We sat in the blind and watched dawn unfold over the duck pond, listening to the rich cacophony of morning bird songs, the deeper background tones of the bullfrogs. We chatted in soft voices, smoked, chewed, and spat streams of tobacco juice into the water.

I asked Barney what it was about the sport of duck hunting that kept him so obsessed over so many years and why he had never developed the same passion for upland shooting. I had asked similar questions of other gunners across the country, and had been surprised by how many of them were inarticulate about their love of sport. It is not something easily defined or explained, even to the hunter's own satisfaction.

"I just don't get the same lift out of hunting upland birds as I do with ducks," Donnelley said. "For me there's a mystique to waterfowl hunting that simply isn't there in upland gunning. I really learned about duck hunting when I went to college in Louisiana and I got to know a lot of Cajuns and Acadians down there; they spoke French and they were trappers and ran trotlines. They were wonderful, interesting, colorful people, who excelled at what they did and who basically lived off the land. Some of them became very good friends of mine. They were superb duck callers. We would hunt the marshes in pirogues. It was very romantic. And it was from them that I learned about the artistry of duck hunting."

The ducks started coming in at daybreak. Barney, who is a master, worked them in expertly with a duck call, while Hobaugh used a whistle, another effective calling technique. The first flock circled, and came back in, setting their wings and gliding in for a landing over the decoys. "Okay," Barney whispered, and we stood up in ambush.

It takes a long time for a duck coming in on final approach with his wings set to reverse direction, to get his wings back under him and lift up again. They are lumbering and vulnerable in this position and after months of upland shooting, seemed like preposterously easy targets. I say this not to denigrate the sport of duck hunting, which is a different kind of art altogether, one of deception in which through the use of decoys, blinds, camouflage, and duck calls, the hunter tricks the birds into coming to him rather than going out in search of the game. But the first time I stood up out of the blind that morning, to see the ducks hovering over the decoys, their breasts exposed to us as if in willing sacrifice, I shot a double, for me the simplest possible litmus test to determine the difficulty of any game shooting.

"Hey, Ferg!" said Reuben, unduly impressed. "When did you get to be such a good shot?"

"Just now, Reub."

Sonny, Hobaugh's young golden, ran up and down the bank; he seemed uncertain about going in the water. Finally, Bill waded out and coaxed the dog in, and between the two of them they retrieved our ducks.

"He's just a young dog," Barney explained.

It is bad manners to run down another man's dog, but Sonny was clearly not a dog who enjoyed his work, and I felt quite sure that Sweetzer, novice or not, could perform at least as well.

A flock of green-winged teal came in next. Serious duck hunters like Donnelley tend to be less interested in shooting teal because they will come into decoys without having to be called. They are one of the more plentiful species of duck and, to this hunter's way of thinking, the most sublime on the table. The teal soared in directly over the blind, banking above us, fixed wings slicing the air with a *whooshing* noise like the Blue Angels in formation, sans engines. I love the sound a flock of teal make on a windless morning at dawn as they bank in unison over a blind, their wings set; and though my heart remains in upland gunning, I will always occasionally be a duck hunter if for no other reason than to hear that sound.

Teal are small ducks and very swift flyers, and a double on flaring teal is a more sporting proposition than one on, say, huge, lumbering mallards hovering over the decoys like tin targets in a shooting gallery. But I did not shoot a double on that first flock of teal that morning because to do so would have put me over my legal limit. I shot one, and thus, ten minutes after dawn on my first morning in Texas, my shooting day was officially over.

As we were picking up our decoys later that morning, I inquired of Bill Hobaugh—who has a doctorate in game biology and is one of the country's foremost waterfowl experts—about the lower daily bag limits on ducks (three per hunter) and whether these might help arrest declining populations.

"The limits are meaningless," Hobaugh said. "They're set low in order to placate the non-hunting public, who want to believe that lowered bag limits can protect waterfowl. The fact is that bag limits have nothing to do with population declines. It's directly a function of habitat loss, specifically the loss of breeding grounds up north."

"Okay, but for the sake of argument, let's say that with ducks already in trouble due to the loss of habitat, gunning pressure at least contributes to declining bird numbers. Other than the outcry from duck hunters, what would happen if you closed the duck hunting season altogether for a few years in order to give the ducks a chance to recover without that added pressure from gunning?"

"I'll tell you exactly what would happen," Hobaugh said. "Without the revenue from duck hunting licenses and waterfowl stamps, state and federal wildlife agencies would lose millions of dollars in funds for wetlands protection and creation. Then, of course, all the funds from Ducks Unlimited, which is the organization that really does more than anyone to fight waterfowl habitat loss, would also dry up—no pun intended—because if they aren't going to be allowed to hunt, a lot of duck hunters would stop contributing their time and money to the cause. So the net result of closing the duck season would be accelerated loss of wetlands and even lower duck populations. In short, it's a lousy idea."

That afternoon, Barney and Reuben went out deer hunting. As I have no interest in deer hunting, other than to eat the proceeds, I was given a sack of decoys and dropped off at another pond with Sweetz. This was to be Sweetz's consolation for having been left behind that morning. Even though I'd already filled my day's duck limit, I was told that at this pond geese were likely to come in. There is a seperate bag limit for geese, which have actually proliferated in the past few years—a great success story in game management—to the point that some golf clubs secretly hire paid exterminators to come in under cover of night and shoot, poison, or otherwise eliminate the geese because the birds poop all over the greens, and golfers hate goose poop on their golf balls. Though I'll kill a goose occasionally to eat, I'd certainly never kill one for pooping on a golf green, and in my opinion anyone who does should be forced at gunpoint to eat said golf ball, rolled first in fresh goose poop.

I set out my decoys. It saddens me that these days duck decoys are such soulless objects, manufactured of hard molded plastic rather than meticulously carved out of wood. Now the old wood decoys are prized as collectibles for the artistry and craftsmanship they represent, and command outrageous prices at antiques stores and galleries. Even anti-hunters are known to collect them feverishly, though certainly not for their original utilitarian purpose of luring ducks to their demise. Perhaps in the future, people will collect these vulgar plastic versions, but I doubt it.

Sweetz and I climbed down in the pit blind, which was sunk in the water, and I pulled the corn stalks over us to obscure us from waterfowl flying overhead. Sweetz didn't know quite what to make of this, but she was game, sitting quietly beside me on the narrow bench, peering out through the cornstalks with some curiosity. Then we waited. . . .

Behind us an oil well pumped loudly and rhythmically.

We waited some more. . . .

The sky was overcast and gray, and there was plenty of it, this part of Texas so flat that it appears concave.

Overhead a flock of geese flew by. Way overhead. They didn't even glance at our pond.

I consulted my watch. Seventeen minutes had passed so far. Only one hour and thirty-three minutes to go before Barney and Reuben would pick me up.

Sweetz quickly grew bored and whined crankily. She wanted to go to sleep, which is how Labs deal with boredom, but the bench wasn't wide enough to accommodate a sleeping position and every time she tried to lie down she would slip off into several inches of ice-cold water at the bottom of the blind. The only thing worse to a Lab than having nothing to do, or being alone, is not being able to go to sleep. She finally managed to doze off in a sitting position, leaning against me, her head on my shoulder.

A duck hunting axiom: The longer you sit in a duck blind, the colder it gets.

I was heartened momentarily by the heavy rushing sound of wings above us. *Swoo, swoo, swooo* . . . Sweetz woke briefly and we both looked up to see one lone goose winging purposefully by, way out of range and clearly with no intention whatsoever of stopping here. Sweetzer went back to sleep.

I pulled a paperback book out of the pocket of my jacket; I had been in duck blinds before.

I was due to meet Barney and Reuben on the road at the appointed hour and just before dusk Sweetz and I climbed up out of the blind. So far I don't think she was that impressed with this waterfowl hunting business. I gathered the decoys and we were walking across the field toward the road when hundreds and hundreds and hundreds of geese got up in waves out of the surrounding fields, the noise of their wingbeats and the primal din of their honking filling the evening sky. We stopped and watched reverently. If you've ever witnessed the spectacle of thousands of geese getting up all around you at sunset, you will know what hunters know: that we are lucky to live in such a graceful and magnificent world as this, a world of such wildness, richness, and bounty. Shame on us for screwing it up.

The geese circled overhead; I almost toppled over backward watching them, and then they all set down on the pond for the night.

Sweetz and I waited by the road next to the garishly lit oil station, which pumped with noisy persistence. Barney and Reuben were late picking us up, and night had fallen by the time I saw their headlights coming toward us. As I climbed in the car, they explained that they'd been late because Reuben had shot a deer and had to dress it out. It was a doe, legal game in

Texas, parts of which, like so much of the country, are seriously overpopu-
lated with deer. When he dressed out the doe he found that she had twin
fetuses in her womb. This is a sobering discovery, for better or worse, an
experience you're not going to have at the meat counter at Safeway. Reuben
was a little quiet on the ride home.

That evening for dinner I cooked quail I brought with me from Alabama, browned quickly in a skillet and roasted in a hot oven, served with
garlic mashed potatoes and a game sauce. Barney grilled a venison backstrap on the barbecue.

At the table Barney practiced his duck calls, as has been his habit for the
twenty-five years I have known him.

"This is a lonesome hen," he said, and he blew his lonesome hen call.
"You know, there are some forty different dialects in the duck language,"
he explained. "To learn those and to use the right one, to be able to call to a
duck and have him respond to your call, and turn him in the air and bring
him in and shoot him cleanly and then have your dog retrieve him—to me
there's nothing about upland hunting that can compare to that experience. . . . Although, I have to admit this quail tastes pretty good."

"I'd really like to take Sweetz out with us tomorrow morning," I asked.
"How about it?"

"Maybe if Hobaugh doesn't bring Sonny," Donnelley answered non-
committally. "You know, a young, inexperienced dog can be a real pain in
the ass in a duck blind."

But Hobaugh did bring Sonny again the next morning, and once again
Sweetz was left behind in the camper. I could hear her mournful howls as
we walked down to the duck pond in the dark.

That afternoon Barney and I plucked and dressed the day's bag of teal,
wigeon, gadwall, and mallards. We breasted a few of the larger ducks and
threw the carcasses into the bushes for the coyotes that would come in for
them. Barney liked to hear their song near the house. Raccoons, owls,
hawks, and buzzards also come in to feed on the offal and the carcasses.
And finally the ants pick the bones clean.

That night for dinner Barney barbecued the backstrap of a feral pig he
had shot on the ranch, while I fried squirrel that he had also killed.

"Tomorrow I'm bringing Sweetzer hunting with us," I announced over
dinner. "It's the last day of the season and her last chance to retrieve a duck
this year. If she causes any trouble in the blind, I'll bring her back in."

"That might be all right," Donnelley reluctantly agreed, "because
Hobaugh's not hunting with us tomorrow."

And so the next morning, a Sunday, the last day of the Texas duck season, Sweetz came in off the bench, a raw young rookie eager to show her stuff. After my insistence upon bringing her out, I hoped she wasn't going to embarrass me in front of Donnelley, who in his long duck hunting career had seen some of the country's outstanding duck dogs. He once raised and trained his own line of yellow Labs, but had given them up when he married his second wife and moved to south Florida because he didn't think that was good country for Labs. He hadn't owned a dog since.

It was warmer and muggy that morning; it had rained the night before. We walked to the duck pond before daylight. Decoys were set out and we positioned ourselves in the blind. We could hear the ducks coming in before it was light enough to see them—the heavy sound of their wings on the damp morning air, the whispering noise as they set down on the dead calm surface of the water. As the sky lightened in gradual increments, we could see their ghostly shapes swimming among the decoys in the mist, a heartbreakingly beautiful scene.

Sweetz sat in the water at my side, behind the camouflage netting stretched across the opening of the blind. She was calm and attentive, interested in the proceedings, her ears pricked alertly forward. So far so good. I was not going to shoot the first few flocks that morning, but would handle her.

Dawn finally, the water like a mirror, the birds still coming in, setting their wings over the decoys. "Okay," Barney whispered, and he and Reuben stood up out of the blind. I remained seated with a hand on Sweetzer's back to steady her. They fired and three ducks folded. Sweetz watched them fall. I peeled back the curtain. "Okay," I said to her, and she bounded enthusiastically out of the blind, leaping in the water, swimming strongly. So far so good. She came to the first few decoys. This can be a difficult moment for young dogs, who if they've never seen them before can be frightened by decoys, but Sweetz merely nudged one with her nose, ascertained that it was not the real thing, and swam on. She passed too close to another decoy and the string caught around her leg. This experience frequently panics inexperienced dogs, causing them to fold altogether. But Sweetz remained intent on the dead duck floating on the water ahead of her, and she simply kept swimming toward it, towing the decoy behind her, the string still hooked across her shoulder. "I'll be damnned," Donnelley said, impressed. Already I was proud of her.

Sweetz reached the first duck, gathered it in her mouth, turned in the water, and swam back toward us, whuffing and snorting through her nose. She delivered the duck to me; I unwrapped the decoy string from her leg and sent her out to retrieve the next bird.

"You have a duck dog there, man," said Donnelley. "Why didn't we bring her out sooner?" I was very pleased. There was nobody on earth I would rather have my dog impress on a duck pond than Barney Donnelley.

Sweetz performed beautifully the rest of the morning, marking dead birds and retrieving them, swimming down cripples; she even took a couple of rudimentary hand signals though we had not practiced these in many months. Donnelley was more and more impressed, and proclaimed her the best first-time dog he'd ever seen, and he'd seen a lot of dogs. "With a natural duck dog like that," he said, "you're going to have to take up duck hunting in earnest. Forget that upland shit!" I was prouder and prouder.

And there was no question that Sweetz was in her element here, her genetic code imprinted by generations of breeding so that though she'd never retrieved a duck before today, she looked like she was born to it. And she was. Like watching a thoroughbred race horse, or a cutting horse, or a cow dog, or a pointing dog, it is wonderful to see an animal do what it was bred to do, what it loves to do more than anything on earth. I decided that morning that I would have to do a bit of duck hunting in future years, if for no other reason than that Sweetzer's genes demanded it.

Reuben had to catch a plane from Houston back to Chicago that afternoon, and after we saw him off at the ranch in his rental car, Barney and I went out for a final dove hunt. He was going home to his new family in Florida the next morning, and I was hitting the road again. We ate doves for dinner our last night together, just the two of us, a quiet bittersweet evening, as the last day of the season tends to be. Donnelley's life has been measured in a real way by duck seasons, and now he felt that he had reached that age "when each season could be your last."

"You know what I like about duck hunting, Jimmy?" Barney asked me that night over dinner. "A few years ago a duck banded in Port Aransas, Texas, was killed eighteen days later in Vladivostok, Russia. Now imagine the country that duck covered—the wheat fields, the rice fields, the marshes, the prairie, the plains. That duck flew across the North Atlantic Ocean. Imagine that! It's a powerful thing to think about, isn't it?"

BARNEY DONNELLEY'S
GRILLED WILD DUCK

(Those who don't like the taste of wild duck often complain that it tastes like "liver." This is usually because they've never eaten it properly prepared. As red-meated fowl, wild duck, and goose, must be treated like beef, not like chicken, served medium-rare to rare. Donnelley likes his fairly rare, as do I. Like most game bird recipes for the grill, this one is extremely simple and simplicity is exactly what is required for ducks.)

Prepare a bed of hot coals—wood or coal. Place whole ducks in a large pan of soy sauce and 1 stick of melted butter. Season with ground pepper. Grill back side down first, letting fat flare in the fire, until skin is nearly charred—about 15 minutes (more or less, depending on heat of coals and size of ducks; less time is obviously required for teal than for mallards). Periodically roll ducks in soy/butter mixture, or baste them with it, while turning and cooking on both breast sides. If you're going to overcook, better to err on the backside rather than the breast. And remember, you can always put an undercooked bird back on the grill, but you can't save one that's been overcooked.

32

THE KING RANCH

For all that I, for one, am never overeager to visit him, and if it were not for the grouse and the partridge, I should probably have dropped his acquaintance altogether.

Ivan Turgenev

Sweetz and I both went in the shop in Columbus, Texas, as did the camper. After over four months, fourteen thousand road miles, and eight hundred or so miles of busting brush, slogging through swamps and deltas, tramping the forests and fields of the American uplandscape, this hunter's road was beginning to take its toll—on man, dog, and machine alike. I dropped Sweetz off at the vet; she required minor surgery to have a golf ball–sized abscess on her nose lanced and drained, an infection that resulted from her battle with the swamp rat in Alabama. The camper went to the mechanic for routine service, while I retired to a local clinic to be treated for a persistent eye infection, caused, I believed, by a briar scratch on an Alabama quail hunt. The sun hadn't shone since I'd arrived in Texas, and I'd also been unable to shake a bad cold that had benefited from several days in a duck blind.

In the waiting room of the doctor's clinic, I thumbed through an issue of *Sports Illustrated*, where I found a piece written by my friend Bob Jones in Vermont about his young Lab, Jake. In the piece was a photo of Sweetz taken during our visit in November. I tipped the magazine toward an old gent seated next to me, like a proud parent showing off a baby album. "Say, this is my dog—Sweetzer. In *Sports Illustrated*. A celebrity!" The old man smiled wanly. He had tubes in his nose and a portable respirator at his feet.

I insisted that the doctor and the nurse look at Sweetzer's photo, too. And the receptionist. It's not every day your dog's picture appears in *Sports*

Illustrated. I'm not sure they believed me at the clinic, but the receptionist said I could have the magazine anyway.

The doctor wrote out a prescription for my eye. He didn't seem to think it was an infection caused by a briar scratch. He thought I'd developed an allergy. I suffered from severe asthma as a child but had more or less outgrown most of my allergies over the years. The doctor asked a few questions.

"From what you're telling me," he said, "I'd say you're having an allergic reaction to one of two things. Possibly both of them."

"Yes?"

"My guess is that you're allergic to dog hair and/or bird feathers."

I picked Sweetzer up at the vet, showed him her photo so that he would know he had a famous patient, and then checked into a motel, the first and only night we would spend in a motel on the entire trip. She was still pretty woozy, wobbly in the legs from the anesthesia, and I had to carry her up to the room and lay her down on the bed. Though she only weighs about sixty pounds, carrying a sedated Lab is the equivalent of carrying your own weight in wet mattresses. I tried to show her her photo, but she seemed less interested in her new celebrity.

I made a drink, phoned my wife, told her to buy a half dozen copies of *Sports Illustrated*, ordered some truly dreadful food from room service (particularly repulsive after having eaten virtually nothing but fresh game for months), took a hot bath, turned the television on, and crawled under the covers next to Sweetz, who was snoring, drooling, and twitching in a deep, drug-induced stupor. We were a pair of worn-out, beat-up hunters. The bed was wonderful, the first time in days that I had felt warm and dry. I fell asleep, dreaming of Sweetz swimming toward me with a duck in her mouth.

Much refreshed, we headed south. The rain continued—rain, fog, and endless damp. In a pay phone at a campground on the Guadaloupe River, I watched nervously as the water rose to the banks. An entire set of lawn furniture floated past; obviously pilfered by the high water from a down-stream patio, it bobbed festively on the surface. The river lapped over the banks and swirled around my shoes. I was talking to a man whose phone number I had been given by a mutual acquaintance, regarding a possible quail hunt. For all their self-proclaimed largess, Texans are notoriously niggardly with their quail hunting, virtually the entire state locked up in private leases. And for all of its immense size, there is very little public hunting land in Texas. "Jim," said the man on the other end of the line, speaking in a slow drawl that sounded like *Jaaam*, "I'm sure you're just a real nice fella, but frankly, I'd sooner invite you into my wife's bedroom than onto my quail lease."

"But I don't want to get into your wife's bedroom," I explained. "I want to go bird hunting."

"I'm afraid that's the best I can do, son."

South. Across the San Antonio River, the Mission River, the Nueces, my direction somewhat aimless, chosen, in addition to the fact that I'd heard they had good quail hunting down here, largely as a climatic measure; I was hoping to find some sun to bake the dampness out of my bones. The rain continued.

I stopped periodically at pay phones to call another number on my rapidly dwindling list of contacts; I'd made the mistake of coming here cold and now I was down to the really obscure longshots—friends of friends of the vaguest of acquaintances. After better than a dozen phone calls the only invitation I had so far was into that fellow's wife's bedroom.

At a pay phone off the road outside Alice, Texas, I got hold of a man who worked for an oil company in Corpus Christi and who suggested I head down to Mexico, where there was some good quail hunting just over the border. He was just back from there. "They use Mex kids to flush and retrieve the birds," he said. "I tell you what, they're better than any bird dogs I've ever hunted behind. They don't miss a trick. And you only have to tip them three bucks apiece at the end of the day. It's the best deal going."

This reminded me of the conversation I'd had with the woman at the Christmas party in south Florida. Personally, I'll stick with dogs for my bird hunting.

Bingo: A retired game biologist in Kingsville, Texas, named Bill Kiel, who once worked for the legendary King Ranch, gave me the phone number of a man by the name of Paul Visel, who managed the El Coyote Ranch, belonging to the Bass family. Kiel explained that Visel also operated a kennel of English pointers that he hired out to bird hunting leases all over the region. I phoned Paul Visel, who couldn't have been more accommodating and very kindly invited me out to the King Ranch where he was presently putting on a hunt for a group of wealthy sportsmen on a lease owned by a large oil and gas concern. Though it was made clear that the invitation was strictly to spectate and not to hunt, I felt lucky to have stumbled onto it. While the narrator might prefer to be driving around the country in a horse-drawn carriage, like our man Turgenev, stopping along the way to hunt where the land looks right, I was at least a century late for that, and in Texas one takes invitations where one can get them.

*   *   *

Richard King, an entrepreneurial steamboat captain, came to these parts in 1847 to ply the waters of the Rio Grande, and made his first fortune running contraband cotton to Mexico during the Civil War, purchasing his product with worthless Confederate paper money and selling it for gold and pounds sterling. King bought his original 15,000 acres in 1853 for the modest sum of $300.

Today, the King Ranch is the largest private ranch in America, sprawling over 825,000 acres in south Texas, an area, company spokesmen like to point out, bigger than the entire state of Rhode Island. To my mind, such comparisons to little Rhode Island actually diminish the true immensity of the King Ranch—somewhat like saying that Texas is bigger than Great Britain. Big deal; everything's bigger than Great Britain (except Rhode Island). More to my liking are such statistics as this: the boundaries of the King Ranch are enclosed within 2,000 miles of fence, enough to stretch from Kingsville, Texas, to Boston, Massachusetts.

Paul Visel had arranged for me to hook up with one of his dog trainers at the El Coyote Ranch offices in Kingsville. At one time, most large private ranches in Texas quail country maintained their own bird dog kennels and employed their own full-time dog trainers, but increasingly these men have been replaced by professionals like Visel, who runs a kennel of over a hundred pointers which he supplies, along with dog handlers, to conduct hunts on ranches all over south Texas—a kind of hunt by hire, *Have dogs, will travel*. Bird hunting has not been immune to the marketplace pressures that have overcome all other sports in our times. Quail hunting is big business in Texas—exclusive, and very, very expensive, some of the large leases running into the hundreds of thousands of dollars per year.

That afternoon I rode out to the King Ranch with David Shumaker, a displaced southerner from Ecru, Mississippi—a stocky man in his late thirties with thinning blond hair, a blond beard, and small bright blue eyes. Shumaker wore knee-high laced snake-proof hunting boots outside his pants, and had a round belly hanging over his belt, narrow hips, and a quick, energetic, duck-footed stride. He was very polite in the manner of so many southerners, addressing all the women in the office as "ma'am," and me as "sir." "Yessir," he would say in answer to my questions, or "nossir," until I insisted he call me by name.

We entered the King Ranch through an elaborate security gate operated by Exxon, which leases the mineral rights on the ranch and maintains 2,700 oil and gas wells across the vast property. A large neon sign, displaying the day's inspirational message, towered over the parking lot at company headquarters inside the gate. *Awareness is essential*, it said—a rather Zenlike communication from corporate headquarters.

Functioning much like a separate state or country (in fact, the security gate puts one in mind of a border check)—though considerably more profitable than most—the King Ranch is a diverse concern with its own industries (gas, oil, cattle, farming, recreation), towns, housing developments, schools, museums, shops, etc. The state even comes complete with its own citizenry known as *Kineños* (King's people), fourth- and fifth-generation descendants of the residents of an entire Mexican village whom Richard King relocated here in the 1850s when he required large numbers of workers to run his vast and growing empire.

A truly multiuse operation, the ranch is intensely, and for the most part quite well managed—but for some recent signs of serious overgrazing due to a severe two-year drought. In spite of the obvious presence of twentieth-century industry, the ranch maintains a certain exotic, untamed feel to it. Known on early maps as the Wild Horse Desert, and the Desert of the Dead (El Desierto de los Muertos), perhaps it is the sheer vastness of the dry, scrubby country, the flat, endless expanse of mesquite, huisache, cactus, grassland, and plains—and all that sky—that offers the implacable sense of wildness.

Too, there is an incredible richness and abundance of wildlife here. The King Ranch might also well be considered the largest privately held wildlife preserve in the United States. Driving in, we spotted a huge flock of Rio Grande wild turkeys on the side of the road; hundreds of white-tailed deer (which due to minerals in the soil grow disproportionately large antlers, making them favorite targets of trophy hunters who pay many thousands of dollars to come here to shoot one); a roving band of javelina (the only native wild pigs of the New World—thuggish-looking creatures with coarse, bristly hair and viciously curved upper tusks, sometimes used to eviscerate hunting dogs); a feral sow with a litter of squealing piglets; and, of course, on the domestic side, the famed King Ranch Santa Gertrudis cattle, originally bred here, the first American beef breed of cattle, and as cattle go, a rather handsome creature, with deep, burnished, reddish brown hides. Later, on another section of the ranch, I would see a herd of grazing nilgais, a large dark-colored antelope introduced from India some years ago and now thriving in this pocket of the country.

For all its abundance of wildlife, the land of south Texas is hard, spare, and for the most part colorless, especially in the winter and especially in these drought years. There was very little grass to speak of this year and what hadn't been grazed down already was sparse and toasted brown. A pair of green jays squabbled noisily on the side of the road as we passed, their shocking green, blue, and yellow plumage reminiscent of jungle parrots. Even the lack of color possessed a certain drama—the leafless January mesquite trees twisted and spiny against a dull gray sky. Overhead a Mexican hawk circled—a stout black-bodied raptor with broad wings and a sandy-colored head.

I asked Shumaker the names of plants, bushes, trees, and wildlife as we drove in; I felt like a tourist in a strange land, and had the sense of being on the African veldt here—an immensity of landscape that a painter would be hard pressed to capture.

"This is hard country on dawgs," Shumaker pointed out. "On men, too. There's a saying down here: 'If it don't bite you, it'll stick you and sting you.' " Indeed, it would seem over the next few days that virtually everything that grew or lived in this country came armed with razor-sharp weaponry capable of piercing or tearing flesh and hide. There were the long needlelike, poisonous thorns of the ubiquitous mesquite, the tusks of javelina, the tails of scorpions, the fangs of rattlesnakes, the pincers of fire ants, and most recently the stingers of killer bees.

We drove into a lovely little hacienda-like compound, set in a watered oasis of trees and greenery. Nearly tame deer (the same that sportsmen pay so handsomely to shoot), drank unmolested from a water hole fifty yards in front of the ranch house. Shumaker explained to me that this section of the ranch, twenty thousand acres all together, was leased by a large oil and gas company as a recreational retreat for executives and their guests. Presently, the members of a private hunting and fishing club, one of whom was a company bigwig, were visiting the ranch for a weekend of quail hunting.

"I won't be going out hunting with you this afternoon," Shumaker said.

"Why not?" I asked.

"I just train the dogs." He smiled. "I'll tell you the truth, I'm kinda on probation. I ain't much good with the guests. Some of them rich fellas get real arrogant and I won't stand for their shit, especially when they start telling me how to handle the dogs. Most of 'em don't know their asses from an anthill. But maybe you'd like to come out with me tomorrow morning and watch me train."

"Sure. I'd like to see that."

We continued on past the hacienda and down the road to the kennels, which were full of lean, houndish English pointers, who greeted our arrival with much crazed barking, braying, panting, and leaping in their cages, all of them anxious to be chosen for the afternoon hunt. Shumaker ushered me into the adjacent hands' quarters, a dingy, malodorous trailer, full of dirty laundry, unwashed dishes, and Salvation Army sofas upon which in the dim light I was able to make out a few young men lounging with their boots off watching a movie on the television. Brief introductions were made, and I went back outside with Shumaker to help him load dogs, while the others finished their movie.

I rode along for the afternoon hunt in one of the trucks with several members of the sporting club, which represented a cross section of American business concerns—an oil man from Texas, a CEO from Arizona, an attorney from Florida, an accountant from Georgia, a voice-over actor from a prominent Pennsylvania family. The club was an exclusive organization formed in 1946 for and by gentlemen of means, who enjoyed hunting and fishing around the world. Their guide and dog handler that day was a young local man by the name of Bruce Roberts, a sincere, clean-cut lad in his early twenties. Recently graduated from college where he had been a star baseball player, Roberts's social and diplomatic skills were clearly better suited to dealing with these guests than were Shumaker's.

It was a pleasant group of gentlemen, primarily conservative Republicans ("There aren't too goddamn many liberals in the club!" one of the crusty older members joked), avid, and for the most part accomplished, sportsmen and more than competent shots. One of them had brought along a rifle to pot coyotes in case we happened across any during our afternoon outing. "If you don't see any coyotes," joked another, the owly, bespectacled lawyer from Florida, who, though dressed in hunting attire, still gave the impression that he was wearing a bow tie, "shoot a goddamn Democrat!"

A kind of variation of the old mule-drawn wagon hunts of the South, south Texas–style quail hunting is undertaken with customized trucks in place of wagons. The hunters ride up top on bench auto seats mounted over the dog kennels, while the trucks follow a network of roads cleared through the mesquite and brush. Certain areas along the road are regularly overseeded with grain to attract the quail, which come in to feed. There are two pointers on the ground at a time, for half-hour intervals, and the dog handler stands on the running board, flushing whip in hand, or walks in front of the slowly moving truck, directing the dogs. This style of motorized hunting is the only practicable way to hunt this country, given the vast space involved and, even this time of year, the generally sultry weather, which can easily overcome big running pointers. Roberts and his driver today, another friendly young local man named Jon Whitenton, conduct hunts virtually every day of the quail season, and with that kind of constant gunning pressure, in order not to do irreparable damage to local quail populations, they need to be able to cover some ground and hunt different sections of the lease every day. In any case, you're not going to get sportsmen of this nature to do much in the way of walking.

And it wasn't such a bad way to see the country, or the shooting action, I had to admit, riding up on my seat above the kennels, watching the dogs quartering on either side. "We have a dog locked up over there," someone would notice, and the shooters would descend from their perch and walk in on either side of Roberts, who swished the ground with his whip in order to put the birds up. Sipping a cold beer from the cooler on the back of the truck, I had done enough hunting on this trip to enjoy my role as spectator, and I had the best seat in the house. After shooting the covey rise, the sports would hunt up the nearby singles before everyone climbed back on the truck to drive to the next point. I congratulated the deserving Republicans on their excellent shooting and asked them if it concerned them that so much of the prime hunting grounds in America were being tied up in private hands.

"I think we got a goddamn socialist among us!" joked the Florida lawyer.

"Sport is not for the masses," explained their Texan host, somewhat sententiously. "That's the way it's always been. And always will be. We're very proud of our private ownership system in Texas. It's the landowners who protect the land and provide the habitat. If it weren't for the landowners there would be a lot less wildlife." He may have been quite right, of course, and I had seen evidence of the truth of what he said time and again across the country. But for those of us among the masses, it can seem a disheartening truth nevertheless.

Having pegged me as a socialist, or at best a bleeding-heart liberal, the little lawyer from Florida seemed to enjoy baiting me with his bigotry. "I stopped riding the buses when they started integrating them," he said with his owlish smile.

I couldn't help but notice that none among the group of sportsmen asked me if I would like to shoot one of the covey rises that afternoon.

That night I parked the camper down by the "cowboy camp," an old Alamo-style building with the name *Ovanito* and the dates 1854–1934 inscribed on the arched entranceway. Originally built to provide shelter for cowhands looking after the herd, the building had been beautifully renovated and decorated and now served as housing for favored employees, as well as guests of the ranch.

It was dusk by the time I reached the cowboy camp, the evening cool and overcast, with intermittent drizzle. I took a walk with Sweetz and gathered some dry mesquite branches with which I built a fire. I let it burn down to coals and then grilled a pair of duck breasts for dinner. I ate them with the last of my wild rice, purchased in Minnesota all those months and miles and all that country ago.

*　*　*

Early the next morning, I hitched a ride down to the kennels to meet David Shumaker. After a full week in Texas, I had seen precisely five minutes of sunshine, and it wasn't to be on that morning either. For the second day in a row, I had to leave Sweetzer behind in the camper.

Professional dog trainers tend to be an odd lot—often eccentric, almost always opinionated, frequently a tad cranky, and, as is the case with writers and artists, having a higher than average incidence of alcoholism in their ranks. Certainly the best of them are artists of a sort, with hunting dogs as their medium, and quite frequently they get along better with the animals than they do with their fellow man. Though I'd seen plenty of fine dog work over the past months, and spoken to a number of professional trainers, I'd yet to see a real pro in action, doing what he did best—training dogs.

That morning we took out the pointers that Shumaker or the other handlers felt especially needed work—generally inexperienced young dogs or dogs that hadn't been hunted recently. Some had been purchased from other kennels or started by different trainers and they all tended to have different problems and shortcomings, which it was Shumaker's responsibility to identify and correct. Some of the dogs had been trained with electronic shock collars by trainers with heavy trigger fingers and tended to be overly timid about ranging too far. Shumaker liked his dogs to hunt "big." "I want a dawg to git out and eat up some real estate," he explained, "because I got a lot of real estate." Others dogs wouldn't hold a point or refused to back another dog on point, or had taken to busting and chasing birds; still others ignored the whistle to come in.

Over the years, dog trainers have devised a wide array of training and disciplinary techniques to instill hunting skills in bird dogs, but many of these techniques have been driven to the brink of obsolescence by the advent of the electronic shock collar. Shumaker trained without a collar, preferring a more old-fashioned, hands-on approach. To the layman (and certainly to a representative of the ASPCA), his methods might seem like a kind of canine chamber of horrors, and let me just say that you won't find anything quite like them in the Monks of New Skete's dog training book.

Besides the standard beating with his flushing whip, Shumaker picked dogs up by the ears (à la Lyndon Johnson) until they howled. He dangled them off the ground by the collar until they were choked into submission. He held their mouths closed and plugged their nostrils with his fingers (the resulting lack of air and sense of impending suffocation frightening them into docility). Occasionally, he peppered a running dog in the ass with a well-placed blast from a shotgun. He even had a little harness and pulley affair with which he could string up particularly recalcitrant dogs in a tree so that they twisted in the wind like hanged men—this latter method another scare tactic, as dogs hate to have all four feet off the ground.

It's quite true that this cruel and unusual punishment wasn't pretty to watch. Some of the dogs bayed pitifully while being disciplined, but for the most part pointers are a tough, hard-headed bunch who can take a good deal of such "correcting" and seconds later be right back about their hunting business. The life of a professional hunting dog is no picnic—these are not pets—but the alternative is even bleaker: young dogs who show no aptitude for the hunt in their first year or so of life are simply culled, that is, put down.

It takes a particular temperament to be a dog trainer, perhaps funda-mental to the job a certain dispassion and lack of sentimentality. Yet however seemingly brutal his disciplinary tactics, Shumaker seemed to care genuinely for his dogs and praised them fervently when they per-formed well. "That ol' liver dawg is layin' out pretty good now," he said toward the end of the morning, in the vernacular unique to the sport, as he watched one of his students with proud satisfaction. (Translation: the dog was working at what he considered to be a proper range.) "Now a lot of trainers if they had a collar on her would bump her right now" (shock the dog for being *too* far out), he continued, "but that's just about how I want a dawg to lay out."

We broke for lunch.

"You like to cook?" Shumaker asked me as we drove back in to the kennels.

"Yes, I do."

"You like to eat game?"

"Sure do."

"I'm working on a book of my own," he confided shyly. "A book of game recipes." He pulled an old tattered, cracked leather briefcase out from under the seat of the truck, the kind of briefcase that school kids used to carry—with the leather flap and little brass clasp that is always broken. "I wondered if you could take a look at it for me, maybe give me some advice about how to go about getting it published."

"I'd be happy to take a look at it."

He pulled a dogeared, handwritten manuscript out of the suitcase. "I need to get this typed up," he said, handing it to me sheepishly. It was a touching gesture of confidence, and I felt sad for Shumaker. I knew from spending time with him, and with some of the other employees the day before, that he didn't fit in down here, that he had no real friends. More than just his Mississippi accent was different. I'd heard that he'd already been fired twice for his abrasive manner with guests, and there were rumors of other troubles.

"I've always liked to cook," Shumaker said. "When I was a boy my family had a hog farm up home." He smiled nostalgically, clearly homesick. "We used to go in there and hit one a them eighty-pounders on the haid, and then we'd slow cook 'em over coals in the pit. . . ." He smacked his lips loudly. "Mmmm, man, I want to tell you, it don't git no better than that!"

We dropped the dogs back off at the kennels, watered them, and hosed out cages. After lunch in the hands' dining room off the kitchen of the main lodge, we took out another bunch of dogs. This time Bruce Roberts and John Whitendon joined us and we all carried shotguns in order to shoot a few birds over the dogs. There was some obvious tension between Roberts, head guide and dog handler, and Shumaker, head trainer, over respective handling and training methods—perhaps some underlying professional jealousies—but it was a pleasant afternoon, and we put up some birds and saw some good dog work. One of Shumaker's young dogs "layed out" a bit too far and we lost her, not an uncommon occurrence in this big flat country where the mesquite grows so thick in places that it's impenetrable. Sometimes dogs, all of whom wear identification collars, are found days later by motorists or by cowboys many miles away; sometimes they're struck by cars or trucks on the highway; and sometimes they're never found, victim to one or another of the considerable hazards in this wild, inhospitable land.

We searched for the lost dog until dusk without success, and then drove back in to drop the others off at the kennels. Roberts and Whitendon had kindly invited me to join them for dinner and a night on the town in Kingsville; Shumaker, conspicuously, had not been included. I exchanged addresses with him and told him to send me a copy of his cookbook when he got it typed up; possibly I could advise him about getting it published. "I'd better go back out and look for that dawg," he said softly, and he drove off alone into the failing light.

The next morning dawned clear and sunny over the cowboy camp, color pooling back into the country with the rising sun. The sun felt splendid, changing the world and immeasurably lightening my recent gloomy mood. I'd declined the invitation to town with the young guides, after all, in favor of an early night, and I woke feeling refreshed, my seemingly perpetual cold finally abated. Sweetz and I set out for a walk into the open country.

Almost immediately we jumped a pack of javelina out of a brushy draw and Sweetz took after them just as she had lit out after the nutria in

Alabama. Shumaker had described to me the damage the beasts can do to a dog with their razor-sharp tusks, and told me that every year he lost a pointer or two in a bloody and almost always losing fight.

Now one of the javelina, a large boar, stood his ground, as the others scattered squealing at Sweetzer's approach. I whistled frantically for her to stop and broke into a run. The boar, grunting, moved quickly and menacingly toward her on tiny stick legs, and Sweetz had the sense, and just enough timidity, to stop short of him, to wheel with tail between her legs and run back to me. I was nearly close enough and was prepared to shoot the boar if I had to, but he turned and disappeared into the brush. Sweetzer's dreams would be populated by a whole new cast of villains.

DAVID SHUMAKER'S TEXAS QUAIL
(OR DOVES)

Pluck birds. Open carcass by cutting up backbone with game shears. Remove intestines. Stuff cavity with wedges of onion, jalapeño, and bell peppers. Wrap birds with bacon, secured by toothpicks. Grill over hot mesquite coals.

33

A SHORT HUNTER'S
ETHICS QUIZ

I loathe aristocracy. Game was put on this earth for every man. I'm just part of the natural balance.

Charley Peace (*nom de guerre* of a modern-day
English game poacher)

Let us imagine, for the sake of argument, that the hunter is wandering across the countryside with his dog. He carries a gun; he is on private property—let's pretend he's on the King Ranch in Kleberg County, Texas. It is a gorgeous sunny day, the kind of day that makes the hunter rejoice to be alive on earth at this moment, to be in the field in this place—the arid, scrubby, game-rich desert country of south Texas.

Approaching a grove of huisache trees and assorted brush, the hunter is startled to see an entire flock of Rio Grande wild turkey gobblers milling about like idle urban teenagers; they poke around in the dirt, scraping and gobbling. This time of year, before spring breeding season, gobblers and hens are segregated in separate flocks, turkeys preferring the company of members of their own sex until such time as their hormones call. Somehow this particular flock of gobblers, maybe twenty birds altogether, haven't spotted the hunter or his dog yet, and, lucky for the hunter, the dog hasn't gotten wind of the birds, either. The hunter motions the dog silently back in and kneels behind a thorny goatweed bush. This is an exciting moment for the hunter. His heart pounds. He thinks of roast wild turkey. He calculates that if he is stealthy enough he could circle around the edge of the brush and put himself in position to actually shoot one of the gobblers. He has never shot a wild turkey before—in fact, he's never hunted them before, because his interest lies mainly in hunting those species that can be hunted in partnership with a dog. Turkeys, although one of the great success stories of modern game management, proliferating around the country in greater numbers than since the turn of the century, are not one such species.

But there is a small matter of legality for the hunter to consider. Consulting the Texas game hunting regulations, a copy of which he dutifully carries in his game bag, he finds that, indeed, the fall turkey season is open for another two days. However, in order to legally shoot a wild turkey, the hunter must possess a special turkey permit. He does not have such a permit, and, at this point, it is certainly a bit late to think about running off to town to obtain one.

At the same time, the hunter is aware that he is on private property, the hunting rights leased out, and that rich men, who do have valid turkey permits, pay enormous sums of money to come here for the privilege of shooting a Rio Grande wild turkey. Of course, the hunter hasn't paid a nickel for such a privilege, and in any case couldn't afford to do so, nor, as mentioned, does he have the requisite turkey permit from the state. Yet here he finds himself, in the viselike jaws of temptation, yards away from an entire unsuspecting flock of wild turkeys.

So here is our hunter's ethics quiz: Finding himself in this situation, does the hunter—who, incidentally, has all his life obeyed game laws, never shot over his limit, and has always considered himself to be a true *sportsman*:

A. Stealthily work himself into shooting position and make an incredibly accurate (if lucky) head shot, thereby cleanly killing his first wild turkey, while in the same instant crossing the line and becoming the lowliest of all forms of fallen sportsman—a POACHER?

B. Stand up and reveal himself to the flock of gobblers, waving his arms and shouting, flushing the birds and thereby abiding by state game laws as well as the laws of private property and the unwritten code of true sportsmanship?

MARINATED MESQUITE GRILLED WILD TURKEY BREASTS AND THIGHS

(This recipe is also suitable for domestic turkey breasts and thighs.)

Make a marinade of:
³/₄ cup good olive oil
2 tbsp. dijon mustard
¹/₂ cup white wine
juice from ¹/₂ lemon
¹/₂ cup fresh chopped cilantro (or basil)
¹/₂ cup fresh chopped Italian parsley
6–10 finely chopped cloves of garlic
1 tbsp. (or more) red pepper flakes
a sprinkling of salt
plenty of ground black pepper

Marinate turkey breasts and thighs in above mixture for a minimum of 3 hours (or overnight). Grill over medium-hot mesquite coals, being careful not to burn, and basting regularly with the marinade. Depending on the heat of the coals, and the thickness of the breasts and thighs, 15–20 minutes should be sufficient grilling time. Be very careful about overcooking as, with any bird, wild or domestic, this will dry out the meat. This dish is excellent accompanied by yellow rice and grilled red peppers, which can also be marinated and basted with the same mixture.

34

A LIFE OF CRIME

As problematic a task as hunting, meditation always runs the risk of returning empty-handed.

Ortega y Gasset

Once you cross the line there's no going back. The next day I was farther north, in the town of Comanche, Texas. My five-day Texas hunting license had expired but I was still in the state, and had even managed to line up another hunt here. I went into the grocery store to buy a new license.

"I'd like to buy a five-day nonresident hunting license, please."

"There is no five-day license," said the woman behind the counter. "We only have licenses for the whole year, and they're fifteen dollars."

"No, that's for a resident. I'm a nonresident."

"You don't live here?"

"Nope."

"You need an out-of-state license?"

"That's right. I need a five-day nonresident hunting license. They cost twenty-five dollars."

"Why pay twenty-five dollars for a five-day license when you can get a license for the whole year for fifteen dollars?"

"Because I'm not a resident of the state of Texas. That's why."

"Well, I'll have to ask Marge about that. She usually does the hunting licenses. . . . Is Marge still in the store? . . . Say, Marge, come up here, will you. This man wants to buy a five-day hunting license."

"Oh, they don't have licenses for five days," said Marge. "They only have them for the whole year."

"No, you're mistaken. I bought a five-day license last week."

"Here?"

"No, in Columbus. They're twenty-five dollars."

"But you can buy a license for the whole year for fifteen dollars."

"Not if you're a nonresident, you can't."

"Oh, you're not from Texas?"

"No, I'm not. That's what I've been trying to explain. I don't live in Texas. I need a nonresident hunting license. A five-day nonresident hunting license."

"But they don't have five-day licenses. They only have licenses for the whole year."

That's how a life of crime is perpetuated.

A slender moon hung over Comanche, the sky a strange steel blue before dawn, a sheen of frost covering the ground. I liked this country, which seemed less monotonous than south Texas—hillier, lusher, and more diverse. I drove up to Breckenridge to meet the Simmons brothers—Jim and Kevin—at McDonald's on the strip. It seemed an odd place to be sitting around having breakfast in hunting attire.

Jim Simmons is the production manager of an oil company in Fort Worth; his younger brother Kevin, vice-president of a bank in Breckenridge; their friend Stan the local GM dealer—nice guys, longtime hunting partners, jocular, refreshingly middle class. Not that I have anything against wealthy Republicans—some of my best friends are wealthy Republicans (well, one or two of my best friends, anyway)—but at some point one begins to long for the company of some "just plain folks," guys who have mortgage worries like the rest of us and don't rely on being "taken care of" by an army of guides, outfitters, and third-world servants (as in "*They really know how to take care of you here*"), guys who find their own places to hunt and have to clean their own birds at the end of the day.

Being native sons of these parts, my hosts had good contacts with local landowners, and we drove to our first hunting spot of the day and unloaded dogs and guns. They had nice-looking dogs—three setters and a Brittany (Babe, Kate, Jo-Jo, and Major) among the three of them—which they had trained themselves and of which they were obviously and justifiably proud. These men had been hunting together for years and liked to tease each other about the others' dogs and brag on their own. "One thing that all bird hunters have in common," said Kevin, a slight, boyish-looking man who looked far too young to be a bank vice-president, "is that they all think they have the best dog."

I had Sweetz with me. The boys immediately teased me about quail hunting behind a Lab (which reminded me of Danny Lahren's remark

back in Montana), and for shooting a double shotgun: "The first thing we
need to teach you about Texas quail hunting," Jim instructed, "is that you
need a pointing dog and you need more bullets in your gun." They all
carried autoloaders with the plugs out, allowing five shots apiece.

We spread out across the hills, working high and low, up and down
through mesquite, prickly pear, jumping cactus, flying cactus, and live
oaks. There was broomweed and ragweed, grassy creek bottoms and rocky
hillsides. Periodically, Sweetzer came limping back to me to have cactus
spines pulled from her feet.

These guys were hard, tireless walkers, and, I was soon to see, excellent shots, and their dogs were good, too—altogether an extremely efficient
hunting team. They covered the ground, and found the birds.

Watching everyone converge on a point, I hung back on the edge as the
covey got up and they unloaded their guns. It sounded like this: *bam, bam,
bam, bam, bam, bam, bam, bam, bam, bam, bam, bam, bam, bam, bam*. So
many shots that I forgot to shoot. Anyway, in the face of this kind of
firepower, it seemed entirely unnecessary. Birds rained from the sky,
feathers floating slowly down in the sudden still aftermath. The dogs had
plenty of work to do gathering dead birds. Sweetz was having a great time,
and she was not particular about whose birds she retrieved to me. The men
razzed one another about their respective shooting; they were competitive
in the easy way of old friends and partners. I witnessed yet another manner
of dispatching a cripple—they simply yanked the head off. It's my least
favorite method, bloody, and there seems something undignified about a
headless bird in the bag.

Later that day a bag count determined that a collective limit had been
shot, the hunt was proclaimed over, and we drove to a parking area off the
road where the birds were cleaned—heads and feet and wings snipped off,
skins peeled, cavities cut open with game shears, intestines flipped into
the garbage cans without ever having to touch them—a neat, surgical,
assembly-line operation. These guys knew their stuff. I held back four
quail in the feathers for myself. I like to age them for a few days in the
refrigerator before I clean them, and I like to pluck rather than skin. The
boys thought this was very odd, and I could tell they found it highly
disgusting to leave intestines in a bird. "I've never heard of that," Jim said
skeptically. "Maybe I'll try it sometime." He was only being polite; I knew
he wouldn't.

The truth is I enjoy cleaning birds. I find it relaxing and somehow
integral to the whole hunting process. I like to take my time with it; I like
just looking at them there in the feathers in the refrigerator for a few days,
picking them up and admiring the beauty and perfection of feather patterns. When I clean them I like to examine crop contents, and several days

later when I cleaned these birds in Oklahoma, I would find that some had been feeding on the rubbery petals of a red cactus flower. This seemed wondrous and astonishing to me, those bright red petals in their crops. Nor do I mind touching bird intestines—indeed, I like the rich, pungent smell. For months my hands had smelled like the inside of birds—a smell of wildness and life.

But to each his own. Bird hunting is pursued in many ways and enjoyed for many different reasons, both in the field and on the table. As we were saying our good-byes that afternoon, back at the McDonald's parking lot where I left the camper for the day, I asked the men how they best liked to cook their quail. At the end of the season, they told me, everyone brought their birds out of the freezer and they invited a bunch of friends over and held a big cookout in which they grilled the quail on the barbecue. Often they stuffed the cavities with jalapeño peppers first. "Kills the *waaald* taste," Kevin explained.

And then Sweetz and I were back on the road—the country racing by—headed north, across the Clear Fork of the Brazos River to the Prairie Dog Town of the Red River, where we camped near a historical marker commemorating the night the outlaws Bonnie and Clyde careened off the road into the stream here, murdered in cold blood the man who came along to pull them out, and later escaped after a shootout with the law.

The next morning we crossed the Salt Fork of the Red River, then the North Fork of the Red River, leaving mesquite country behind and entering the shortgrass prairie just past the Canadian River. Near the border, around the town of Perryton, the farmland began to take on the overly neat appearance of monoculture, plowed all the way to the edge of the road, not a thin blade of grass left, not enough cover for a sparrow, let alone a game bird. Herds of plastic deer grazed on the lawns of the farmhouses, the only wildlife adaptable to this man-made habitat. The prairie chickens, so prolific here in the last century, were long gone.

We were headed for Oklahoma. I had no contacts there or hunts lined up, but I felt the need of a few days of unplanned solitary wandering—hunting on my own time, at my own pace with only my own dog. There was no hope of finding public land to hunt in this part of Texas but I'd located a large splotch of it on the map in the Oklahoma panhandle and that's where we were going.

I nosed around for a while in the town of Beaver, Oklahoma, went to the laundromat and the grocery store, and asked some questions of the local citizenry regarding bird hunting opportunities in the area. I went to all the likely places—the hardware store, the cafe, the sheriff's office. This is the way hunters used to get information about unfamiliar country, and there seemed something quaint and old-fashioned about the approach. Unfortunately, now that there are so many hunters and less available country, most locals are considerably more taciturn about giving out hot tips.

As I was filling out the license application and once again forking over my nonresident fees at the local oil and gas supplier, which for some reason handled hunting licenses here, I got talking to the owner of the establishment, a very tall, thin fellow named Jim Madden, a bird hunter himself. Oklahoma, he told me, had a more democratic history regarding hunting access than did its big neighbor to the south (it's no secret that Oklahomans are disdainful of Texas and Texans, and vice versa), and that his state was resisting the inexorable forces of "paid" hunting. Unfortunately, Madden explained, the practice seemed to be spreading over the border like a cancer as more and more farm and ranch lands were being leased to private groups. Madden told me about a consortium of physicians from Oklahoma who had recently tied up a large ranch in the area, fifty-two thousand acres, which they leased for one dollar an acre. "How can I compete with that?" he asked, adding flatly: "I'll hang up my gun before I pay to hunt."

For the next few days I hunted the Beaver River Wildlife Management Area, seventeen thousand acres of mixed shortgrass prairie and sand hills; gently rolling open country of sage and grass above a long winding river bottom, sparsely treed with bare cottonwoods, salt cedar, willow, tamarisk, elm, and locust. A remnant population of greater prairie chickens—for which there is a very short hunting season, now closed—survives here.

Quail season was still open and I camped for several days on the crest of a hill overlooking the river, lovely solitary days spent hunting alone, wandering the sand hills and the red dirt arroyos that cut down to the river, which was frozen along the edges, and—in some places—clear across. The landscape was vast and spare—buffalo country—the weather wintry after the sun set, well below freezing by morning, but crisp and sunny during the day, perfect walking and hunting weather. Sweetz and I covered many miles.

The hunting was less than spectacular; it was late in the season and the birds had been hunted hard all year; what coveys we found and the few birds killed were well earned. Whatever her innate shortcomings as a flushing dog in such big country, Sweetzer hunted beautifully in Oklahoma, like an old pro, keeping in just the right range, quartering and investigating every likely bit of cover, and diving enthusiastically into each plum thicket, their leafless branches a beautiful shade of purple. Though I had a general direction in mind, I had no particular course plotted and more or less followed Sweetz, deferring to her superior nose and bird sense. By now she knew better than I where to look for birds.

On the second morning, Sweetz flushed a covey of quail out of the grass against a hillside. I was in an awkward position that didn't offer a shot and we watched the birds set their wings and sail over the contour of the hills. We marked them down around a small stand of cottonwoods below. Walking in on them, she put several singles up again and I knocked one down but when we went to look for it we could not find it. I must have only broken a wing and the bird was running because several times Sweetz seemed to get on its trail and then lose it again. I hate to lose a cripple; it taints the rest of the day. We searched for an hour, hunted for a bit, came back and searched some more, but we couldn't find that bird.

The next day we started in a different area but by late morning had worked our way back to the same cottonwood stand, coming up on the other side of it this time. There I found the remains of a quail, possibly the one I had shot—a few feathers and a freshly picked skeleton, precisely and delicately stripped of flesh. I picked up one of the legs, the foot still attached, the fine skein of bone and cartilage translucent and oddly beautiful against the sky. A hawk or an owl must have made a meal of the bird. I kept the leg, and put it in my totem bag.

Late the following morning, our last there, Sweetz got birdy on the edge of a bowl of shortgrass. I hurried to keep up with her as I had learned to trust that stiff wagging tail and loudly snuffing nose. A single quail came whirring up out of the grass, then two more, then three, followed by the rest of the covey, perhaps a dozen birds in all. I shot both barrels and knocked down two birds. I should never admit to this but it was my first true double on quail on this trip, and other than Sweetzer, who promptly retrieved the birds, I had no witness. I sat down to rest and take a drink of water and to admire the pair of quail, both males, lying side by side in the grass. I squirted a stream of water to Sweetz from my plastic bottle; it was dry in this country and she opened her mouth eagerly to receive it. "Don't forget this part when you write your memoirs, Sweetzie—14,699 miles later and your partner finally shoots his first double on quail."

That's all I wanted to shoot that day—my larder was full—so we just walked and saw the country. I spent an hour or so sitting on a sand hill overlooking the river bottom, Sweetz snoozing in the sun beside me. There were quail tracks in the sand on the hill, and I spent a long time studying their dainty imprints.

Before I left Oklahoma, I spent a half day in the company of the biologist who managed the Beaver River Wildlife Area, a young native Oklahoman with the marvelous name of Wade Free, which sounded to me like some sort of exotic high-water fly fishing move. Free drove me around the wildlife area and showed me some of the ongoing work they were doing to restore the land and improve its carrying capacity for wildlife—prescribed burning, controlled grazing, discing the soil, and replanting native grasses and weeds—all to simulate the natural state of the country when the buffalo were still extant and before so much of the land had been altered by overgrazing and poor agricultural practices. Just beyond the perimeters of the wildlife area there was substantial evidence of such land abuse on some of the private holdings, and looking at the two side by side, it took no expert to recognize the difference between the healthy, healing, managed land, and the overgrazed, overfarmed, dead land, much of which had been succeeded by yucca and exotic weeds due to long-term suppression of the native grasses.

We drove down to check on the progress of some fencing that Free's men were doing—trying to keep a neighbor's cattle off the wildlife feed-plots. The management area works in conjunction with its neighboring landowners, providing free grazing and other economic incentives in exchange for which the farmer is required to plant and maintain one crop for wildlife, a crop he is not allowed to harvest or graze. This is an equitable arrangement for all parties and most of the local ranchers and farmers willingly cooperate. Inevitably, there are individuals who have learned to take advantage of these programs, and we happened to run into one such fellow that day.

The farmer, whom we shall call Floyd, was approaching in his pickup truck across the field from the other direction. "Oh, hell," Free said under his breath, "I was really hoping not to run into Floyd today. Wonder what he'll ask for this time."

Floyd was one of the neighboring landowners under contract with the WMA to farm one hundred acres of the area and to maintain his fences so that his cattle didn't get on management area land. He drove a brand-new pickup truck, spotlessly clean, the cleanest ranch vehicle I've ever seen.

The two trucks pulled up alongside each other, and Free and Floyd turned off their engines. They nodded and smiled at each other and a long silence ensued as both men squinted out across the prairie. They clearly had an adversarial relationship, barely concealed beneath tight, wry smiles.

Floyd looked like he was dressed for a Saturday night dance; he wore a brand-new, perfectly blocked Stetson, and a spotlessly clean, impeccably ironed white snap-button shirt. He was just about the tidiest rancher/farmer I'd ever seen in the middle of a work day, and, in fact, didn't look like he did much physical labor. Even his fingernails were perfect, as if he'd just had a manicure.

Free's fears were well founded. After some perfunctory small talk, Floyd worked around to his request—it seemed that he wanted the Wildlife Management Area to install a new twenty-thousand-dollar sprinkler system for him so that he could increase his alfalfa production.

Free laughed with thinly veiled disdain. "Now maybe you can explain to me, Floyd, how we're going to benefit from you being able to water your alfalfa better and triple your production?"

"Okay, I'll tell you," said Floyd, who'd obviously been studying the matter. "I'll only be able to cut alfalfa up until December and after that the wildlife can use it."

"Uh-huh," said Free, nodding. "Well, I'll tell you what Floyd, I'll make you a deal. We've done for you for the last four years and now you do something for us. All we ask is that you grow one itty-bitty crop for us. In four years you haven't managed to do that yet. And your fences are always down so your cattle are all the time getting in on our crops. You grow us a decent crop, keep your cows off it, and then we'll talk about that sprinkler system."

I was beginning to understand that the reason Floyd was so immaculately neat, without a speck of dirt under his fingernails, was that the way he really made his living was not so much by the honest sweat of his brow while he toiled at the venerable vocations of ranching and farming, but by an uncanny talent he had cultivated for filling out the various federal and state subsidy application forms, a mazelike labyrinth of paper work with which Floyd had made himself intimately familiar. You could hardly blame him for it; this occupation is considerably more profitable than ranching and farming.

Here's how one of Floyd's farm scams works: Floyd signs up for a United States Soil Conservation Service (SCS) farm program whereby he is paid $20 an acre by the agency to grow a crop that he must leave standing for wildlife. He grows the crop and collects his payment. Shortly thereafter, Floyd's cattle mysteriously get through a hole in the fence, and even more mysteriously Floyd doesn't notice this for several weeks, until his cattle have grazed down the entire wildlife plot. Even if the SCS catches his cattle in the plot, Floyd simply pleads ignorance and moves them off, until the next time that they accidentally get through the fence. At the very worst, and only after being caught repeatedly at this offense, Floyd will be assessed a small fine. In the meantime, in effect, he has been paid twice for that crop.

This is a more complicated scheme, so stay with me here: There is excess wheat on the world market, so, in order to use up surpluses, the SCS gives free wheat seed to Floyd to plant, say, 100 acres, and they also pay him $10 an acre to plant the seed. By the terms of this arrangement, though he is paid for the entire 100-acre crop, Floyd is allowed to harvest only half the wheat—the other half he must leave standing or plow under so as not to flood the market with yet more wheat. Again, and entirely by accident, Floyd's cattle get through the fence and graze down the whole 100 acres of wheat before he's managed to harvest the 50 acres. Floyd goes to his insurance company and claims disaster—his cows got in and ate all his wheat, he explains. The insurance company reimburses him for the value of the entire 100-acre crop, even though he's already been paid for it once by the government, and notwithstanding the fact that he's also grazed his cattle on it. Thus, in effect, Floyd has been paid three times for this crop.

But even that is not enough for Floyd. Now he goes back to the SCS and tells *them* that he's had a disaster—the cattle have eaten all his wheat down and he wants permission to plant oats in that same field. By the terms of this particular program he is not allowed to plant oats unless he's had a disaster, which, of course, he now has. Floyd is given permission, plants his oats, and, come spring, puts his cattle in to graze those oats.

The following spring he declares disaster once again because that oat field which, of course, was grazed down by his cattle, comes up as volunteer wheat, which Floyd claims choked out his oats. And so on and so forth—an endless bureaucratic shell game in which Floyd always knows under what shell the pea is concealed.

"He's a beggar," sighed Wade Free, shaking his head, after we drove away from our encounter with Floyd. "But he's real good at it. Real good. He's one in a million."

35

THE SPORT OF KINGS

When his Majesty (the Great Khan) has resided the usual time in the metropolis, and leaves it in the month of March, he proceeds in a north-easterly direction, to within two days' journey of the ocean, attended by full ten thousand falconers, who carry with them a vast number of gerfalcons, peregrine falcons, and sakers, as well as many vultures, in order to pursue the game along the river. The Great Khan follows the chase in a pavilion borne upon the backs of four elephants, a conveyance rendered necessary to him during his hunting excursions, in consequence of the gout, with which he is troubled.

In the pavilion he always carries with him twelve of his best gerfalcons, with twelve of his favorite officers, to bear him company and amuse him. Those who are on horseback by his side give him notice of the approach of cranes or other birds, upon which he raises the curtain of the pavilion, and when he espies the game, gives direction for letting fly the gerfalcons, which seize the cranes and overpower them after a long struggle. The view of this sport, as he lies upon his couch, affords extreme satisfaction to his Majesty. . . .

Marco Polo (circa 1298)

We made a stab north from Oklahoma to Coldwater, Kansas, for a short quail hunt with an old friend and gentleman sportsman, George Purnell. I could feel the barometer plunging and I was out of sorts all afternoon, hunting listlessly and worried about being caught by a storm this far north this time of year. As if sensing my mood, Sweetz, too, was ill-behaved and inattentive, embarrassing us both in front of Purnell and his fine English pointers.

I camped for the night on the banks of Lake Coldwater, still unable to shake a certain sense of trepidation. It was way off-season and I was the only camper, the prestorm evening quite beautiful with the sky a stunning red at sunset. Enormous flocks of Canada geese circled in to land for the night, filling a patch of open water in the middle of the lake, while hundreds of

ducks set their wings and dropped their feet like landing gear to put down
on the ice, skidding comically and crashing into one another before coming
finally to a stop. Then they began the long march to another patch of open
water at the inlet where they would spend the night. Watching their funny,
duck-footed waddle en masse, I wondered how I could possibly kill so
wonderful a creature. I watched them through my binoculars until it was
too dark to see.

The storm blew in around midnight, a high, cold wind rattling and
shaking the camper, pelting it with icy snow. Unable to sleep, I worried for
the ducks and geese, and about the drive tomorrow; with Sweetz under the
covers with me, I remembered a young boy lying in bed with his little
terrier, Sugar, thirty years ago in the Midwest, worrying for his parents and
for himself. I would like to think that boy was free, at large at last in the
countryside; but still he worried.

Snow swirled on the ground the next morning but the worst of the storm
had blown through overnight. I was walking Sweetz and watching the
ducks on the lake through my binoculars when a couple of men drove up in
a new Buick. They stopped and I went over to talk to them. They had a
carton of Salem cigarettes on the seat between them and they were both
smoking and drinking coffee, evidently out for a Sunday morning drive.
The driver introduced himself as the owner of the Gambel's store in town,
and expressed his surprise at finding a camper out here this time of year; he
wanted to know what brought me. I told him. "Maybe you'll put us in your
book," the store owner said, hopefully. "Maybe you wouldn't mind men-
tioning that Lake Coldwater is the only place in southwestern Kansas
where you can water-ski."

Southward again, we angled back across the Texas panhandle (some dog-
ugly, denuded, used-up agribusiness land there, land that does not look
remotely birdy), coming to rest finally just over the border in the vaguely
eerie sand plains country of eastern New Mexico.

Too small to be called hills, the dunes and ridges hereabout have the
look of a light choppy sea against the sky, seem to dance and shimmer on
the horizon; they are not precisely pretty, definitely an acquired taste in
country. And there is plenty of horizon in these parts, almost nothing but
the sand choppies, as they are sometimes called, to disturb it—that and a
few clumps of elm trees marking the old homestead sites on virtually every
section. The homesteaders came here, plowed up the thin prairie soil, and
tried to plant corn and various other crops, but freed from its anchoring
grassroots, the topsoil blew away on the wind. The same thing happened in

parts of west Texas, where now they grow cotton on the dead land and where on a windy day you can still see the billows of topsoil coming up behind the tractors, headed for the jetstream. There are few game birds in such country.

But in other parts of west Texas and here in eastern New Mexico, only a few miles from the border, one of the last huntable populations of the once plentiful greater prairie chicken are still resident. As in Oklahoma, the short gun season on prairie chicken was well over by the time of my visit and, in any case, I came not to hunt them but to watch them hunted by another predator—a bird of prey.

Jim Weaver lives in the back of the beyond of this strangely haunting country—some miles beyond the end of the road past Lingo, New Mexico. Weaver is a former technical associate for the Laboratory of Ornithology at Cornell University and former president of the North American Falconers' Association. He moved here a few years ago for no other reason than that it is the last best place in the United States to fly birds of prey on prairie chickens for a few months out of the year.

Weaver wasn't around when I pulled in to his place, past a fenced pasture where the visitor is greeted by a flock of a dozen or so Australian emu—a member of the ostrich family—huge, fantastical birds whose presense in this already surreal landscape seemed somehow not at all out of place. I parked and Sweetz and I walked up to the fence to look at the emus. Three-toed, duck-footed, and geekish, they ran at us threateningly with weird swaying motions, at once graceful and clumsy, like imaginary creatures designed by a special effects man for a Steven Spielberg movie. They weaved and feinted and made a strange angry hissing noise at Sweetzer. Some of them (the females, I learned later) swelled their necks and issued a booming sound like a bass drum—clearly a warning. Not that they had anything to fear from us. Indeed, these were perhaps the first birds Sweetz had ever seen that she had no interest whatsoever in adding to her life list of retrieves. They were way out of her frame of reference, and she seemed unwilling to acknowledge that they were even birds. She kept her head averted, as if frightened to look at them directly, and cast furtive, sidelong glances their way.

I watched the emus, and looked out over the shimmering plains, musing on the distinct possibility that perhaps Mr. Weaver was a tad bit eccentric. A moment later, the man himself roared up in a jeep and climbed out holding a string of dead rabbits. He strode briskly over to introduce himself. Weaver bears an uncanny resemblance to the actor

Clint Eastwood, a resemblance reinforced by a muscular build, a taciturn no-nonsense manner, and the long-barreled .22-caliber pistol he wore in a shoulder holster—his rabbit gun.

I followed Weaver into the steel shed, where he had his office and kept his prize falcon, a gyrfalcon/peregrine hybrid. They are stunning-looking animals that command attention, and this one had sleek mottled bluish gray plumage and clear, yellow eyes that watched me dispassionately. "Where did you get him?" I asked in a quiet voice.

"I made him," answered Weaver, a man of few words.

Weaver dressed and skinned his rabbits while I pestered him with questions about this extremely arcane form of game bird hunting. The "oldest sport on earth," falconry originated among the Mongols of Central Asia around 2000 B.C. Introduced to Europe by A.D. 560, the sport flourished there for centuries—the sport of kings, emperors, sultans, czars, and popes.

The wide popularity of falconry did not survive the invention of gunpowder, and today the sport is pursued with considerably less fanfare than in the time of the great Kublai Khan. There are only about three thousand falconers and hawkers in the United States, of that number considerably fewer who own birds and hunt regularly, and only a handful who pursue the sport with anything like the single-minded dedication of Jim Weaver, who, of his passion for falconry, says simply, "It's ruined my life."

In spite of the esoteric nature of falconry, the small number of people who actually pursue it, and the fact that relative to the shotgun it is hardly an efficient method of taking game, the sport remains controversial in this country—much maligned and misunderstood.

"We're the only group of people who are allowed to keep live wildlife in this country," Weaver explained, "and a lot of people don't like that. You're allowed to kill it, but you can't keep it."

In order to become licensed to legally own and fly a bird of prey, one must apprentice to a master falconer for a full two years, which might help explain why the sport has never caught on with the hunting public, even the most cretinous of whom can own and use a shotgun on game with a minimum amount of training and knowledge.

"For only three thousand practitioners," Weaver continued, "we have an exceptional battery of regulations and legislation to monitor ourselves, as well as to protect the raptors. Every once in a while we go through a thing where we wonder if the public is well informed enough about the sport, and do we want to bother trying to inform them—would they understand anyway? The arguments are so overwhelmingly pro-falconry, but some people just don't want to hear them."

Long popular in the Middle East, particularly in the Persian and

Arabian gulfs, not the least of falconry's public relations problems in the United States is our own cultural and political xenophobia regarding the Arab world. There is something about those photos of the shiek in desert headgear with manned falcon on gloved arm that tends to promote a bad image of the sport in this country.

While historically an important means of supplementing the comparatively Spartan diet of the Persian Gulf region, the Arabs' continued passion for falconry comes with no commensurate notion of conservation or of the most basic principles of game management—their motto in such matters: Allah will provide. In the past couple of decades as oil-rich shieks, princes, and emirs find themselves with ever greater purchasing power and plenty of leisure time, the huntable game in the region has been drastically depleted, both with hawks and with shotguns. As a result, these days Allah isn't providing much of anything in the way of game and Arab hawkers are having to take their show on the road—to India, Pakistan, or wherever else there is still something to hunt.

In 1981 the U.S. Fish and Wildlife Service (USFWS) launched a widely publicized undercover "sting" operation called "Operation Falcon." The purpose of the sting, which targeted members of the tiny North American Falconers' Association, and primarily peregrine falcon breeders, was to uncover the alleged American and Canadian black markets in endangered and protected raptors. The USFWS had it in mind that falconers were routinely robbing nests and/or illegally selling birds to wealthy international patrons (Arabs included), and the agency spent several years and hundreds of thousands of dollars of taxpayer money trying to prove this. The end result of their abortive entrapment effort, in which their own agents did most of the nest robbing, as well as conducting most of the illegal sales, was that the law enforcement division of USFWS was severely reprimanded by a House subcommittee and those officials responsible forced to apologize to the North American Falconers' Association. Jim Weaver, then president of the association, testified before the subcommittee.

That evening Weaver invited me to dinner at the adobe house he himself built on his ranch, and he served prairie chicken killed earlier in the season by his hybrid tiercel (male falcon). My contribution to dinner was a six-pack of Budweiser longnecks and an hors d'oeuvre of crabmeat and jalapeño pepper fritters brought from Texas.

Weaver's own commitment to conservation was such that he had stopped hunting local prairie chickens this year due to unusually low populations as a result of a spring drought. But as I had never seen a manned falcon in action, he agreed to fly his bird for me the following afternoon.

Weaver was more talkative over dinner, a bright, urbane, well-traveled man (having only recently been to Alaska and Africa), with an intimate and comprehensive knowledge of wildlife and wildlife issues. He was further proof of the rather obvious fact that quite often the most interesting people live in the least fashionable places. Whereas urbanites sometimes imagine living in the country as an escape from the "real" world, it is anything but. Men like Weaver, who care deeply about wildlife and the natural world, are in the position of witnessing, on an almost daily basis, the ongoing depredations that are being visited upon the land and upon wildlife: the historically bad agricultural practices, the ignorance and greed of landowners and federal agencies, the vanishing habitat and ruined land.

"In many ways," Weaver pointed out over dinner, "it's easier to live in a place like Manhattan, where one's primary concerns are dinner and the theater.

"Sometimes I look around," he added, smiling, "and I wonder what the hell I'm doing here."

Weaver refers to the burgeoning antihunting community in America as "the minders of other people's business," and one suspects that another reason he lives out here is simply to be left alone.

Few Americans realize that it was the fraternity of falconers and falcon breeders, under the auspices of the North American Falconers' Association, who in the mid 1960s were largely responsible for launching the Peregrine Fund and thus saving the endangered peregrine falcon from almost certain extinction as a result of pesticide (DDT) use. The organization and its members not only helped focus world and national attention on the dire plight of the peregrine, they raised funds for scientific research and provided manpower in the field as well as critical breeding stock for the massive recovery and species restoration program. As a direct result of the efforts of a couple of thousand individuals, peregrine falcon populations have been stabilized and the bird now thrives in greater numbers in the United States than at any time since the 1950s. Roger Tory Peterson, world-renowned naturalist, wildlife author, and bird expert, calls it "one of the most remarkable conservation stories of our time." Under the circumstances, it would seem difficult to begrudge these few people the pursuit of their ancient venatic art form.

Weaver's rooster woke me the next morning at 4:15 with his premature crowing. I cracked the camper door open and tried to explain to him that he was supposed to wait until dawn, but he only crowed with renewed enthusiasm and started pecking the camper; it was obvious that I wasn't going back to sleep.

It was a frigid morning, with a sliver of waning moon still in the sky and a dust of snow on the ground. The wind came up shortly after daylight, blowing the snow in curls over the dunes. Weaver had business in town and we wouldn't be flying the falcon until evening, so Sweetz and I took a long walk around the ranch. I carried my gun as there were also quail in this country.

The country didn't get any less strange being out in the middle of it on foot, and in fact, I found it a bit melancholy, which may have had to do with the wind moaning across the plains. Weaver was trying to restore some of the native grasses and institute agricultural practices that would be beneficent both to the wildlife and to the land, hoping to save what remained of the topsoil on his place and at the same time increase his game populations. He also raised some beef cattle.

We didn't find any quail, but had a fine walk and saw the country, and wandered upon a wonderful little adobe cabin on the prairie where I took brief sanctuary from the wintry wind. The cabin—small, Spartan, nearly monkish—belonged to the writer Dan O'Brien, who lives in South Dakota and is a friend of Weaver's and fellow falconer. O'Brien wrote a lovely book about the sport, called *The Rites of Autumn*, published in 1988.

Weaver's old setter, Dan, accompanied us, and he and Sweetz had a good run together. On the way back I shot a rabbit, as I like to eat them, and after I shot it, I let it lie on the ground for a while until the body cooled and the fleas bailed out. I put it in my game bag and skinned and cleaned it back at Weaver's shed.

The wind had layed down by afternoon, and Weaver and I drove out to an alfalfa field where the prairie chickens come to feed in the evenings. Weaver sent his English pointer out to quarter the field and released the falcon from his arm. He had apologized in advance for what he thought was going to be an unspectacular flight. Appreciation of this rarefied sport is strictly in the eye of the beholder, and to the critical eye of the expert like Weaver, a great flight is only achieved when any number of variables come together in perfect sync: the falcon soaring so high in the air that it is nearly invisible; the dog pointing and holding the birds; the man walking in to make the flush at just the right instant to maximize the falcon's chances; the falcon spotting the birds at the right time, picking one out and committing to it in a perfect "stoop," and taking it cleanly.

To an untrained eye such as my own, the fact that the falcon was presently circling the alfalfa field overhead, watching us and clearly participating as a partner in the hunt, seemed a remarkable enough feat. This served, too, to put my own puny efforts with a shotgun into proper perspective.

Within minutes, the dog went on point across the field and Weaver and I broke into a run to reach him. Weaver kept one eye on the falcon circling in the sky as we ran and even called out to it at one point in order to get its attention. The falcon heard him and turned. Upon reaching the dog, I hung back, while Weaver, gauging the right moment, walked in to flush the birds. A small flock of eight or nine prairie chickens got up; they are swift, strong flyers, capable of flying long distances once they gain airspeed. The falcon picked one out, folded its wings, and went into an angled stoop. Gyrfalcons being the largest and fastest of falcons, and peregrines the most aggressive and athletic, this particular hybrid was the aviary equivalent of a Stealth fighter plane—in a full stoop capable of flying 200 mph. Despite the fact that as a novice spectator I might not be able to appreciate all the finer esthetics of the sport, the sight of that bird in a stoop raised goose bumps on my arms.

As Weaver hadn't been hunting his falcon, like an athlete during the off-season, the bird had gained two or three critical ounces (equivalent to twenty or thirty pounds in a human being). Nor was the well-fed tiercel especially hungry, and when it reached its prey, it pulled up short and almost casually strummed the chicken on the back with its talons, as if playing a game of tag, before veering casually away. A few feathers floated in the air, but the prairie chicken, unharmed, flew on.

At last—catch-and-release hunting.

36

CITIZEN OF
THE LAND

The farmer attends only to what is good or bad for the growth of his grain . . . , the rest remains outside his vision and, in consequence, he remains outside the completeness that is the countryside. The tourist sees broadly the great spaces, but his gaze glides, it seizes nothing, it does not perceive the role of each ingredient in the dynamic architecture of the countryside. Only the hunter, imitating the perpetual alertness of the wild animal, sees everything. . . .

Ortega y Gasset

South and west, the prairie fell away to desert: Portales, Ruidoso, Mescalero, Alamogordo, Las Cruces. Poetry in the names, but the real romance lay outside town, in the rimrock and sand, the hard white desert rock, rising into mountains and surprisingly verdant valleys. After a short trip north into the Nimbres Mountains of the Gila National Forest to see the land where the young Aldo Leopold got his start in game management (and where early in his career he recommended extermination of wolves and other predators, a heresy that he recanted later in life), we came to rest in Rodeo, New Mexico, hard against the border of Arizona. I liked the country right off—a broad expanse of scrubby plains with long mountain ranges on either side that reminded me somewhat of a southwestern version of my home country in northern Colorado.

I was supposed to meet an old friend down here, a burly, bearded painter named Doug Baer. I hadn't seen or talked to Baer in several years, nor had any of his other old friends. I had heard rumors that he had holed up in an abandoned rent-free homestead cabin in the Badlands of South Dakota, on the heels of a bad romance that relieved him of all assets and set the hounds of creditors upon him. I had looked for him when I went through that country months ago, but couldn't find him; nor had the creditors, who rarely go to the trouble of tracking insolvent artists to such remote places as the Dakota Badlands. I had heard Baer got some good work done while he was there.

Through a mysterious process of telephone calls to several states, I finally managed to track Baer down, and had arranged to meet him in Rodeo for what would ultimately be my last few days of hunting this long season. The trip was winding down, time running out. I did not want it to end.

There was a decidedly scruffy border atmosphere to this part of the country, land of illegal immigrants and a booming drug smuggling trade, a kind of wide-open, anything-goes feeling that seemed to match the harsh desert landscape. Anonymous abandoned vehicles with no license plates were canted at odd angles off the highway, and occasionally the hunter wandered upon the wreckage of an airplane that had gone down in mysterious circumstances. Locals have many tales to tell.

In the desert just outside Rodeo, a sign on a trailer, its roof secured by tires, grandly proclaimed *Chateau Guillaume*—Bill's Castle. The town itself was tiny and sleepy and looked to have gone through several cycles of boom and bust. There was a post office, a small general store with a soda fountain and one gas pump, a bar, an old church converted into an art gallery, and a number of abandoned buildings, most of them crumbling back to earth. Several generations of junked cars were lined up neatly in a yard in the middle of town, and looked like a museum display telling the tale of Detroit. Things refuse to rust in this dry desert air.

I parked by the boarded-up train station across the street from the tiny post office, made a sandwich, and enjoyed the quiet rhythms of the town. People came and went from the post office—mainly weather-beaten locals in unfashionable vehicles with noisy mufflers. An old ranch couple with a full load of hay on their truck drove by at about 6 mph; they sat right beside each other in the cab of the pickup like a couple of teenage lovers. Two pregnant mongrels, one black and one yellow, waddled together across the highway, as if commiserating in their maternity.

I may have dozed off there sitting in the sun.

I spent my first night parked on the banks of Cave Creek under a lovely white-barked canyon sycamore in a deserted campground in the Coronado National Forest of Arizona. In the middle of the night, a black bear brought out of hibernation by the unseasonably mild weather bumped the camper before shuffling off into the darkness. At least, that's how I remember it. I know I didn't dream it, though Sweetz slept through the whole thing. The next day, when I let her out for her morning constitutional, her hackles rose up on her neck when she caught the scent. Some watchdog.

I never knew how these things were going to work out, and I was actually somewhat surprised that Baer arrived in Rodeo that same day. I called the phone number he had given me that belonged to his rancher friends, the Millers, and drove out to the ranch to meet him. I arrived in time for a picnic lunch and afterward the Millers took me on a tour of the ranch.

Bill Miller, Sr., and Bill Miller, Jr., are third- and fourth-generation ranchers, respectively, salt-of-the-earth men who provide community and a sense of permanence to the land; they seem to offer ballast to the otherwise transient and frequently outlaw feel of the region. Besides ranching, Bill, Jr., a tall, wry, easygoing man, is also a pilot and flies a monthly inspection tour of a natural gas pipeline out of El Paso. His father is a small, slight, inquisitive gentleman with a ready smile. I recognized on our tour of the ranch that the Millers were stewards of the land in the highest sense of the term—the kind of folks Thomas Jefferson had in mind would take care of things.

In this book I have been critical of some ranchers and farmers across the country. Encouraged by the federal government, some are guilty of heinous crimes against the earth, and nowhere more than in parts of the Southwest where the land is simply too delicate to tolerate overuse and bad management. Aldo Leopold witnessed the depredations from cattle grazing here seventy-five years ago, and since then things have gone from bad to worse. More recently, the late Edward Abbey made a blanket condemnation of the industry's practice of grazing public lands; he called (however tongue-in-cheek) for an open hunting season on range cattle. The Millers know of Abbey and despise him. Do not get them started on the subject of environmentalists. They believe that the movement is trying to put them out of business, and they are currently involved in a bitter court case with environmentally minded neighbors—the new breed of gentleman ranchers who don't ranch, and would like to put some of those who do out of business.

"I've been an environmentalist all my life," said Bill Miller, Sr., in his soft voice. "You couldn't ranch this country for all the years that my family has and not take care of it. You'd go out of business. This land is in better condition now than it was fifty years ago." Indeed, the Millers know every blade of grass on the place, and they nurture the land with a kind of spiritual care and fervor. In dry years, they take their cattle to market early rather than risk overgrazing the fragile range. The country is not only their livelihood but their life.

Driving around the place that afternoon, we came upon a herd of deer. Though they see deer nearly every day, Bill, Jr., stopped the jeep and he and his wife, Carol, watched the herd with the kind of reverence and wonder that is usually reserved for tourists who have never laid eyes on a deer before. As the sun dropped down that evening over the mountains across the plains, Bill parked on a rise so that we could all admire the scene as the valley shaded pink before us. "Not bad, is it?" he asked in a voice of real admiration and respect. He'd been watching sunsets here for fifty years but each was still special to him.

For the next few days, we would hunt three species of native quail (harlequin, Gambel, and scaled) on the Millers' ranch, which spills across the state line of New Mexico into Arizona. Quail populations were down this year, by now a familiar refrain of this trip, but that made our hunts no less enjoyable. Low bird populations tend to be a self-regulating factor for conscientious sportsmen and land managers, and the Millers hadn't been hunting much this season, saving their few coveys for our visit. Even then we hunted sparingly, a bird here and a bird there, each pointed covey, each hard-earned bird killed, specific and precious.

In the evening, Carol Miller fed us wonderful country meals—baked hams and home-baked pies—and we talked for hours around the dinner table. These were just the people I had imagined visiting and sharing meals with when I first dreamed this trip, lying in bed as a boy all those years ago. This was the American family I had in mind, and there seemed a wonderful sense of having come full circle.

I killed my first scaled quail, a lovely pale gray bird, on my first shot on the first morning of hunting in the flats; one of those nearly perfect situations where everything—even, remarkably, the shooter—works. The covey had already been broken up by a hawk and the single bird was pointed for me by one of Bill's fine Brittanies, Nell.

Afterward we hunted Cottonwood Canyon, where Baer walked in on Prissy's point on a steep hillside and made a fine shot on a going-away Gambel quail, a beautiful brown and gray bird with a curved black head plume. From below, Bill, Jr., and I had an excellent view of the shot. Bill didn't carry a gun, but handled his dogs, who were truly superb and whom he had trained himself and of whom he was obviously proud. We had his dad's dogs with us, too—Rusty and Penny.

"You know," Bill confided in me, "sometimes when I'm watching my dogs holding a point, it almost brings tears to my eyes, it's so beautiful. I just love these dogs." You think ranchers are by nature hardhearted and inured to the sentimentality common to animal lovers? That's only because you've never heard Bill Miller talk baby talk to his beloved Brittanies.

Baer came down off the hillside with his quail in hand, which he brought over to show me. I'd never seen a gambel before, and what I remember is the way Baer so gently smoothed the bird's ruffled feathers back, a loving gesture, made with the artist's delicacy of touch. Baer is a veteran of the Vietnam war, where he served as a sniper. We don't talk much about it.

Baer grew up in North Yellowstone, Montana, where the rites of passage into manhood included learning to be a good shot, knowing how to take care of yourself in the outdoors, and killing a deer. His childhood had no connection to the popular culture so many of us grew up with, especially suburban midwestern boys such as myself—no connection to TV or professional baseball heroes. Some mornings there would be a grizzly bear in the yard of Baer's house and he would be late to school on account of it. He would take a note signed by his mother to the teacher: "Grizzly made me late." When he moved to Chicago to attend art school, Baer learned that such tales had no currency in the broader world, particularly the urban art world. He may as well have been a foreigner without the language. It was a solitary time and Baer stopped telling the stories, which entered his art. He became a very fine wildlife sculptor. He understands figures and shapes, the muscled roundness of the natural world that is the model for everything else.

In the field, Baer was constantly stopping, stooping down to pick things up off the ground, things that told some tale, suggested some small natural drama. We hunted higher up into Cottonwood Canyon, which became narrower, steeper, and rockier as we went. "God had a bushelful of rocks left over," Bill, Sr., had explained, "and that's where He put them." We were looking for the third species of quail—harlequin (commonly known as Mearns'), often called fool quail because they hold so tight on the ground, refusing to fly, that sometimes horses and cattle actually step on them. Cowboys worry about having a covey get up underneath their horse, spooking it, and many have been bucked off that way in this country. Mearns' also put out almost no scent, making them notoriously difficult for dogs to locate.

Earlier, at the elder Miller's house, nestled in a lush oasislike setting at the base of the Peloncillo Mountains two canyons over, I had seen their incredible collection of metates—the ancient corn grinding stones of the prehistoric Indians who once inhabited this region. The metates had all been found on the ranch over the years, a number of them here in Cottonwood Canyon. Because of the year-round spring that ran through the canyon and nourished the cottonwoods after which it was named, this had been a favorite place for human beings to take up residence in the otherwise arid land.

As we climbed, Bill, Jr., told us more about the rich history of the canyon. He showed us an old corral built entirely of stones by a fellow who used to break horses up here fifty years ago. The worn snubbing post was still visible in the center of the corral. A little farther up we came to the remains of an old windmill and well, said to have belonged to some enterprising moonshiners who inhabited the canyon for a while, and a bit farther on, an old cabin foundation where a Basque sheepherder once lived.

Farther up yet we stopped to rest along the spring, beneath an old oak tree under which Bill told us lay the graves of three young cowboys killed by Apaches. Under this same oak tree, a strongbox full of the proceeds from a train robbery was also said to have been buried. The robbers were caught, convicted, and served their time, the story went, came back twenty years later, dug up the strongbox, and reclaimed their spoils. Bill, Sr., was just seven years old and he remembered seeing the men riding back down the canyon with bulging saddlebags.

That morning we put up one covey of Mearns' that came buzzing up like firecrackers out of a manzanita bush alongside the spring. They are smaller and even faster than bobwhite, or any of the other quail species for that matter, and they seem to rise straight up in the air and then peel off, vanishing. I fired both barrels and missed, as did Baer.

We walked back down to the mouth of Cottonwood Canyon, four Brittanies and a Lab quartering ahead, and ate lunch by the vehicles while weary dogs flopped in the shade.

The next afternoon, hunting across the highway in Arizona, we got into a large covey of running Gambel quail, notorious among southwestern bird hunters for that characteristic. It is said that one needs to wear running shoes to hunt Gambels. Here's how it was according to a last journal entry.

> The Brittanies, running and pointing, running and pointing, could never quite hold the birds. I could see the quail dashing like road runners ahead of us, from sage bush to sage bush, darting and hiding and darting, making their shrill cries. Their scent was everywhere and Sweetz too was chasing them, but of course she was under no genetic compunction to stop and try to point them. Baer, Bill, and I had spread out across the plains, and were also jogging through the sage in hot pursuit. It was great fun, unlike any hunting I'd done yet; I was laughing as I ran. Finally Sweetz caught up to a bird and pushed it into the air where it made a tactical error, looping back toward me. I shot it and Sweetz retrieved it.

We spent our last afternoon on Horseshoe Creek in Arizona, a broad canyon that opened up into a lush, gorgeous park. I was headed home first thing the next morning and this would be the last hunt of the year, the last of over one hundred days in the field this longest season. It had long ago occurred to me that I would never again in my life make a trip like this; never again hunt this many days or this many game bird species in this many places, or see so much country in one season. I had known from the beginning that this day was coming, and now I wasn't sad about the end of the road. Now I had lived it.

As we were walking through the high meadow a Mearns' quail got up like a buzz bomb out of the grass at my feet. Here, at the end of my trip, I would like to reward the loyal reader, who has been so patient with my shooting flubs across the country, with an eloquent description of how I mounted my gun with lightning-fast reflexes, smoothly swung, fired, and cleanly dropped the quail. But I can't lie to you, and in any case, by now you would see right through it. The truth is, startled once again out of a reverie by the proximity of the flush, I rocked back on my heels, fumbled with the safety, and mounted my gun in agonizing slow motion, already aware as I pulled the trigger that I had let the speedy little bullet of a bird get too far out. I missed cleanly.

I marked the bird down and Baer and I walked in on it. The quail got up again and peeled off to Baer's side and he killed it. The sun was setting over the rimrock above the canyon, the sky turning the strange, striking iridescent pinkish purple that often precedes a storm. Between the two of us, Baer and I had killed only three birds in a hard, full day of hunting in two states. We pulled them out of our game pouches to look at them, as hunters sometimes do at the end of the day. Entirely by accident we had one bird of each of the three indigenous species—one Mearns', one Gambel, one scaled quail. We laid the three of them down side by side on a rock, the light on the canyon walls changing shades with each moment. How extraordinary those three quail seemed, how perfectly beautiful the variances of color and form, the differently and exquisitely patterned feathers. We gazed at the quail reverently and softly smoothed their breast feathers before putting them back in our game bags.

There is nothing more to be said about this hunter's season. Baer and I walked back down the dirt road at the base of the canyon in the dusky light. Sweetzer ran ahead.

37

HOME

And here at last is your hut. Through a window you see a table, with a white cloth, a candle burning, supper. . . .

Ivan Turgenev

Well below zero on a snowy night, the first day of February, Sweetz and I pulled back up in front of our cabin in northern Colorado. It had been a two-day drive home, the longest drive yet as there had been no stops along the way to hunt.

Home country seemed like another world from the one we had left behind in the Southwest—frigid with over a foot of snow on the ground. My wife was still in Florida, and I had phoned ahead to ask my friend Don Reed to come by and light fires in the fireplace and the kitchen cookstove. I had no electric power but the cabin was warm and snug by the time I arrived; I lit candles and a kerosene lamp.

I had brought a bundle of mesquite wood with me from New Mexico, and I laid a pyramid of sticks on the fire. I cleaned three quail—one Mearns', one Gambel, and one scaled. The Mearns' had a crop full of small brown tubers, which they dig from the ground with a special spur that grows on one foot. The palmful of tiny tubers went into my totem bag.

When the mesquite wood had burned down to red coals, I grilled the three quail—basted with olive oil, crushed garlic, and pepper flakes. With them I grilled five varieties of southwestern peppers—red, yellow, and three shades of green—running the gamut from sweet to hot. I drank Mexican beer and ate this festively colored meal with my fingers in front of the fire. I fed the quail carcasses to Sweetzer.

Then—exhausted, spent, and sated—we curled up together on the rug before the fire. The snow fell steadily outside, huge white flakes drifting past the window. We fell asleep and dreamed our dream of hunters.

SWEETZER'S TRIP LIST:
Birds retrieved, 1990–91

Sage grouse
Blue grouse
Sharptail grouse
Pinnated grouse (lesser prairie chicken)
Ruffed grouse
Chukar partridge
Gray (Hungarian) partridge
Ring-necked pheasant
American woodcock
Bobwhite quail
Scaled quail
Gambel quail
Harlequin (Mearns') quail
Mallard
Green-winged teal
Gadwall
Northern pintail
American wigeon
Mourning dove
Common snipe
Central Park pigeon

TOTAL: TWENTY-ONE SPECIES

BIBLIOGRAPHY AND
SUGGESTED READING

The following books are recommended to anyone interested in upland bird hunting (and related subjects), nature, the outdoors, conservation, wildlife biology, natural history, or literature (the lines between these categories are not always well delineated). Of course, there are many other interesting and instructional books available about bird hunting and the author apologizes in advance for the inevitable omissions.

Bodio, Stephen. *Good Guns*. New York: Nick Lyons Books, 1986.

Bourjaily, Vance. *The Unnatural Enemy*. New York: Dial, 1963.

Bowlen, Bruce. *The Orvis Wing-Shooting Handbook: Proven Techniques for Better Shotgunning*. New York: Nick Lyons Books, 1985.

Cade, Tom J., James H. Endersen, Carl. G. Thelander, and Clayton M. White, eds. *Peregrine Falcon Populations: Their Management and Recovery*. Boise, Idaho: The Peregrine Fund, Inc., 1988.

Elman, Robert, and David Seybold, eds. *Seasons of the Hunter.* New York: Knopf, 1985.

Evans, George Bird. *An Affair with Grouse*. Bruceton Mills, W. Va.: Old Hemlock, 1982.

————. *The Upland Shooting Life*. New York: Knopf, 1971.

Foster, William Harnden. *New England Grouse Shooting*. New York: Charles Scribner's Sons, 1942.

Grooms, Steve. *Pheasant Hunter's Harvest*. New York: Lyons & Burford, 1990.

Gullion, Gordon. *The Ruffed Grouse*. Minoqua, Wis.: NorthWord Press, 1989.

Hastings, Macdonald. *Robert Churchill's Game Shooting.* Traverse City, Mich.: Countrysport Press, 1963, 1971, 1990.

Hamsun, Knut. *Pan.* New York: Farrar, Straus & Giroux, 1956, 1984.

Hemingway, Ernest. *A Farewell to Arms.* New York: Charles Scribner's Sons, 1929.

Hill, Gene. *Shotgunner's Notebook: The Advice and Reflections of a Wingshooter.* Traverse City, Mich.: Countrysport Press, 1989.

Hinman, Bob. *The Golden Age of Shotgunning.* Prescott, Ariz.: Wolfe Publishing Co., Inc., 1982.

Johnsgard, Paul A. *Grouse and Quails of North America.* Lincoln, Nebr.: University of Nebraska Press, 1973.

Jones, Robert F., with photographs by Bill Eppridge. *Upland Passage: A Field Dog's Education.* New York: Farrar, Straus, Giroux, 1992.

Leopold, Aldo. *A Sand County Almanac: With Essays on Conservation from Round River.* New York: Ballantine Books, 1970, 1989.

Mackenzie, John P. S. *Game Birds.* London: Harrap Publishing Group, 1989.

Matthiessen, Peter. *Wildlife in America.* New York: Viking Penguin, Inc., 1959, 1987.

McIntosh, Michael. *Best Guns.* Traverse City, Mich.: Countrysport Press, 1989.

Mitchell, John G. *The Hunt.* New York: Knopf, 1980.

Norman, Geoffrey. *The Orvis Book of Upland Bird Shooting.* Piscataway, N.J.: Nick Lyons Books, Winchester Press, 1985.

Norris, Dr. Charles. *Eastern Upland Shooting.* Traverse City, Mich.: Countrysport Press, 1989.

O'Brien, Dan. *The Rites of Autumn.* New York: Atlantic Monthly Press, 1988.

Ortega y Gasset, José. *Meditations on Hunting.* New York: Charles Scribner's Sons, 1972, 1985.

Peterson, Roger Tory. *Peterson Field Guides: Western Birds, Eastern Birds.* Boston: Houghton Mifflin, 1990.

Polo, Marco, with Manuel Komroff, ed. *The Travels of Marco Polo.* New York: Liveright, W.W. Norton & Company, Inc., 1926, 1933, 1953, 1982.

Proper, Datus C. *Pheasants of the Mind: A Hunter's Search for a Mythic Bird.* New York: Prentice Hall Press, 1990.

Reiger, John F. *American Sportsmen & the Origins of Conservation.* New York: Winchester Press, 1975.

Rue, Leonard Lee, III. *Game Birds of North America.* New York: Harper & Row, 1973.

Ruffer, Jonathan Garnier. *The Big Shots: Edwardian Shooting Parties.* London: Debrett-Viking, 1977.

Tolstoy, Leo. *Anna Karenina.* New York: Bantam Books, 1960.

Turgenev, Ivan. *A Hunter's Sketches*. Moscow: Progress Publishers, 1979.

Valdène, Guy de la. *Making Game*. Livingston, Mont.: Clark City Press, 1991.

Vance, Joel. *Upland Bird Hunting*. New York: E. P. Dutton, 1981.

Watson, E. T. *King Edward VII as a Sportsman*. London: Longman, Green & Co., 1911.

Woolner, Frank. *Grouse and Grouse Hunting*. New York: Crown Publishing, 1970.

Wolters, Richard A. *Game Dog: The Hunter's Retriever for Upland Birds and Waterfowl*. New York: E. P. Dutton, 1983, 1987.